Adam & Eve

The Spiritual Symbolism
of Genesis & Exodus

Samuel D. Fohr

ADAM & EVE

The Spiritual Symbolism of Genesis & Exodus

Fifth, revised and enlarged edition, 2017

Fourth, Third, and Second editions,
Sophia Perennis et Universalis, 2005, 2001, 1997
First edition, University Press of America, 1986

Series editor: James R. Wetmore

For information, address:
Philosophia Perennis
84 Main St, Peterborough, NH 03458
jameswetmore@mac.com

978-1-62138-262-1 pb
978-1-62138-263-8 cloth
978-1-62138-264-5 ebook

Cover Image:
Unknown Romanesque Painter, German
(active 1125–1250 in Hildesheim), wooden ceiling (detail),
St. Michael's Church, Hildesheim, Germany
Cover Design:
Michael Schrauzer

CONTENTS

TO RENA,

WHO HELPS TO COMPLETE ME

Acknowledgments

I WOULD LIKE TO THANK the following publishers for permission to quote copyrighted material: The Jewish Publication Society for passages from their series of translations, *The Torah*, copyright 1962 (second edition, 1967), *The Prophets*, copyright 1978, and *The Writings*, copyright 1982; The University of Chicago Press for passages from Moses Maimonides' *The Guide of the Perplexed*, translated by Shlomo Pines, copyright 1963; the Paulist Press for passages from *Gregory of Nyssa*: *The Life of Moses*, translated by Abraham J. Malherbe and Everett Ferguson, copyright 1978 by The Missionary Society of St Paul the Apostle in the State of New York.

I am indebted to Professor George Mavrodes for demonstrating the unreasonableness of typical modern arguments against the existence of the spiritual realm. I also owe much to the late Professor David Noel Freedman for all he taught me about the Bible and for his support of the publishing of the first edition of this book. I gratefully acknowledge the help I received from the late Swami Bhashyananda, former head of the Vivekananda-Vedanta Society of Chicago, in learning about the Hindu tradition and especially Advaita Vedanta. I thank H.E. Shyalpa Rinpoche for all he has taught me about Tibetan Buddhism.

I must especially thank my late father, Henry Fohr, for his expert translations of many of René Guénon's works that had not been translated when this book was first published. Without his help this book could not have been written. I am happy to report that twelve of these translations have been edited and published by Sophia Perennis.

I would like to express my gratitude for the work of the late Lynne Chiles, who typed all drafts of the first manuscript, put up with many little changes that were made in it, and provided many excellent suggestions for improving it; and my gratitude to Sharie Radzavich for typing sections of the second manuscript.

Finally, I would like to thank Cecil Bethell for proofreading the second edition of this book (as well as indexing and proofreading many volumes of the Guénon series), and James Wetmore for his exceptional help in getting this edition into good shape and the patience he has shown in the light of many last minute changes and additions I have made in it.

All translations form Genesis, Exodus, Isaiah, Ezekiel, Job, Daniel and Psalms are from the Jewish Publication Society translations mentioned above. These translations are based on the oldest complete Hebrew version, the Masoretic Text.

All translations of verses in the New Testament are from *The HarperCollins Study Bible: New Revised Standard Version* (New York: HarperCollins, 1993).

Preface

THE SYMBOLISM OF THE BIBLE has been expounded from at least 200 BC by Jewish writers and by both Jewish and Christian writers throughout the Christian Era. In addition, there has been no lack of Islamic commentators on those parts of the Old Testament which have been incorporated into the Qur'an. Particular mention can be made of Philo, Origen, St Gregory of Nyssa, and St Augustine in ancient times, Maimonides, Al-Ghazali, and Al-Arabi and Meister Eckhart in the Middle Ages, and René Guénon in the twentieth century. Unfortunately, in spite of all the symbolic interpretations of scripture which have been available for over 2,000 years, most believers are unaware of this dimension of the text they consider sacred. Past studies of biblical symbolism have had two characteristics. First, they were geared more for the specialist (or the elect) than the layman. Second, with the exception of Philo, Meister Eckhart, and to some extent St Augustine, they treated the symbolism of the Bible on a piecemeal basis. This second point is not meant as a criticism. The aim of a writer like Guénon was to examine certain symbols wherever they occurred in religions and other spiritual traditions throughout the world. If such symbols occurred in the Bible then they were explained in that context. While the others were not concerned with explaining the symbolism of traditions other than their own, with the exceptions noted, they picked their subjects carefully rather than aim at comprehensiveness. It is our goal to bring the symbolic dimension of Genesis and Exodus to the attention of the typical believer, and to do so in an organized manner which is accessible and rewarding to the specialist and layman alike.

Guiding our examination will be the idea that God or the Godhead is Reality, or as it is often put, the Ultimate Reality. The Bible, like all spiritual works, is geared to bringing about in us a correct apprehension of Reality and its relation to ourselves. Some people view God in personal terms (with or without form, e.g., as the merciful judge) and others view God in impersonal terms. But most view God in both ways, the first because it makes God easier to relate to, the second because it is awe-inspiring and thus makes God worthy of worship. In the end, it is the impersonal that must take precedence, for the personal is inherently finite in conception.

Reality is to be understood as *one*, or better *non-dual*. For the doctrine of non-dualism is not that there is one reality as opposed to two or many realities, but that there is just *Reality*. This seems to be in direct contradiction to our normal experience, since if we open our eyes and look around we see a world of separate things. But if Reality is non-dual, then either we are not seeing the Real, or not seeing It as It ultimately is but in some illusory way. Now it so happens that within Hinduism there is a school with the very name of this view of Reality, namely Advaita Vedanta, but it can be found implied or directly stated elsewhere. For instance, the Buddhists say that *samsara* (the changing impermanent world) is *nirvana* (understood as the ultimate unconditioned Reality), and sometimes that both have a more ultimate root or essence. And within Islam, the *dhikr* of the Sufis, *La ilaha illa 'Lla*, has the outer meaning that there are no other gods but Allah, but also the inner meaning that there is nothing other than God. Similarly with the twice stated declaration of Isaiah 45 in the Jewish tradition that 'I am the Lord and there is none else.' Finally, in Christianity we have the following from St Bernard of Clairvaux in Book 5, Section 3 of *Five Books on Consideration*:

> Again, what is God? That without which nothing exists. Just as nothing can exist without him, so he cannot exist without himself: he exists for himself, he exists for all, and consequently in some way he alone exists who is his own existence and that of all else.[1]

If indeed Reality is non-dual, then we should expect this view to be expressed in all authentic spiritual traditions, for they all have been inspired by that same Reality. Furthermore, we should expect

1. Bernard of Clairvaux, vol. 13, *Five Books on Consideration* (Kalamazoo, MI: Cistercian Publications, 1976), pp155–156.

to find the same subsidiary spiritual truths expressed in all of these traditions. So readers should not be alarmed by explanations of the meaning of something in one authentic tradition using terms drawn from another such tradition. To be more specific, we will often explain Biblical passages by referring to spiritual traditions outside the orbit of the Judeo-Christian tradition. We will do this because we believe it can result in a clearer and deeper understanding of these passages than would otherwise be the case, and because, as we have already stated in a different way, it is one God who speaks through all of these traditions.

Evidently Meister Eckhart, a Christian, felt similarly about the matter, for in explicating Biblical texts he cited Christian, Jewish and Muslim sources, as well as Plato, Aristotle, Cicero, Seneca and Proclus – 'pagans' all.

From the last comments it should be clear that although this book is primarily about the stories in Genesis and Exodus, it is also an exercise in comparative spirituality. Guénon's writings are a kind of Rosetta Stone for such an investigation, and we hope to add a little to his great accomplishments.

Readers of the 1986 edition of *Adam and Eve* may have felt that the writing had an edge to it. We do not apologize for that. What needs to be said should be said in no uncertain terms. This new edition presents the material of the first edition, but with chapters 10–12 moved up to 3–5. In some cases what was formerly in the footnotes appears in the main part of the text. Changes generally appear in the form of additions to the original text, but in many cases ideas have been expressed in a clearer way, and we trust that the new edition will achieve its aim more effectively than the old.

1

Introduction

What's in a Word?

The discussion of any matter will involve the use of certain key words. In the case of spiritual symbolism, the list will include 'religion', 'mysticism', 'initiation', 'exoteric', and 'esoteric'. Our views on the meaning of these terms as well as their extension may not be in sync with those of most Western scholars of religion, but we think there is good reason to reconsider the accepted wisdom.

If the writings of René Guénon in the first half of the twentieth century and those of Wilfred Cantwell Smith in the second half of the century have taught us anything, it is that we should not assume the spiritual traditions of other cultures are quite similar to our own. To put it another way, we should not read into their traditions various aspects of our own. Applying terms from our Western spiritual traditions as they have existed in modern times to Eastern spiritual traditions and so-called primitive spiritual traditions does a disservice to the latter groups. In particular, the free application of the words 'religion' and 'mysticism' to non-Western traditions is a symptom that we are not approaching them on their own terms.

In this section we want to concentrate on the word 'religion'. It is a fact that, no matter how different they are from one another, spiritual traditions from all over the earth are called religions. There are even some who feel that if we refuse to describe a certain spiritual tradition as a religion we are thereby demeaning it, or practicing some sort of 'cultural hegemony'. But what is really gained by calling Judaism, Christianity and Islam religions, and also calling Hinduism, Buddhism and Taoism religions, when the truth is that the first group is markedly different from the second? And if one brings in primitive or tribal spiritual traditions, there is even less reason to call them all religions. By applying the term 'religion' to all of these traditions one is glossing over their differences. A modern westerner understands the word 'religion' in a certain way. By applying the same term to the spiritual traditions of the East and primitive traditions, the westerner may assume certain things about these traditions which are false. As William Herbrechtsmeier writes in an article titled 'Buddhism and the Definition of Religion: One More Time',

> Western observers have frequently exported ideas about religion into foreign contexts where they do not fit the conceptuality of the peoples they study.[1]

Or if he is very objective and does not export any such ideas, the westerner may view these other religions as inferior to the religions of the West. It is most likely that all these traditions include a belief in something beyond the natural world—a spiritual or supra-natural realm—on which the natural world somehow depends for its existence, with emphasis on 'somehow'. But we should not let this sameness cover up the multitude of important differences between them.

Let us look for a moment at how modern Western scholars have divided up the spiritual traditions of the world. Jonathan Z. Smith has catalogued the various ways.[2] At first they were divided into 'nature' (what I have called 'primitive') and 'ethical' religions. The latter were divided into 'national/nomistic' and 'universalistic' religions. Only Christianity, Buddhism and Islam were considered universal or world religions. The national/nomistic religions included Judaism, Confucianism, Brahmanism, and Jainism. No doubt Shintoism should have been included in the latter category. One writer divided the world religions into prophetic—Christianity and Islam, and mystic—Buddhism. But along the way, the list of universalistic religions rose from three to seven, as if not to slight anyone, with many of the so-called national religions included. Without going further into Smith's article and without mentioning

1. *Journal for the Scientific Study of Religion*, 1993, vol. 32, no. 1, p1.

2. 'A Matter of Class: Taxonomies of Religion', *Harvard Theological Review*, Oct. 1996, vol. 89, no. 4, pp 387–404.

the telling criticisms he makes of the various modes of classification, let us just work with what we have. Note that the so-called nature religions are considered quite different from the rest. Actually, even these primitive (in the sense of coming from societies without a written language) spiritual traditions recognize a reality beyond nature. But that is almost all they have in common with the rest of the spiritual traditions which were mentioned. So why refer to them as religions? Then again, if Taoism, Judaism, Brahmanism (Hinduism), Jainism, Confucianism and Shintoism are so different from Christianity, Islam and Buddhism, why call all of them by the same name? Actually, while Judaism started as a national religion it became a universalistic proselytizing religion, and gave birth to Christianity and in a way to Islam (which began as a tribal religion)—all three being considered the Abrahamic religions. So it should be classed with the other two. On the other hand, Buddhism has seemed different from the other two, occasioning articles like the aforementioned one by Herbrechtsmeier. While the author chooses to count Buddhism as a religion, we think this is misleading.

Besides all of the above considerations, there is another reason for viewing Judaism, Christianity and Islam as a different type from the primitive spiritual traditions and those of the East. Eastern traditions are often called philosophies. This is ironic considering that philosophy is an invention of the West. But it points up the fact that westerners really do see the spiritual traditions of the East as quite different from those of the West. This is yet another reason for not using the same terminology for both.

Finally, there is the history of the term 'religion' and equivalent terms in other languages, which Wilfred Cantwell Smith has discussed in great detail.[3] To begin with, it is a Western word which to this day has no equivalent in the languages of any Eastern spiritual tradition, much less in the languages of the various primitive traditions. It does have an equivalent in Arabic, namely *din*. And it seems that Islam was the first surviving spiritual tradition to recognize itself as a religion, that is, as an 'institutionalized entity', 'an objective

3. *The Meaning and End of Religion* (Fortress Press, 1991), chaps. 2–4. Cf. also Josephson's *The Invention of Religion in Japan* (Univ. of Chicago, 2012).

something', 'an overt institutional phenomenon', 'a reified entity', 'a self-conceptualized definable entity', 'an exclusive membership community', 'a system, an intelligible entity susceptible of objective conceptualization', to use some of Cantwell Smith's phrases. Although there were tentative moves in this direction by Judaism and Christianity before the existence of Islam, it was not until the very beginning of the modern epoch during the Renaissance that these two began to see themselves in such a way. As Smith states:

> At a pre-reified level, for a concept of religion signifying that inner personal orientation for which there are a number of alternative or correlative words even in Western languages—piety, reverence, faith, and the like—it would seem that other cultures also have their designations. That some persons are 'religious,' devout, God-fearing, is an observation that has been widely made throughout the world. Although I have not made a systematic investigation, I believe that parallels or rough counterparts to the adjective 'religious,' as applied to persons, are to be found in a variety of cultures.... When we move from considering this personal quality of life to thinking rather of an organized system, the conceptualization that envisages a series of entities in the world each of which is called a religion, then this unanimity of mankind vanishes. It would seem that few have shared this particular analysis of humanity's religious involvement.[4]

When we add to this the idea that only one of these organized entities can be the way to God, we are definitely limiting ourselves to modern times and the Abrahamic tradition.

But what is most noteworthy is that there is no word corresponding to 'religion' in the Hebrew Old Testament or in the Greek New Testament or even in Latin. The Hebrew Bible definitely describes a faith tradition and community—but not a religion. You might say it is a difference between an attitude and an institution. The word 'religion' derives from the Latin 'religio', but even in ancient times there was debate over its original meaning. Some derived it from 'religare', which meant to bind and which is the basis for the word

4. Ibid., pp52–53.

'ligament'. Anyone conversant with the Hindu tradition would immediately see a connection here with the Sanskrit term 'yoga' which is related to the word 'yoke'. But other commentators derived 'religio' from 'relegere' which meant to be careful or take care and is the opposite of 'neglegere' from which comes the word 'neglect'.[5] If we accept the latter derivation, we have almost a synonym for 'sacred'—that which should be treated carefully. But this is a long way from the meaning that the word 'religion' has today.

As we observe the march of history over the last five-thousand years we see more and more the effects of what René Guénon called the solidification of the world, something we will refer to again in the chapter on Cain and Abel. Just as loosely connected city-states and feudal fiefdoms joined up into nations with rigid boundaries to which all the inhabitants were supposed to swear allegiance, so rather flexible and somewhat dissimilar faith communities formed themselves into institutions with rigid belief systems. There is a correspondence between nationalism and militant religiosity, a matter we will return to later in the chapter.

The hardening of a faith tradition into a religion includes a change that is very important for anyone interested in understanding spiritual symbolism. For that symbolism involves the esoteric side of the tradition rather than its exoteric side. But the esoteric side of a tradition is slowly forced out by its rigidification into a system. In the West, the result has been a disappearance of the esoteric within the sphere of Christianity, with the possible exception of the hesychastic practices under the aegis of the Orthodox Church. Within Islam, Sufism has been under attack for centuries by the religious authorities, and is under greater pressure today than ever before. Kabbalism still exists in the sphere of Judaism, but up until very recently touched the lives of few Jews. And some of what passes for Sufism and Kabbalism in Western countries today is not the true coin, if we may speak this way. In Eastern spiritual traditions the esoteric side is still very much alive. But then these traditions are not so rigid, and it has been said that we should not even use such names as 'Hinduism', 'Buddhism', 'Taoism', 'Jainism', and 'Shintoism'

5. Ibid., pp 204–5.

to refer to them, since these names, invented by people in the West, carry the implication of something comparable to Western spiritual traditions. Following the ideas of Guénon, we can describe these Western traditions, or religions, as comprising a dogma, a moral code and a set of rituals or prescribed practices. The dogma, or set of beliefs to which everyone must assent, includes the view that we are all creatures of and separate from the supernatural God who created the world, and that the proper goal of life is to be with God forever after earthly death. The moral code is seen as something handed down from on high by a potentate. The rituals are primarily congregational. Eastern and primitive traditions fail to match up in one or more ways. One of the main differences between the esoteric and exoteric approaches is that the Ultimate Reality (or God) is viewed as essentially impersonal in the former but as essentially personal in the latter. This has led some of those who define 'religion' as the belief in super-human beings (a rather crude way of putting the matter) to deny that Buddhism is a religion. Actually all of the Eastern traditions could be lumped together with Buddhism in this regard. However, they all have a personal as well as impersonal side which Western scholars sometimes refer to as their religious and (mistakenly) philosophical sides.

What matters for our purposes in this book is that in going back to Genesis and Exodus, and sometimes to the Gospels, we are returning to the pre-religion forms of the Judaic and Christian spiritual traditions, to a time when their esoteric sides played a larger role than later in their history.

The Esoteric and the Exoteric

Whatever the terms 'esoteric' and 'exoteric' may designate in the thinking of some people, it is clear that first and foremost they refer to the two main ways of approaching God that are open to human beings. As the etymologies of these words indicate, one way is internal and the other external. That is to say, one may strive for the inner realization of one's essential identity with God, or one may take up the devotional attitude of a loving servant doing the master's bidding. Implicit in the second attitude is the idea that God is totally external and other, while the first involves the idea that really knowing ourselves is tantamount to knowing God. Both attitudes can be present in a person, and from the standpoint of our individuality we must never cease to view ourselves as servants. But the esoteric approach involves an attempt to see ourselves from another standpoint in which our relationship to God will be viewed accordingly.

Another way of making clear the difference in viewpoints is to compare their stands on the relations of humans, God and the world. From the dualistic exoteric perspective God and humans exist within the world with God 'up there' and us 'down here'. From the non-dualistic esoteric perspective humans and the rest of the world exist within God. As stated in Acts 17:28, 'In him we live and move and have our being.' This latter perspective is made very clear in Kabbalism which holds that God withdrew into Himself or created a space within Himself in order to provide a place for the world. In a statement reminiscent of St Bernard's comment on God in the Preface, Philo expresses this relationship between the God and the world in the following way:

> There is a third signification [of place] in keeping with which God himself is called a place [*Ha-Makom*], by reason of His containing things, and being contained by nothing whatever...for He is that which He Himself has occupied, and naught encloses Him but Himself. I, mark you, am not a place, but in a place; and each thing that likewise exists; for that which is contained is different from that which contains it, and the Deity, being contained by nothing, is of necessity Itself, Its own place.[6]

And at the very beginning of his *Confessions*, St Augustine, addressing God, states, 'I exist in you,' and 'you contain all things within yourself.'[7] This reversal of the usual way of thinking of things must seem strange to the typical believer.

6. Philo, *On Dreams* [De Somnis], trs. F.H. Colson and G.H. Whitaker (Cambridge: Harvard Univ. Press, 1968), bk I, sec. 11, lines 62–64, p329.

7. *Confessions*, bk I, sects. 2 and 3, translated by R.S. Pine-Coffin (Baltimore: Penguin Books, 1961). In explicating the idea that 'all things are in God,' Meister Eckhart goes even further and says, '. . . man in God is God.' Meister Eckhart, *Teacher and Preacher* (New York: Paulist Press, 1986), p209.

There is another description of the esoteric-exoteric distinction which may seem at variance with our own. It is that the esoteric encompasses what is secret and reserved for initiates while the exoteric is open to the public and meant for the masses. But there is no incompatibility here. Such a description is correct, but is only part of the truth, and certainly does not give us the defining characteristics of the two approaches.

It has been said, not without good reason, that a religion is an essentially exoteric phenomenon. For if we consider Judaism, Christianity, and Islam, it is obvious that for many centuries they have stressed the devotional approach. However, besides the presence of esoteric groups within the sphere of influence of these religions (Kabbalists within Judaism and Sufis within Islam, as well as various groups within Christianity at least up through the Renaissance), we must also point to the esoteric character of many of the writings which are recognized by them as canonical. Some of the most striking passages occur in the Gospel of John[8] and those interpreters with an especially exoteric bent have a great deal of trouble explaining these passages and rather try to avoid them altogether. Yet such ideas are like a building's supporting columns, which cannot be removed without the whole edifice crumbling.[9]

Exoterism and esoterism are present in a more balanced way in the spiritual traditions of the East such as Hinduism and Buddhism. In both traditions there is the way of the householder and the way of the monk. In Hinduism the householder is expected to fulfill the duties of his status in life and take part in certain rituals as a way of gaining birth in a higher sphere of Existence or (more usually) of gaining a better birth in his next reincarnation. In both cases he sees himself as serving God. The monk, on the other hand, is aiming by inner spiritual practice to attain realization of his Godhood. Now the situation is really more complicated than this since there are all

8. John 14:18–21 and 17:20–23, and with these in mind 10:30.

9. These passages reflect the original esoteric (and thus initiatic) character of Christianity before it became a source of spirituality for the masses. On this change cf. René Guénon, *Insights into Christian Esoterism* (Hillsdale, NY: Sophia Perennis, 2004), chap. 2.

kinds of householders and all kinds of monks, but the general point still holds.

The mainly exoteric nature of religions is shown by the stress placed on worshiping God publicly and following God's commandments. Indeed, the typical believer of today thinks that living a good life (as defined by scripture and/or religious authorities) and attending services at synagogue, church or mosque are the keys to salvation. It is to be noted that both of these practices have to do with the outer life of the believer, i.e., with what is external to him. And we may add that the God he is supposed to love and worship as well as the Heaven he is supposed to reach are also taken to be external to the believer.

A good way of distinguishing the exoteric from the esoteric approach to God is to examine what each has to say about the subject of holy war. From the exoteric viewpoint, which has been that of organized religion, a holy war is something completely external in which 'heathens' are converted, or put to death, or at least put to flight. From the esoteric viewpoint a holy war is something that goes on within a human being and involves a sort of inner conversion and death. In fact, the waging of the inner war constitutes the whole of esoteric practice.[10]

In the esoteric approach the emphasis is not so much on outer activity as on inner activity with the goal of gaining knowledge of one's innermost being, for God is understood as constituting the center point or heart of the believer. Basically this approach involves two initiatic deaths and rebirths which have as their goals the perfection of the human state and the 'escape' from its limitations.[11] Thus the journey to Heaven is an inner one which does not have to wait on bodily death. This is the central point of Dante's *Divine*

10. On this subject we read in the Buddhist *Dhammapada*, 'One man on the battle field conquers an army of a thousand men. Another conquers himself—and he is greater' (P. Lal, tr.; New York: Farrar, Straus & Giroux, 1967; p75). Rumi devotes a section of the *Masnavi* to the esoteric understanding of holy war. And, going back to ancient Greece, there is little doubt that the war which Heraclitus glorified was first and foremost the inner one.

11. The goals of the two rebirths can also be described as building the ego and overcoming the ego. The typical human being of our age hardly possesses an ego

Comedy in which Dante portrays himself as journeying to the Celestial Paradise while still 'in the flesh'.

In fact, immortality is understood in a completely different way in exoterism and esoterism. One problem with the exoteric approach is that it tends to understand everything in crude spatio-temporal terms. Thus salvation is understood as living forever in a place called Heaven. On the other hand, salvation from the esoteric approach is more properly called liberation or deliverance, what the Hindus call *moksha*. It involves penultimately a residing in consciousness at the still center point of one's being (the point of the 'actionless activity' of God), and ultimately an awareness of one's essential identity with God. In either case one achieves a sense of eternity (or timelessness), which is the esoteric understanding of 'immortality'. St Augustine refers to this state in the latter part of his *Confessions*:

> Try as they may to savor the taste of eternity, their thoughts still twist and turn upon the ebb and flow of things in the past and future time. But if only their minds could be seized and held steady, they would be still for a while and, for that short moment, they would glimpse the splendor of eternity which is for ever still.... If only men's minds could be seized and held still: they would see how eternity in which there is neither past nor future, determines both past and future time. Could mine be the hand strong enough to seize the minds of men? Could any words of mine have the power to achieve so great a task?[12]

This great task is the goal of meditational practices prescribed in esoteric paths all over the world as a way of inner development. These practices may include the repetition of phrases or sentences as well as visualizations, but all of these serve as means to the end mentioned by St Augustine.

---

and lives his days in inner chaos. Only by overcoming the flesh—which constantly pulls him in different directions and thereby fragments him—can he develop a unity within himself, even if it is a unity which is to be surpassed. Sri Ramakrishna, a Hindu saint of the nineteenth century, talked of unripe and ripe egos, and stated that when the ego is ripened it will fall of its own accord.

12. *Confessions*, bk XI, sect. 2.

At once it will be objected that we have misunderstood those who engage in the typical religious or exoteric approach to God, for they too are concerned with the inner life, seeking inspiration through prayer. We can readily admit that this is true to some degree, but we must also say that many who think they have found inspiration are deluded. We are referring to the practitioners of what can be called emotionalistic religion, for they have mistaken heightened emotional states for inspiration. It may well be that certain very inspired people down through the centuries often experienced heightened emotional states, but we should not confuse or equate these states with inspiration. Besides, even real inspiration should not be confused with realization which is the true goal of the esoteric approach, a point we shall come back to further on.

It will also be objected that those who take the esoteric approach are merely being self-centered. This is a simplistic view which does not hold up under close scrutiny. In fact, it can be said that the goal of the exoteric approach is to save oneself, whereas the goal of the esoteric path is to lose oneself, as mentioned in Matthew 10:39. There is little doubt that many who think they are on the esoteric path are laboring under delusions. But there are those who are truly preparing themselves for a time when they can be of inestimable value to the rest of the world. We must keep in mind the phrase 'physician heal thyself'. It is impossible to be a 'force for good' in the world if one is basically dreaming one's way through life, and is filled with egoism and overwhelming desires and the negative emotions they engender. All the 'shalt nots' in the world cannot remove the thoughtlessness and inner turmoil that causes outer strife. While exotericism deals almost entirely with the outer man, esotericism addresses itself directly to the inner man and is able, indirectly, to effect the outer life.[13] The matter is sometimes put in terms of *being* and *doing*. It is said that in order to do one has to be. On the esoteric path, the spiritual master helps us to be by prescribing meditational practices and correcting us at every turn. The latter is to make us

13. In Abraham Joshua Heschel's words, 'The good is the base, the holy is the summit. Man cannot be good unless he strives to be holy' (*The Circle of the Baal Shem Tov* [Chicago: The University of Chicago Press, 1985], p xxxii).

more mindful and the former is to help us realize our true nature. The result is that we are able to act on the world and not just react to it, at the mercy of circumstances.

The anthropologist Mary Douglas sees the emphasis on either outer or inner religious practices as reflecting the type of society to which a person belongs. She asserts that highly structured societies with sharp boundaries tend to stress ritual whereas less structured societies with amorphous boundaries stress asceticism and individual inner states including trances. Again, those on the periphery of structured societies will stress inner states.[14] Her view may be seen as a variation of Emile Durkheim's bottom-up view of religions as reflecting the structures of their societies (or of religions being the images of their societies). But why not say that the structure of societies reflect certain spiritual realities, which we believe is the case where traditional societies are concerned. Douglas mistakenly lumps together all kinds of trance, and looking at the larger picture, all kinds of non-ritual behavior typically called religious. But leaving this aside, her thesis is belied by the facts. Within Islam and Judaism, the exoteric and esoteric approaches to religion have existed side by side for centuries, with the same people partaking of both. The Hindu and Chinese societies have been very structured and ritual-oriented. Yet over the centuries many people in these societies decided to become monks and nuns engaged in an inner journey. The same is true of traditional Christian societies down through the ages. And these monks and nuns were *not* drawn mainly from the fringe elements of these societies—the dispossessed and alienated. No doubt Mary Douglas would charge that we have over-simplified her thesis, and would have some counters to the examples we just gave. But unless she is willing to make all sorts of questionable assumptions which would reduce her thesis to one which is true by definition and hence empty, she cannot make it stick. Favoring the interior life over external ritual is not merely a matter of the type of society one lives in or even one's place in that society.

14. *Natural Symbols* (New York: Pantheon, 1982), chaps. 4–11.

Before going any further in contrasting the esoteric and exoteric approaches to God it is necessary, in order to avoid misunderstandings, to point out that mysticism is an exoteric or essentially religious development. Unfortunately, the term 'mystic' has changed meanings over the centuries and this has led to a great deal of confusion. The mystic who took part in the ancient mysteries was definitely engaged in an esoteric venture, but for the most part, those called mystics in the Judeo-Christian tradition have been squarely within the province of exotericism. There have been exceptions to this, but we are concerned with the general rule. A practitioner of the esoteric way takes an active posture with respect to his spiritual development. There are definite practices which are guided by a spiritual master. The master begins his guidance with a formal initiation (called 'taking refuge' in Buddhism) whose essential aspect is the transference of spiritual influence to the disciple. This allows the disciple to begin to make actual something that was previously only potential. It charges the disciple's spiritual battery which normally exists in a run-down state in our present age. In contrast to all of this the typical mystic adopts a rather passive attitude, praying and hoping for Divine inspiration and often being subject to various visions. These visions, like all special experiences arrived at by whatever means, are quite different from the realization sought by someone on the esoteric path.[15] Then too, the mystic views himself as separate from God, although he seeks to be united to Him. The mystic is the artist of the soul, and is inspired much in the way a poet, painter or composer is inspired. Only his inspiration takes his life as its canvas.

15. For a discussion of the sorts of special experiences produced by the ingestion of psychedelic drugs, and the relation of these to spirituality, see Samuel D. Fohr, 'Shamanism for the Twenty-First Century: Spirituality and the Quest for Special Experiences' in the *Journal of Drug Education and Awareness*, vol. 1, no. 1, 2003, pp13–34. As to the effects of ingesting psychedelics, all indications are that it is the drugs doing the talking, not God. However, there are definitely such things as religious experiences or experiences of the Divine, and William Alston has written about them in *Perceiving God* (Ithaca, NY: Cornell University Press, 1991). But these experiences are not the goal of either the exoteric or esoteric path, and can constitute a hindrance to reaching the goal if too much attention is paid to them.

Unity and Division

The word 'believer' for a practitioner of religion is quite suggestive, and contrasts sharply with 'knower' which is an apt description of one who has made progress on the esoteric path. And it is not a matter of the latter knowing what the former only believes, for the subject matter is different in the two cases. In the case of the believer we are in the realm of dogma whereas in the case of the latter we are in the realm of that sort of knowledge where knower and known are one—where it is a matter of realizing, remembering, recollecting our true nature. There is no doubt that belief is of central importance for those on the exoteric path, since the holding of certain beliefs is considered necessary for salvation in all of the major faiths. Now there are certain beliefs that are surely very central from the religious perspective, e.g., that the universe is a creation of God, that (in this context) the believer is a creature, and that God is perfectly good. But there are other beliefs that are insisted upon in many of the religious sects that are not at all central, e.g., that the universe is approximately 6,000 years old, that it was given its form in six days, and that the story of Adam and Eve is an historical account.[16] In addition to these, there are particular doctrinal matters having to do with key concepts and practices which are also stressed. The end result is a sort of recipe theory of salvation according to which if you believe such and such and do so and so you are saved. Not surprisingly, the different religions, as well as sects within the religions, put forward different recipes,[17] a matter which, though not serious in itself, can lead to serious consequences. This is especially so when members of a particular religion or sect believe that their own faith and its sacred texts are somehow

16. As a way of countering evolutionism, such dogmas are quite ineffective, as they concentrate on superficial matters and not the basic idea that intelligence, far from being the end product of the formation of the universe, was there at the very beginning.

17. On this subject see Frithjof Schuon's 'The Two Paradises' in *Islam and the Perennial Philosophy* (London: World of Islam Festival Publishing Company, 1976), and his 'Alternations in Semitic Monotheism' in *Christianity/Islam: Essays on Esoteric Ecumenicism* (Bloomington, IN: World Wisdom Books, 1985).

devalued by being put on the same level as other spiritual traditions and their sacred texts.

As members of these different groups tend to identify themselves by adherence to the full set of their beliefs (their complete dogma), religions and sects tend to divide people. This is exacerbated by what we might call the meta-religious belief according to which the believer's particular salvation recipe is the only one which will work.[18] All of this results in a we-they dichotomy where the 'we' are taken as saved and the 'they' as damned. Thus the exoteric approach carries the idea of winners and losers into the sphere of salvation. It is as if salvation is the prize of a special kind of Olympic games entered by various religions. Since there can be only one overall winner it means that many whole groups *must be losers.* And on the principle that 'he who isn't with us is against us,' hostility is developed toward other groups, a hostility that results in one of two outcomes. The 'we' may try to convert the 'they' by reasoning or by force, or the 'we' may decide that the 'they' are somehow less than human and can be slaughtered like animals. Thus in some cases religion has had effects similar to those of extreme nationalism or ethnic identification. One is forced to conclude that each of the various religions is a method of exclusivity.[19] In a book which details his travels in the region of Tibet, Marco Pallis recounts, 'One young lama told me that they were taught from childhood not to speak ill of other religions, but on the contrary to treat them with every respect.'[20] On the other hand, in the West we are taught to speak ill of other spiritual traditions and even to ascribe them to the working of the devil. Those who judge 'Whoever is for the Lord' (Exod. 32:26) by the acceptance of their particular set of beliefs have

18. The Christian form of this belief is typically buttressed by a reference to the Gospel formula 'I am the way, and the truth and the life' (John 14:6).Unfortunately, this statement is not understood rightly. Jesus can be so described because he is an example of what in esoteric doctrine is called 'Universal Man', of which more in chapter 4. The Islamic version of this claim is supported by declaring Jesus a prophet and Muhammed the 'Seal of the Prophets'. But newer prophets do not negate the teachings of the older and new covenants with God do not erase previous ones.

19. This formulation is due to Rena Fohr.

20. *Peaks and Lamas* (New York: Alfred A. Knopf, 1949), p75.

something less than love in their hearts, whatever may be the lip service they give to the concept.

Martin S. Jaffee[21] has put the matter starkly by reminding us that the three great monotheistic religions—Judaism, Christianity, and Islam—have more than monotheism in common. What he calls the 'elective' monotheism of the three faiths involves two quite separate beliefs: (1) God is one and unique, and (2) There is only one proper faith community which is thereby unique in its own way. That second belief makes everyone outside the community into the evil Other which is either to be brought into the unique community or destroyed, the latter either by the community members or God. He concludes with the chilling comment, 'On the plane of history, the capacity of God to love intensely and exclusively is translated, as often as not, into the human capacity to hate intensely.'[22]

Jaffee's comment holds not only for the three great faiths but for the often antagonistic sects within them. Even the smallest sect may believe that it alone constitutes the unique faith community, and thus that most of its erstwhile co-religionists are members of the evil Other. Some of these sects have proselytized peacefully, but others have exhibited a totalitarian bent (reflecting the ideological age in which we have been living since the French Revolution) as well as a puritanical disposition. And as H.L. Mencken wrote, 'It must be confessed that man's inhumanity to man is almost intolerably distressing.... The moral bully is the worst of all. Puritanism is completely merciless.'[23] Like the humanism they are meant to combat, these movements are a completely modern invention. And like humanism, they are idolatrous in that their purveyors recognize no higher authority than their own minds, their own thoughts. Recognizing no authority beyond themselves, there is no action of which they are incapable when dealing with those outside their groups, or

21. 'One God, One Revelation, One People: On the Symbolic Structures of Elective Monotheism' in the *Journal of the American Academy of Religion*, vol. 69, no. 4, Dec. 2001, pp735–775.

22. Ibid., p774.

23. H.L. Mencken, *Minority Report* (Baltimore: The Johns Hopkins University Press, 1997), p23. Mencken's avowed atheism and closet bigotry do not vitiate the truth of his comment.

those within their group who do not follow the official line to the last detail. In light of all that has just been said, there is no use hiding from the fact that the exoteric approach to God, being essentially divisive, can easily lead to hatred and violence. On the other hand, the esoteric approach tends to unite people, for the tenets of esotericism are shared by all of the major religions as well as all other true spiritual traditions.[24] Different groups are not seen as enemies but as seeking God in their own way.[25]

There is no question here of watering down religion to its lowest common denominator, something which is being done, in quite a different way, in our own time. The esoteric side of religions is their most profound and spiritual part and involves the recognition that just as 'holy war' has an inner meaning, so does 'chosen people'.

Writers like the aforementioned Mary Douglas have decried the contemporary rejection of ritual in the religions of the West, as well as the accompanying emphasis placed on inner experience. She says that this state of affairs has led to a lack of commitment to common symbols. She remarks that doctrinal differences are down-played, and the result is a group of indistinguishable sects. Where before people gained justification of their existence from the performance of set rules, now they can only find it in performing good works. Thus religion is reduced to an ethical system.[26] While we can agree with the author's views on what amounts to the secularizing of religion by reducing it to do-goodism, this is certainly not what we are advocating. The traditional exoteric approach to God stressed rituals which embodied certain symbols. Rituals and symbols are not ends in themselves but tools to reach other goals. No doubt they

24. We mean to include here such traditions as Hinduism, Taoism, Buddhism, and Ch'an (or Zen) Buddhism, which are essentially esoteric in nature.

25. This view is hardly new, being enunciated in Ancient Rome by those outside of the Judeo-Christian tradition.

26. *Natural Symbols*, chapters 1–3. René Guénon had already described this situation half a century earlier in his book *The Crisis of the Modern World* (Hillsdale, NY: Sophia Perennis, 2001). In chapter 5, 'Individualism', he writes of 'the degeneration into moralism', 'the dissolution of doctrine', religion's sinking into 'sentimentalism' [emotionalism], 'religiosity', or 'vague and sentimental aspirations unjustified by any real knowledge.' (p 61)

help order societies and provide a framework in which to live. They also help aim us in the direction of God. In this latter function they must continually be transcended if we are to make spiritual progress. Rituals and symbols may be abandoned in two different ways. One way is that outlined by Mary Douglas. The result is that we are cast adrift in a morass of spiritual impoverishment and an over-concern with good works. The concomitant emphasis on inner experience will involve either the intellectualizing (in the modern sense of the term) or the emotionalizing of religious life. The second way involves going beyond all duality and form, including the good-bad duality, and emphasizing the kind of inner experience that is the *sine qua non* of the spiritual life. The latter does not involve curbing the divisiveness of religions by asking them to give up their rituals and particularizing doctrines so they can all join together in a kind of insipid religious soup. Rather it is a matter of rising above their divisiveness by realizing that essentially they are all aiming at the same goal.

In describing the esoteric path we have mentioned spirituality and spiritual development rather than religiosity. The use of the word 'spirituality' has led social commentator Wendy Kaminer to express concerns like those of Mary Douglas in a different way. 'Spirituality,' she says, is 'a term frequently used to describe the vaguest intimations of supernatural realities.' She goes on,

> Spirituality, after all, is simply religion deinstitutionalized, and shorn of any exclusionary doctrines. In a pluralistic marketplace, it has considerable appeal. Spirituality embraces traditional religions and New Age practices, as well as forays into pop psychology and a devotion to capitalism.... You can claim to be a spiritual person without professing loyalty to a particular dogma or even understanding it. Spirituality makes no intellectual demands on you; all it requires is a general belief in immaterialism (which can be used to increase our material possessions).[27]

27. 'The Last Taboo,' *The New Republic*, Oct. 14, 1996, vol. 215, no. 16. See also chapter 1 of her *Sleeping with Extra-Terrestrials* (New York: Pantheon Books, 1999). We should mention that Wendy Kaminar is writing from the atheistic viewpoint.

Kaminer's view has been echoed by many others. Rev. Donna Shoper has written,

> Unfortunately, the garb of spirituality is a bleached, if companionable substitute for faith. Amateurish tai chi and yoga, quasi-Buddhist meditation, and New Age prayers are a far cry from the ancient practice of the Sabbath. [She adds], it's not surprising to find a highly personal spirituality replacing institutional religion. We are so mired in the self that we are losing sight of the sacred.[28]

And on the subject of New Age factor in 'the present explosion of Jewish spirituality,' Rabbi Arnold Jacob Wolf has commented, 'The consequence may be religious narcissism instead of patient struggle.'[29] It would seem that if the esoteric path is connected with spirituality then we are really dealing with a sort of watered-down self-centered and eviscerated religion. Such observations are not surprising given the way the word 'spirituality' is thrown around these days. Like all traditional terms it has been devalued. Truly spiritual practices may not be 'institutional' (i.e., congregational), but neither are they undemanding intellectually or any other way. Nor are the goals of spirituality selfish, amorphous or airy.

It is at least interesting that a study of religion on American College Campuses found that students

> ... preferred to use the words 'spirituality' and 'spiritual' instead of 'religion' and 'religious' [to describe their attitudes and practices, and] understood 'religion' to mean institutions and organizations [but] took 'spirituality' to mean a personal experience of God or ultimate values.... Furthermore, more often than not, 'spiritual' and 'spirituality' connoted a quest, a journey, something not yet completed, whereas 'religion' and 'religious' signified something completed, fixed, handed down. [The authors conclude that] most of the undergraduates we encountered ... could

28. 'Me-First "Spirituality" is a Sorry Substitute for Organized Religion on Campuses'. This is the 'Point of View' article in *The Chronicle of Higher Education*, Aug. 18, 2000.

29. 'Against Spirituality', in *Judaism*, vol. 50, no. 199, Summer 2001, p365.

> be characterized as spiritual seekers rather than religious dwellers, and many of them were constructing their spirituality without much regard to the boundaries dividing religious denominations, traditions, or organizations.[30]

All of this may sound like a self-absorbed quest for authenticity dragged into the realm of religion, but seeing oneself on a quest is preferable to the self-righteousness that often accompanies those who believe they have arrived at their destination. After all, can anyone claim that he knows everything and is beyond progress? And even if what most students call 'spirituality' is usually a hodgepodge of vague ideas and unguided practices, the spiritual quest need not be so, and proper guidance exists.

The term 'spirituality' is just one of many to be devalued in our times. The word 'veteran' has received similar treatment. At first it meant anyone who fought in a war, then anyone who had served in the armed forces, then anyone who had worked in a profession for a long time (especially professional sports, perhaps because sports are seen as a kind of war). Today it means anyone who has worked in a profession for a few years. The term 'esoteric' itself has suffered the same fate. A typical mail-order catalog for books listed the following under the heading 'Esotericism': *In Search of Ghosts, A Treasury of Superstitions, The Oracles of Nostradamus, The Runes, Ghostly American Places, Magic and the Magician, Harper's Encyclopedia of Mystical and Paranormal Experiences, Divine Magic: the World of the Supernatural, The Encyclopedia of the Occult, The Power of Gemstone, Voodoo, The Vampire in Europe, The Power of Magic, Malleus Maleficaram* (on witchcraft), *Strange Sects and Curious Cults, Spontaneous Human Combustion, I Never Believed in Ghosts Until... 100 Real-Life Encounters, The Pictorial Key to the Tarot, The Complete Book of Devils and Demons, The Nazis and the Occult, Scotland's Unsolved Mysteries of the Twentieth Century, The UFO Conspiracy, Revelation: St John the Divine's Prophecies for the Apocalypse and Beyond*, and *Abducted: The Story of Intruders Continues*

30. Conrad Cherry, Betty A. DeBerg and Amanda Porterfield, 'Religion on Campus' in *Liberal Education*, vol. 87, no. 4, Fall 2001, p10.

(about encounters with space aliens).[31] It is difficult to know whether to laugh or cry over this list, but whatever one concludes about contemporary civilization from the evident popularity of certain items, only A. E. Waite's book on the tarot could plausibly be said to have anything to do with esoterism. Certainly a perusal of the list must raise the question of the usefulness and propriety of employing the term 'esoterism' or its variant 'esotericism' to describe the higher reaches of spiritual practice, and spirituality in general. It almost seems as if there has been a determined effort from some quarters to devalue the word. On the other hand mere commercial motivation may be the culprit. In any case we will keep the term (at a minimum, for lack of any better one) and turn to further criticisms of the esoteric point of view.

A view that is often expressed by those on the exoteric path is that the various spiritual traditions of the world differ over whether one or many gods are worshipped. It is said that while in Judaism and Christianity people worship one God, in Hinduism and various tribal traditions people worship many. If true, this would certainly count against the esoteric idea that each spiritual tradition is seeking the same God in its own way. In answer one could reply that all spiritual traditions seem to believe in many gods, only some hide this claim by calling their gods 'angels', and 'saints'. Or one could reply that all spiritual traditions believe in a highest or Ultimate Reality, a creator of this world, and where other gods are mentioned they either represent aspects of the One God or serve as intermediaries between God and humans. Again the charge will be made that in Hinduism and tribal traditions male and female deities are worshipped whereas in Judaism and Christianity there is no worship of the female. But this distinction too dissolves under closer scrutiny. On the one side, traditions like Hinduism can be seen as worshipping one God under male and female aspects. On the other, Western religions can be seen as giving a prominent role to the feminine, e.g., the *Shekinah* in Judaism, the Virgin Mary in Christianity. There will always be people in any tradition who actually pray to different personages, whether called gods or saints. But there will also be people

31. Barnes & Noble Catalog H39X205X sent out late-summer of 1997, p38.

in these traditions who believe in only the Ultimate Reality. One should not judge a spiritual tradition by its most childish adherents and their beliefs.

There is a commonly held exoteric view that all of the various spiritual traditions of the world are not up to the same thing in that they do not all promote the same high ethical standards. In particular, the received view is that the spiritual traditions of the East do not involve the high standards of the religions of the West.[32] If true, this would certainly be damning, for the outwardly moral life is a preliminary for any spiritual advancement as well as an indication of such advancement. But this view of the East probably stems from the fact that the social rules of various Eastern cultures were not handed down from on high amidst lightning and thunder. The social teachings of the East, which are the equivalent of our moral rules minus the latter's emotive content, are for all intents and purposes the same as those in the West. In Hinduism there are the Laws of Manu which deal with one's *dharma* or duty. (The word also means righteousness or justice). In Buddhism there are Right Action, Right Speech, and Right Occupation from the Eightfold Noble Path, whose implications are spelled out in the Five Precepts (*panca-sila*), the Four Stations of Brahma (*Brahma-vihara*) or Immeasurables as they are called in Tibetan Buddhism, and the Six Perfections (*Paramitas*). The last group includes *dana* (generosity or giving) which corresponds to the Western idea of charity. In the Chinese tradition we have the general and specific strictures of the *Tao Te Ching* and the *Analects* of Confucius. The concepts of *karma* and ego-less-ness in the East are comparable to those of sin and humility in the West. And on the matter of humility and ego-lessness it is significant that Meister Eckhart, in his 'Counsels on Discernment' (what the Hindus might call 'discrimination'), describes humility as the 'annihilation of self' and 'becoming nothing'.[33] All in

32. G.K. Chesterton was an especially strong adherent of this idea, and it can be detected, surprisingly, in the writings of Hermann Hesse.

33. Meister Eckhart, *The Essential Sermons, Commentaries, Treatises and Defense*, trs. Edmund College and Bernard McGuinn (New York: Paulist Press, 1981), pp280–81.

all there is little reason for the West to boast of moral superiority over the East.[34]

Literal and Symbolic

Adapting Friedrich von Hügel's masterful analysis[35] we may say that all people first become acquainted with religions through their exoteric dimension. It cannot be otherwise since, as we have already said, religion is basically exoteric in character. A majority of people never go beyond this first stage, which we will call the childish stage of belief. It is childish because people are urged to accept what they are told without question, even if what they are expected to believe is highly implausible, e.g., the historical truth of all the stories in the Bible. A significant minority questions the historical truth of these stories as well as the dogmas of their religion. Some of these people, feeling that religion is a tissue of lies, never go beyond this stage and become atheists, or at best agnostics. Or perhaps they do not have quite so strong a reaction and grudgingly accept Bible stories as fictional tales whose purpose is to teach certain lessons. People in this latter group live out their lives in a state of lukewarm faith bordering on atheism. But some realize that there is another dimension to religion and go beyond this second stage. They discover the esoteric writings of those connected with initiatic groups and learn of the inner life and the inner meaning of Bible stories. These people take up the life of the spirit as best they can, and we may call this third stage the mature practice of religion.[36]

34. A good rebuttal of the view of the moral West vs. the amoral East is found in chap. 3 of S. Radhakrishnan's *Eastern Religion and Western Thought* (London: Oxford University Press, 1959). Frithjof Schuon gives a very clear exposition of the Shinto equivalent of morality in chap. 12 of his book *In the Tracks of Buddhism* (London: George Allen & Unwin, 1968). We very much recommend this chapter to the reader, first because it helps explain our general approach to myths and other spiritual stories, and second because it relates the material we cover in chaps. 3–5 to Shintoism. There is a comprehensive review of the ethical teachings of Buddhism in *The Nature of Buddhist Ethics* by Damien Keown (New York: Palgrave, 2001).

35. Cf. his *Mystical Elements in Religion* (London: Dent & Sons, 1923), vol. 1, chap. 2.

36. Some, while not leaving their religion, may join initiatic groups. This will

Cerno Bokar Saalif Taal, a West-African Sufi who taught in the first half of the twentieth century, described three kinds of faith. Obviously, the second stage mentioned by von Hügel will not make an appearance in such an account. But the first and second kinds of faith mentioned by Cerno Bokar correspond roughly to the first and third stages of von Hügel. The third kind of faith corresponds to what would be the result of pursuing the third stage in von Hügel's presentation. Cerno Bokar says there are *sulb* or solid faith, *sa'il* or liquid faith, and *ghazi* or gaseous faith.

> The first degree of faith, *sulb*, is solid faith. It is suitable for the common man—the masses—and for the teachers who are attached to the letter [of the law]. This faith is channelled by prescriptions imposed by a law drawn from revealed texts, be they Jewish, Christian or Islamic.... It is subject to a rigorous determination which admits of no foreign element. It is intransigent and hard like a stone from which I draw its name.... *Sa'il* faith is that of men ... who have set out on the way which leads to truth. The constituent elements of this faith derive from understanding. It values truths from wherever they come, considering neither their origin nor the date of their existence. It gathers and assembles them in order to make from them a body in perpetual movement.... This faith, due to its subtle, liquid nature, is strong and undermines the faults of the soul, erodes the rocks of intolerance and spreads out, taking on a shape which is not fixed as in the case of *sulb* faith ... but borrows the form of its recipient.... *Sa'il* faith ... disciplines the adept and makes of him a man of God capable of hearing, listening to and appreciating the voices of those who speak of God.... This faith is the ante-chamber of

be the case especially where there exist initiatic groups connected with or in the sphere of influence of a particular religion. Others, finding no initiatic groups connected with their religion, will leave it for one to which such groups are connected. Still others, finding a well-developed mystical side to their religion, will pursue that mode of spirituality. Finally, some will leave their religion and join a group belonging to a spiritual tradition which is essentially esoteric. We feel constrained, due to the rise of many aberrant and sometimes violent groups in our own time, to say that when we talk of initiatic groups we are not referring to what today are termed 'cults' or to similar groups which prey on the suggestible.

> truth.... *Ghazi* faith is the third and final form. It is decidedly more subtle, and it is the attribute of a specially chosen elite. Its constituent elements are so pure that, void of all material weight which would hold them to the earth, they would rise like smoke into the heaven of holy souls, expanding to fill them.... On this sublime plane *sulb* faith ... and *sa'il* faith ... both disappear to make place for one sole thing, the Divine Truth which flourishes in the fields of love and Truth.[37]

Thus we have movement from a fixed and literalistic approach to an expansive approach seeking truths wherever they may be found on the path and finally to realizing the Ultimate Truth.

In light of this analysis, what must one think of the view that questioning the historic truth of Bible stories undermines religious belief? If by 'religious belief' is meant unquestioning assent to what one is told, a sort of parroting back of what one has heard with no real inner development, then we must agree that such questioning undermines religious belief, i.e., childish religious belief.[38] On the other hand, if by religious belief is meant a life chosen by oneself based on repentance and conscious spiritual striving, then questioning the historical truth of Bible stories may well be the first step toward religious belief. It is a strange irony that the literalistic view of how one should read the Bible to get the most out of it is not only not true, but is the very opposite of the truth. But more can be said in answer to the above question, for there is an important matter which cannot be avoided. In a way, turning from the exoteric approach to the Bible does undermine religious belief, but not so as to produce a negative result from the spiritual perspective. It under-mines the 'belief' aspect of religions which, as we have said, is responsible for their particular form. Thus the mature phase involves, in a sense, a breaking out of the confines of a religion while still using it as a base. This indeed is what Cerno Bokar described in the movement from the first to second kind of faith. However, from

37. Louis Brenner, *West African Sufi* (Berkeley: Univ. of California Press, 1984) pp170–172.

38. We must be careful to distinguish between childishness and the childlikeness attributed to many saints.

a wider perspective we can reiterate that religions do contain esoteric ideas in their canonical works, and this is especially true of Genesis and much of Exodus, which are the concerns of this book. So by adopting the esoteric perspective which involves interpreting many passages symbolically, we are not really leaving the sphere of religion.

The importance of not adopting a literalistic approach to the Bible is explained very clearly by both Origen[39] and Maimonides.[40] Much of Maimonides' work, *The Guide of the Perplexed*, deals with the perplexities engendered by a literal reading of the Torah, and his comments center on the description of God and His actions. If we were to take the story of Adam and Eve in a crude historical way, we would have a picture of God as a superhuman being who takes walks around the Garden of Eden. Furthermore, we would have to view Him as a vindictive being, jealous of His prerogatives, who punishes people for learning of the difference between good and evil. It is not surprising that a thoughtful person might either throw up his hands at the whole thing, or at least decide that such a God was not worthy of worship. This last reaction was indeed that of the Gnostics, as Origen mentions. They viewed the God described in Genesis as an inferior being to the Most High God.[41] What Rumi says of reading the Koran is relevant here:

> Ibn Muqri reads the Koran correctly, but he hasn't a clue as to its meaning.... It is said that during the time of the Apostle, the Companions who memorized a chapter or half a chapter of the Koran were deemed extraordinary and were objects of admiration. They did this because they 'devoured' the Koran. Now anyone who can devour a pound or two of bread can be called extraordinary, but a person who just puts bread in his mouth and spits it out without chewing or swallowing can 'devour' thousands of tons. It is about such a one that it is said, 'Many a

39. *On First Principles*, especially bk IV, chaps. 2A and 3.

40. *The Guide of the Perplexed*, tr. Shlomo Pines (Chicago: University of Chicago Press, 1963), especially the Introduction and pt. I, chaps. 2 and 5.

41. That this was a misunderstanding will be shown in chap. 3.

> reader of the Koran is cursed by the Koran,' that is, one who is not aware of the real meaning.[42]

And Meister Eckhart writes of 'the theological, natural and moral truths hidden beneath the form and surface of the literal sense,' claiming:

> No one can be thought to understand the scriptures who does not know how to find its hidden marrow—Christ, the Truth. Hidden under the parables we are speaking of are very many of the properties belonging to God alone, the First Principle, and that point to his nature. Enclosed there are to be found the virtues and the principles of the sciences, the keys to metaphysics, physics and ethics, as well as universal rules.[43]

Finally, no less an authority than St Augustine mentions in his *Confessions* what a change took place in his life when he learned from Bishop Ambrose's sermons that one did not have to take the Bible literally:

> First of all it struck me that it was, after all, possible to vindicate his arguments. I began to believe that the Catholic faith, which I had thought impossible to defend against the Manichees, might fairly be maintained, especially since I had heard one passage after another in the Old Testament figuratively explained. These passages had been death to me when I took them literally, but once I had heard them explained in their spiritual meaning I began to blame myself for my despair, at least in so far as it had led me to suppose that it was quite impossible to counter people who hated and derided the law and the prophets.[44]

42. *Signs of the Unseen: The Discourses of Jalaluddin Rumi*, tr. W.M. Thackston, Jr. (Putney, VT: Threshold Books, 1994), pp85–86.

43. *Meister Eckhart: The Essential Sermons*, p94. The whole discussion is found on pp92–95.

44. *Confessions*, book V, section 14. In book VI, section 5, he adds, '... while all can read it [Scripture] with ease, it also has a deeper meaning in which its great secrets are locked away.'

We do not believe there is a clearer or more cogent statement of how damaging a literalistic reading of the Bible can be.

Origen and Maimonides agree that the Bible itself provides hints that certain of its material is to be interpreted symbolically. In his book, *On First Principles*, Origen mentions 'certain stumbling blocks or interruptions of the narrative meaning' which take the form of 'impossibilities and contradictions'. Maimonides likens the stories of the Torah to articles of gold covered by filigree work of silver. The filigree work has small holes in it which can be seen if examined closely. These holes correspond to the indications in the stories that something deeper and of much greater value is hidden within them. We will discuss some of these indications in subsequent chapters.

Neither Maimonides nor Origen deny that the literal meaning of most of the Bible is valuable. The laws and the morals drawn from many of the stories are beneficial externally for societies and individuals alike. We can go further and say that an appreciation of the literal meaning can lead a person to the point where an appreciation of the symbolic meaning is possible, for there are always two stages in spiritual growth, one preparatory and the other active. But we must agree with both Maimonides and Origen that some of the biblical narratives cannot be swallowed in a literal way without harmful effects. We may choose to put them aside, but that is merely avoiding the issue.

Besides providing hints about what is to be taken symbolically, the Bible explicitly refers to the use of symbolic stories for the purpose of teaching wisdom.[45] And once one has become aware that symbolic interpretations of ancient 'historical' texts are commonplace in other cultures, and that certain items which are prominent in bible stories (e.g., the tree and the snake) were almost universally understood to symbolize specific things in ancient times, one can hardly avoid the conclusion that certain parts of Scripture, though they may strike the modern mind as historical narratives, are to be understood symbolically.

45. Cf. Hos. 12:11, Ezek. 17:2 and 21:5, and Prov. 1:6, all cited by Maimonides.

There are many people who are distrustful of symbolic interpretations except where allegories or parables are clearly identified as such (e.g., in Ezekiel and the Gospels). They usually attempt to explain away the 'impossibilities and contradictions' we mentioned earlier. They believe that anyone who interprets Bible stories symbolically is 'reading something into them' and perverting their intended meaning. In light of what we have already said this distrustful attitude is uncalled for. And we may add that attempts to explain away unpalatable aspects of certain Bible stories have been uniformly unsuccessful. Besides invoking hypotheses for which there is no evidence and twisting the obvious meanings of words, they smack of trying to make the best of a bad situation. Instead of all this twisting and turning it behooves us to look beneath the surface of things. If we do, we will find that everything makes sense.

It is important to stress that the literalism and distrust of symbolic interpretations which we have been examining are completely untraditional, being rather late developments in response to the rise of science with its devastating effect on religious belief.[46] Paradoxically, direct statements of spiritual truths, such as the aforementioned, 'In him we live and move, and have our being' (Acts 17:28) are not taken literally.

Individual Symbols and Allegories

It has been said that to those with understanding everything in creation is a symbol. We would like to put emphasis on the phrase 'to those with understanding'. There are no symbols without minds to comprehend them as such, just as there are no sounds (although there may be sound waves) without senses and souls to perceive them as such. This feature of symbols leads to a problem in

46. Cf. Martin E. Marty's article 'Literalism And Everything Else' in *Bible Review*, April 1994. Those who take the Bible in a literalistic way sometimes claim that while they are just reading what is there, others who do not take the Bible in this way are really interpreting it according to their own views. But the literalists do not seem to realize that they are interpreting the Bible themselves. That is to say, they have decided to take all the stories as history. Viewing sacred stories in this way is an interpretation.

expounding the symbolism of the Bible in the present age. But before we explain this more fully it will be well to make some general comments about symbols.

Put simply, symbols are things which stand for other things. That is to say, they are taken by rational beings as pointing beyond themselves. We can most easily divide symbols into two categories: natural and artificial, though it is hard to know where to place numbers. Examples of the former, which are the most important ones as far as spiritual matters are concerned, are men, women, fathers, mothers, children, siblings, heaven (sky), earth, atmosphere, rain, waters, mountains, caves, hearts, snakes, eggs, the sun and its rays, the moon, the stars, trees, flowers, rocks, meteorites, fire, smoke, sexual union, wine, and drunkenness. The most obvious example of the latter are words and pictures, although anything made by people can fall into this category. For instance, the human institution of marriage, which in a way corresponds to sexual union, has functioned as a very important symbol in Kabbalism. And on the level of artifacts we have rope and the hourglass with its reversal of top and bottom. Among the most important linguistic symbols are names, such as 'Cain' (which stands in most people's minds for fratricide and evil in general) and 'Nineteen Eighty Four' (which stands for an oppressive world situation). The most important pictorial symbols include the dot (which really stands for the dimensionless point), various basic geometrical shapes in both two and three dimensions, the cross, the spiral and the swastika. Numbers such as one, seven, and forty, also function as symbols. All that needs to be added to this account of symbols is that in the spiritual hierarchy, the lower can symbolize the higher but the higher can never symbolize the lower.

Much ink has been spilt on the nature of symbols, complicating the issue more than is necessary. For example Karl Rahner has written a long essay on symbolism titled 'The Theology of the Symbol'.[47] After announcing 'Our task will be to look for the highest and most primordial manner in which *one reality can represent another—*

47. This essay forms chapter 9 of his *Theological Investigations*, vol. IV, tr. Kevin Smyth (London: Darton, Longman & Todd, 1966), pp 221–252.

considering the matter primarily from the formal ontological point of view' (my italics), he goes on to say that there are true symbols and derivative or secondary symbols. The second are arbitrary or conventional, but the first are not. True symbols contain the symbolized. The symbolized reveals and realizes itself in the symbol; it is present in the symbol. If this is an accurate summary of his views (which are similar to our own), then since God is present in all of His creation, everything created can function as a true symbol.

We have been focusing on individual symbols, but alongside of them stand symbolic stories, and these too can be natural or artificial. Besides actual episodes in the lives of individual people and nations we can say that the development of our realm of Existence can be seen as a symbolic story. On the artificial level there are what are usually called allegories and parables, where one group of events is meant to symbolize another group of events. It is clear in these cases that the literal meaning of the story is merely a vehicle for expressing the symbolic meaning, or to put it another way, the original story is just an oblique way of saying something else which can be said directly. H. Flanders Dunbar devoted a whole book, titled *Symbolism In Medieval Thought*, to the subject of symbolism, especially as it related to Dante's *Divine Comedy*. But setting aside her interpretations of Dante's writings, her discussion of symbolism is confusing. She says, 'Fundamentally, as far as there is any agreement among men, it is agreed that a symbol is an expression of meaningful experience.'[48] One hesitates to disagree with this definition, since symbols do not exist *in vacuo*, but it does not get us very far. Dunbar goes on to identify three types of symbols: (1) arbitrary or extrinsic (2) descriptive or intrinsic (3) interpretive or insight. Although the first and second correspond roughly to what I have called artificial and natural, her main point about the second is that there is a similarity to the thing symbolized. But the third type really does not seem commensurate with the other two, and in fact is a symbol used to refer to the indescribable. For instance, she paraphrases Thomas Carlyle as describing the insight symbol as 'the

48. H. Flanders Dunbar, *Symbolism In Medieval Thought*, (New York: Russell & Russell, 1961), p6.

union of silence and speech, infinite and finite,' and quotes Frederick Tisdel as saying

> Symbolism ... concerns itself with just those experiences that seem beyond the reach of drama.... In the symbol proper, what we call a symbol, there is ever, more or less distinctly or directly, some embodiment or revelation of the infinite.[49]

But then she says that the same symbol can function in all three ways. It is difficult to make sense of her own analysis, but she is sound about how scripture and nature were interpreted in the Middle Ages:

> It became clear that every fact or event in the realm of nature or of scriptural record might be considered as conveying truths of four kinds. These were analyzed as the literal ... and three 'symbolic' interpretations called allegorical, tropological, and anagogical, all being of the nature of insight symbolism. The symbolic interpretations called allegorical included truths in relation to humanity as a whole, and here the Christian of course included truths in regard to Christ as the Head of humanity. The interpretation called tropological applied specifically to the moral lesson which might be learned from any event.... The final truth was that of anagoge—ultimate truth, belonging neither to time nor to space, such knowledge as had been dear to the Greeks since the formulation of Plato's absolute ideas.[50]

Both Dante Alighieri and St Thomas Aquinas speak of these four ways of explicating writings. The literal sense need not detain us. As to the moral, Dante interprets this in a broad way as including any principle for living a wiser life. Dante describes the allegorical meaning as 'the one that hides itself under the mantle of these tales, and is a truth hidden under beauteous fiction.'[51] The anagogical sense 'signifies again some portion of the supernal things of external glory.' Sticking to his definitions, allegories would correspond to

49. Ibid., pp8–9.
50. Ibid., p19.
51. *Convivio* (London: J.M. Dent & Sons, 1924), Treatise II, chap. 1.

what we have called symbolic stories. As to the anagogical sense, and keeping in mind what Dunbar said about insight symbolism, we would say that spiritual symbolism need not point to the Ultimate or Supernal Reality, although it will at least have to do with the stumbling blocks and aids to realizing it. Turning to St Thomas Aquinas, we find that he is primarily interested in the different ways of explicating scripture. He contrasts the literal or historical sense with the spiritual sense, and adds that 'this spiritual sense has a threefold division.' In giving an example of these senses he refers to the 'Old Law', the Law of Moses or the Old Testament in general, and the 'New Law' or teachings of the New Testament.

> Therefore, so far as the things of the Old Law signify the things of the New Law, there is the allegorical sense; so far as the things done in Christ, or so far as the things which signify Christ, are types of what we ought to do, there is the moral sense. But so far as they signify what relates to eternal glory, there is the anagogical sense.[52]

We find it significant that St Thomas mentions Hugh of St Victor's division of the senses of scripture into three: the historical, the allegorical, and the tropological, with the anagogical included in the allegorical sense.[53] Peculiarly, Dante himself at the beginning of his work mentions only two modes of exposition, the literal and allegorical, seemingly including all three non-literal interpretations under that one heading.[54] We prefer Hugh of St Victor's method of categorization.

Gershom Scholem, evidently following Goethe in his conceptualizations, expresses the view that there are two sorts of non-literal interpretations of Scripture which he calls symbolization and allegorization:

52. *Summa Theologiae*, ques. 1, art. 10, translated by the Fathers of the English Dominican Province.

53. *De Sacramentis*, IV, 4 Prolog (Medieval Academy of America, 1976).

54. *Convivio*, treatise 1, chap. 1. This twofold division is actually repeated in treatise 2.

> The thing which becomes a symbol retains its original form and its original content. It does not become, so to speak, an empty shell into which another content is poured; in itself, through its own existence, it makes another reality transparent which cannot appear in any other form. If the allegory can be defined as the representation of an expressible something by another expressible something, the mystical symbol is an expressible representation of something which lies beyond the sphere of expression and communication, something which comes from a sphere whose face is, as it were, turned inward and away from us. A hidden and inexpressible reality finds its expression in the symbol.... Where deeper insight into the structure of the allegory uncovers fresh layers of meaning, the symbol is intuitively understood all at once—or not at all.[55]

There is an implication in this analysis that allegorization somehow devalues the events of a story. On the other hand, symbolization would understand the events and characters as paralleling something in a higher realm, and thus they are given even greater value. In this way the 'profane' acquires a sacred aspect and everything in the world is seen as symbolizing something on high.

There is much to be said for such an analysis, but the distinctions on which it is based are not as sharp as Scholem would like us to believe. First of all, symbols are not 'intuitively understood all at once—or not at all' unless one wishes to make this true by definition. And in the second place, the inexpressible is also the subject of much allegorization. Truthfully, one should not divide things into the expressible and the inexpressible, for *something* can be said about all spiritual realities and yet there is a remainder in each case that cannot be expressed. Obviously, the higher one goes in the spiritual hierarchy the less one can say. But there is a distinction Scholem misses which is very important from our viewpoint: the difference between individual symbols and stories. Examples of symbols, as Scholem understands them, inevitably involve individual things.

55. *Major Trends in Jewish Mysticism* (New York: Schocken, 1954), lect. 1, sect. 8, p27.

But there does not appear to be any reason for denying that stories too can function symbolically, for they are especially suited to express spiritual growth and degeneration as well as the process by which the world was manifested.

As to the devaluing (implied by the phrase 'empty shell') of the literal meaning of stories when they are interpreted allegorically, we can make the following points. If we decide that a particular biblical story is only an allegory, we have in a sense devalued the events which make it up and the personages involved. However, if the events never actually occurred, nothing has really been devalued. In the case of the parables of Jesus, it is understood that they were invented and no one worries about their literal sense being devalued. In the case of other narratives in the Bible there is great disagreement over whether they were invented or recount events which actually occurred. It is our view that many of the stories are not historical and hence can be properly called allegories. While it is true that some of these stories may contain a kernel of historical truth and that some of the characters in them may be based on people who really existed, this is not enough to deflect us from taking them as allegories. However, even if we agreed that most of the stories to be analyzed recounted historical events faithfully (a matter on which nobody today can have precise knowledge), our treating them allegorically (which does not entail taking them as mere allegories) would in no way devalue them. We would be admitting that the events actually took place but at the same time holding that their spiritual significance lies in what they symbolize.

There is another sense in which it could be claimed that we are devaluing Scripture and it is important enough to be discussed fully. It might be held that we are embarking on a reductionist policy of equating the stories themselves with what we take to be their symbolic meaning. To this charge we must plead 'not guilty'. As in the case of poems and jokes, explanations of biblical stories do not constitute the whole of the original article. After all the interpretations are given there is still something left over which cannot be put into words and which, in a sense, strikes the reader directly. We might call it the power of the story, and it would make little sense for us to deny what is so obviously a reality. Besides, it would be equally foolish to deny, what is also obvious, that the stories function on different levels and thus have meanings which are untouched by our symbolic interpretations.

Now that we have analyzed the nature of symbols we can turn to the problem we mentioned at the beginning of the section. For something to *function* as a symbol (rather than as a mere metaphor or part of a comparison) it must be understood as representing the same or similar things by a group of people. And here is where we run into trouble in analyzing the symbols of the Bible. What was a symbol to people in a different locality at a much earlier time in history may not be a symbol to us today. Or if something still functions as a symbol today it may indicate something entirely different. An example of the former case is 'elder brother'. This has no symbolic function in the West today, but it functioned as a symbol in Israel 3000 years ago. An example of the latter case is 'snake' or 'serpent'. At present in the West a snake is a symbol of temptation, sliminess, and evil, or at best a 'phallic symbol'. But for the ancients it was an ambivalent object, a symbol (among other things) of the earthly, the feminine, healing, prudence, life, immortality, creative energy, death, destruction, and evil.[56]

Here we must pause and say a little more on the nature of symbols, because it seems to us that a basic misunderstanding exists over the matter of 'true symbols'. These supposedly exist independently of their recognition as symbols. For instance, Isaiah Tishby has written:

> There exists a permanent integral relationship between the symbol and the thing symbolized, for a symbol has its symbolic character impressed upon it from the very beginning of its existence.[57]

Such a view is usually combined with the claim that symbols are universal. In contrast there is the statement of Wilfred Cantwell Smith:

56. Although this list may seem to be a *mélange* of disparate elements, many of them are related, as we will go some way toward showing in chapter 5.

57. I. Tishby, *The Wisdom of the Zohar* (Oxford: Oxford Univ. Press, 1991), vol. 1, p285.

> To live religiously is not merely to live in the presence of certain symbols, but to be involved with them or through them in a quite special way—a way that may lead far beyond the symbols, that may demand the totality of a person's response, and may effect one's relation not only to them but to everything else: to oneself, to one's neighbor, and to the stars.[58]

He adds that it is people's 'involvement' with the 'overt data of religious life' contained in a tradition 'that bestows on the data their religious significance, as well as bestowing on the persons their changed lives.'[59]

Pursuing Smith's theme, first, it is highly improbable that there are any universal symbols at this time. Some few are very widespread, but that is not the same thing, and the emphasis is on 'few'. And second, there is no point to saying symbols spring fully-formed from God's mind, as it were, and exist as such in perpetuity. If there is no one to hear a sound caused by the vibration of the air, then no sound is made, no matter how violent the vibration. Similarly, if there is no one to recognize a symbol as such, then nothing is functioning as a symbol, no matter how obvious it may be (e.g., the sun in the sky). Only in the practice of a particular tradition will something carry a person's consciousness from the mundane to the Divine, from the sensible to the supra-sensible or intelligible. It is true, that certain natural objects or scenes may have an effect of exaltation on just about anyone anywhere, but the effect will be diffuse and non-specific. Things are symbols only within a particular spiritual tradition, and can eventually cease to be symbols in that tradition.

Jacques Ellul discusses what he calls 'the process of the obsolescence of symbols.' He mentions that,

> our symbols which have been consecrated by long tradition no longer symbolize anything. They are outdated and fail to convey meaning. The symbol of the water of baptism or the wine of Holy

58. Wilfred Cantwell Smith, *Faith and Belief* (Oxford: Oneworld Publications Ltd., 1998) p3.

59. Ibid., pp3–4.

> Communion is as void for contemporary man as the phoenix or the grail.[60]

But he recognizes that old symbols can take on new meanings, and gives the example of the swastika, saying,

> it has become a symbol once again for modern man, but with a meaning entirely different from the meaning it had three thousand years ago.[61]

To quote Smith again, this time on Islam:

> As with other religious traditions, given symbols have in fact meant different things to different people. Interpretations have varied, from person to person, from century to century, from village to city. Islamic religious symbolism being preeminently verbal, the observer must simply record that the words have had different meanings for various members of the community.[62]

In our study of biblical symbolism we will have to leave people's present-day understanding and immerse ourselves in the ancient and traditional understanding of symbols.

By way of fleshing out what we mean by the traditional understanding of symbols we offer the following indications, very general in nature. Brothers (as well as any set of siblings) represent different components of a person or different tendencies within a person, the latter being related to the former. A whole people often symbolizes a person, and particular individuals within it symbolize components of a person, as well as related tendencies. A physical journey signifies a spiritual journey. Finally, a judgment or punishment of God

60. See following note.

61. The Ellul quotations are from *The New Demons* (New York: The Seabury Press, 1973), pp68–69. The swastika was a traditional polar (not solar) symbol of the circulation of the earthly plane of Existence or of the cosmos as a whole around the World Axis with its two poles (of which more later on). But with this meaning forgotten it was appropriated by an evil group and thus become a symbol of evil. On the traditional meaning of the swastika cf. René Guénon, *The Great Triad* (Hillsdale, NY: Sophia Perennis, 2004), chap. 5.

62. *The Meaning and End of Religion*, p109.

represents the natural result of some human action, and sometimes just the natural progression of events.

One Source and Many Sources

It is sometimes argued that we must believe in the historical truth of the stories of Genesis and Exodus because the whole Torah, or first five books of the Bible, was spoken by God to Moses. The conclusion is a *non sequitur*, but mentioning this argument provides us with a chance to speak about its premise. One of the quirks of contemporary life is that while scientists are learning more and more about the universe, laymen are falling into deeper and deeper ignorance. The gulf as far as knowledge is concerned is widening year by year. While this is generally admitted, very few would think it applied to knowledge about the Bible, yet the gulf in this area is also widening every year. In the last 150 years scholars have found out many important and enlightening facts about the Bible. But unfortunately, very little news of these discoveries has filtered down to laymen. Ignorance of these facts is due mainly to clergymen keeping these discoveries to themselves or choosing to ignore them completely.

It is agreed by most, though not all, Bible scholars that the Torah is a man-made compendium of different sources commonly referred to by the letters J, E, D, and P, standing for Yahwist (Jehovist), Elohist, Deuteronomist, and Priestly, respectively. These were committed to writing roughly around 850, 750, 625, and 550 BC. Thus at the beginning of Genesis we find two creation stories (1:1–2:4A, and 2:4B–25) which contradict each other in some particulars. The first is from the Priestly source and the second from the Yahwist source. Similar contradictions can be found in the Noah and Joseph stories, and duplicate passages can be found in many stories.[63]

Ignoring these findings of Bible scholars has resulted in more of the twisting and turning mentioned earlier. Even some of those who

63. In a footnote to 'The Forbidden Fruit' in *Islam and the Perennial Philosophy*, p196, Frithjof Schuon writes, 'It is not true that the Bible contains divergent "strata", the one "Elohist", and the other "Jehovist"; there is simply a diversity of viewpoint,

know of these findings and do not ignore them have adopted preposterous explanations of the aforementioned contradictions and duplications, e.g., that the authors of the Bible introduced deliberate ambiguities into the text.[64] For some reason they have overlooked the obvious explanation that the variants of Bible stories came from earlier oral traditions all of which were considered sacred by the ancient redactors.[65]

Scholars have also shown that some of the early stories of the Bible are patterned after those of other cultures. Among them are the Adam and Eve story, the flood story, the Joseph and Potiphar's wife story, and the baby Moses in the reeds story. None of these discoveries lessens the value of the Torah, for the important thing is the underlying meaning of these stories and not their historical truth.

We must not make the mistake of underestimating the authors of the narratives found in Genesis and Exodus, and assume that they were naively relating stories they took to be historical. They had many purposes in mind and these narratives function on many levels. One purpose was etiological—to explain the origins of things, be they tribes, practices, items of nature, or the general difficulty of living. Another purpose, connected with the first, was to explain the positions of the various tribes of Israel with respect to each other and the non-Israelite peoples around them. Still another purpose was to promote belief in the One God of creation (monotheism)

---

as in all sacred Scripture.' In answer, it must be pointed out that his positive statement does not support his negative statement. However, if his basic contention is that the so-called 'strata' are not in any way opposed to one another when it comes to essential truths, but rather complementary, we can certainly agree with him.

64. Cf. Edmund Leach's 'Genesis As Myth' in *Myth and Cosmos*, ed. by John Middleton (Garden City, NY: The Natural History Press, 1967); 'Nobody Lives in the Real World' (*Psychology Today*, July 1974); and 'Anthropological Approaches to the Study of the Bible During the Twentieth Century', in *Structuralist Interpretations of Biblical Myth* (Cambridge: Cambridge Univ. Press, 1983). A complete analysis of the correct and incorrect aspects of Leach's general theory and particular applications would require a whole chapter and would be out of place in this book.

65. That the existence of variants of Bible stories points to underlying oral traditions is explained very clearly by the folklorist Alan Dundes in his book *Holy Writ as Oral Lit* (Lanham, MD: Rowman & Littlefield, Inc., 1999).

responsible for every single aspect of the created world as well as belief in the way of life He ordained. And finally, another was to teach certain spiritual truths in a symbolic manner and thus offer a set of directions for the inner journey to God for those with deep enough insight to interpret the symbols.

At any rate, while the whole Torah was not spoken by God to Moses, being instead the result of input from different sources, it was nevertheless inspired by the one ultimate source: God.

One Story and Many Stories

Reading through Genesis and Exodus one often gets the impression that the same story is being told over and over in different ways using different characters. We are not here referring to the duplications mentioned in the previous section. Nor are we referring to episodes which repeat certain motifs, e.g., episodes involving Sarah and Abraham (twice) and Isaac and Rebecca which record the 'she is my sister' motif (Gen. 12, 20, and 26). It is more a matter of certain stories having echoes in other stories. The rivalry between Abel and Cain is echoed by that between Jacob and Esau. Noah's getting drunk after the flood is similar to Lot's getting drunk after the destruction of Sodom and Gomorrah. Abraham's preparing Isaac to die is not all that different from Hagar's leaving Ishmael to die, and God intervenes in both cases. There are parallel captivity stories concerning Joseph. Noah's surviving the flood is echoed by Moses surviving his voyage on the Nile. There are numerous stories of the Israelites backsliding in the wilderness, and also of God providing the Israelites with sustenance. The crossing between walls of water at the Red Sea is echoed by a similar event at the Jordan River (reported in Joshua 3). Finally, Moses' staff provides victories over Pharaoh's magicians and the Amalekites, and both Pharaoh's forces and the Amalekites are completely wiped out.

That themes are repeated in these stories should not be surprising if they are symbolic of spiritual truths as well as those of traditional cosmology. There are in fact two basic triads to be considered. On the world level we have: creation-degeneration-recreation. On the individual level we have: birth-fall-rebirth. The fallen state may be symbolized by captivity or enslavement. Rebirth may be symbolized by passing between walls of water. Along the way there will be various symbols of what must be overcome for spiritual progress, and symbols of the aids to such progress.

Literalism and the Modern Mentality

The mentality which says we must take everything in the Bible as the literal truth and the mentality which says the Bible is a collection of falsehoods ('fairy tales') are two sides of the same coin. We are speaking of that more and more worthless coin: the modern mentality. The authors of the Bible would scarcely know what to make of the current controversy. Both sides show that they have very little idea of what the Bible is about.

We may describe the modern mentality as a factualist mentality. Our obsession with 'objective facts' is worthless for two reasons. One is that we are not passive in observing creation; we mold the world as much as we perceive it. The second is that even when we turn to scientific instruments to tell us 'how the world really is', we run into problems; on the subatomic level we find the observer disturbs the observed in observing it. Thus the realm of facts is one of relative truths. Anything that has to do with temporality and plurality is relative, and this includes morality as well as modern-day science. This last statement should not be misunderstood. Relative truths are truths having to do with the relative, or as Buddhists would say, the conditioned realm. Given the dualistic way we view a reality that is essentially non-dualistic, certain claims are objectively true and others are objectively false, and this goes for the sphere of morality as with anything else. According to what is usually termed natural law theory, humans are such, and the world is such, that in order to attain what they value (i.e., to thrive or flourish), humans must act in certain ways rather than others. Humans value living in groups both because they are social animals and they can live better, more secure, lives in groups. But in order for such groups to exist, humans must refrain from lying, stealing, and murdering. This notion of morality as objective was put forward by Plato in his *Republic* where he explained that a just or righteous society functions excellently while an unjust society tears itself apart. Nevertheless, there is another way of viewing reality which transcends moral strictures. The great Buddhist teacher Padmasambhava summed up the relation between holding the true view of reality and acting virtuously in the following way: 'So descend with the view while ascending with the conduct. It is most essential to practice these two as a unity.'[66] While relative truths should not be treated as absolute,[67] if we have no care even for relative truths, we can hardly be expected to care for absolute truth, and in the case of morality we must reiterate that it is a preliminary for spiritual growth.

Northrop Frye, in *The Great Code*,[68] writes that the primary meaning of the Bible is the literal meaning. But by 'literal meaning' he understands the metaphorical sense of the sentences. He is really getting at the same point we are trying to make in a different way. He is saying that for the ancients, the most straightforward way of understanding the Scriptures was metaphorically. Frye is actually echoing St Augustine's understanding of 'literal', as in his work *The Literal Meaning of Genesis*. St Augustine seems to have in mind the first or primary meaning.[69] There is certainly no reason to equate 'literal' with 'physically descriptive'; this just happens to be part and parcel of the modern turn of mind. We tend to view the ancient writings as expressing the same sort of observation statements with which we are obsessed.[70] This is analogous to dragging a beautiful

66. *Dakini Teachings*, tr. By Erik Pema Kunsang (Kathmandu: Ranjung Yeshe Publications, 1999), p9.

67. Maimonides' reference (in *The Guide of the Perplexed*, pt. III, chap. 51, p619) to the *ignoramuses who observe the commandments* was, it hardly needs saying, not an indictment of following the Mosaic Law. Rather, it was an indictment of those who would treat the Law as the beginning and end of the spiritual life.

68. New York: Harcourt, Brace, Jovanovich, 1982, chap. 3, especially pp59–62. Although writing from a secular or profane point of view, the author at least recognizes a few truths that escape the many who are trapped in the modern mentality, and his book contains some interesting insights into the Bible.

69. St. Augustine, *The Literal Meaning of Genesis*, tr. By John Hammond Taylor, S.J. (New York: Newman Press, 1982). The interpretations which he gives are most often not literal in the sense we mean today.

70. Thus we mistakenly take ancient myths as indicating only the worship of parts and forces of nature. While on this subject we might say that although there is

jewel through the mud. Then, depending on which side we are on, we either praise the mud-caked jewel as beautiful (which is ludicrous) or point out its ugliness (which is beside the point). We are speaking of the mud of modern understanding which is peculiarly anti-spiritual.

From what has just been said we can understand that the higher truths found in the Bible are not hidden in symbols. Thus, all who would invent reasons for their being hidden are engaged in useless activity. That they appear hidden only shows the blindness and ignorance of present-day humanity. And that the literalistic interpretation of the Bible is taken as the most obvious or natural shows the very same thing.

The emphasis on the literalistic interpretation of the Bible is not due solely to ignorance. There is a less 'innocent' reason which plays a great role. By claiming that all of the Bible stories are literally true, i.e., historically true, Jews and Christians are distancing themselves from and elevating themselves above the pagans and heathens. 'Their stories are just stories, but our stories are really true!' Some biblical interpreters are conscious of such thoughts, but others are only dimly aware of them. This pretense about literal truth is an understandable outcome of the idea of one true religion. But what made Judaism and Christianity preferable to paganism was not the falsity of paganism but its degeneracy. The denial of this view implies that God had abandoned the world until the advent of Judaism.

The use of symbols to express the highest truths is what the Buddhists call an *upaya*, an expedient means. For one thing, it is difficult to state truths about the suprasensible. One most naturally turns to language that refers to the sensible, and besides, language itself has this bias. Second, using symbols is the best way of preserving the highest truths for the greatest number of people. Symbolic stories will be passed down from generation to generation regardless of whether or not they are understood, even if only in books few read or take seriously. Third, non-linguistic symbols tend to be more suggestive than language. This suits them especially for the

---

a nature symbolism to many of the ancient myths, there is also a deeper stratum of symbolism which modern interpreters fail to see.

expression of the highest truths since the latter can never really be stated precisely, being beyond the distinctions on which language is based. Fourth, and connected with the last, symbols are a help or aid in bringing the understanding along more quickly and permanently than would otherwise be possible. This is especially true when one is dealing with a general audience rather than a select few who have developed enough to understand the highest truths in a more straightforward manner, although even with the latter, symbols are a help. As Ananda Coomaraswamy puts it,

> It is evident that symbols and concepts . . . can serve no purpose for those who have not yet, in the Platonic sense, 'forgotten'. . . . The need of symbols, and of symbolic rites, arises only when man is expelled from the Garden of Eden; as a means by which a man can be reminded at later stages of his descent from the intellectual and contemplative to the physical and practical levels of reference. We assuredly have 'forgotten' far more than those who first had need of symbols, and far more than they need to infer the immortal by its mortal analogies; and nothing could be greater proof of this than our own claims to be superior to all ritual operations, and to be able to approach the truth directly.'[71]

Finally, nature, from which most symbols are drawn, is an expression of the reality of God. We can say that the whole universe is a theophany or Divine revelation. Should not the plan of nature be such as to suggest our true relationship to God and other metaphysical truths? The most widely acknowledged symbols, which we have already enumerated, are all natural and thus derive from God. In this way, nature becomes a symbol of the supernatural.

As to the hermeneutical principle of this book, it is our view that the same primordial truths, the highest of which are called 'metaphysical' in the West, have been expressed variously in different times and places. Thus, the expression of them in Genesis and Exodus is only one case among many, and it is of help in understanding the narratives in these books to consider those in other venerated

71. 'Symbols', in *What is Civilization?* (Great Barrington, MA: Lindisfarne Press, 1989), pp126–27.

texts. With the tenets of esoterism in mind, we will not be trying to fit the biblical tradition into a doctrinal Procrustean bed, but rather indicating basic metaphysical and cosmological doctrines as they appear within the Scriptures. Our interpretations will never contradict or go against the palpable meaning of any Bible passages. And far from 'reading things into them', we will be in Coomaraswamy's phrase, 'reading *in* them' what they truly contain.[72] Or to use a phrase of the educator Harry Broudy, we will be 'reading with them', that is, coming to them *with* a background understanding of basic metaphysical truths. And we must add that our interpretations will not always be symbolic but sometimes involve noting things presented in a very direct way which are not seen for what they are by the typical reader of today.

72. 'The Interpretation of Symbols', in *What is Civilization?*, p130. Coomaraswamy goes on to say: 'When meanings, which are also *raisons d'être*, have been forgotten, it is indispensable that those who can remember them, and can demonstrate by reference to chapter and verse the validity of their "memory", should re-read meanings into forms from which the meaning has been ignorantly "read out", whether recently or long ago.' (p133)

2

The Meaning of Early Biblical History

We will begin our study of the narratives which take us from Adam to Moses by noting a certain cosmological doctrine which, far from being expounded in symbolic fashion, is presented by the Bible in a rather straightforward manner. This doctrine escapes most readers of the Judeo-Christian tradition because of their linear view of history, a view which is taken for granted in the West. It is rather with what has been called the 'cyclical' view of history that we will be dealing.

Perhaps the fullest exposition of the cyclical view is given in Hindu doctrine. We find there first a doctrine of successive ages called the *Krita* (or *Satya*)-*Yuga*, *Treta-Yuga*, *Dvapara-Yuga*, and *Kali-Yuga*. In Greek mythology these are termed the Golden Age, Silver Age, Bronze Age, and Iron Age. Although we have not found such a complete theory of ages among their writings, there is little doubt that the Sumerians had one as well. And we also find in Taoist and Ch'an Buddhist writings many references to earlier ages when the level of humanity was higher. As hinted by this last comment these ages represent a degeneration of creation, a progression from order to disorder, a tendency toward chaos.[1] The Golden Age is paradisiacal compared to the others, but even it tends to degenerate toward its close. The Iron Age might be called the dark age in comparison to the rest. If the first age is paradisiacal, the last, which is our own, is hellish.

1. If we were to try to fasten on a modern analogy, it would be the increase in entropy in the universe. In the present age, human life itself seems to be heading in

According to the second part of the doctrine there is a general destruction or *pralaya* in the form of a deluge at the end of a complete cycle of ages, which is sometimes connected with a particular astrological alignment. This sets the stage for a new cycle beginning with a new Golden Age, like the turning of an hourglass. There may also be limited deluges in the course of a cycle. The story of Atlantis may well refer to one of these limited deluges. It is unfortunate that many people take the symbolic story of Atlantis as if it were history. This has led the to search the ancient world for some catastrophe corresponding to the story. They will never find Atlantis, for it is a symbol of the progressive degeneration in our cycle of ages.

In Hinduism, each cycle is called a *manvantara* or *mahayuga*, and fourteen of these (seven descending and seven ascending) are said to make up a *kalpa*.[2] For our purposes it is not necessary to go beyond this point in the Hindu doctrine. We will say only that within each cycle the ages last for a shorter and shorter time in the ratio 4–3–2–1, and this shortening is also reflected in the lives of humans within the ages.[3]

In the Hindu tradition each cycle is ruled by a Manu who functions as King of the World. There is a primordial Manu (the Adi-Manu) who rules for the whole *kalpa*, and fourteen subsidiary Manus, one for each *manvantara*, the present one being designated

the direction of more simple lower animals. One need only recall Dostoevsky's comment, in 'The Grand Inquisitor' chapter of *The Brothers Karamazov*, that most humans yearn to form 'a common, concordant, and incontestable anthill' (from the Richard Pevear and Larissa Volokhonsky translation [New York: Vintage Classics, 1991] p257). Those who condemn even the weak nationalism which holds that each nation has a particular identity different from others, and wish to bring the nations together under one world government, are promoting this sort of outcome. Oddly, many of these same people claim to be worried about cultural diversity being eliminated in the current world situation, and wish to limit the products of one culture that can be exported to another.

2. One is reminded of the wheels within wheels of Ezekiel's vision (Ezek. 10:10).

3. On the shrinking of human ages and other related matters, cf. René Guénon, *The Reign of Quantity and the Signs of the Times* (Hillsdale, NY: Sophia Perennis, 2001), chap. 5. St Augustine, in *The City of God* (New York: Penguin Books, 1972), bk xv, chaps. 12 and 14, shows conclusively that the years mentioned early in the Bible had to be of the 365–day variety rather than a much shorter period.

as Manu Vaivasvata. This Manu is the Prototype of man and functions as 'the primordial and universal legislator' and is thus equivalent to the Greek Minos. He combines priestly and royal functions and brings peace and justice to the world. However, it must be quickly said that Manu Vaivasvata should not be viewed as an actual person but as the personification of Divine influence at the beginning of the manvantara.[4]

Current opinion, popularized by writers like Thomas Cahill, holds that the Bible represents a break with the cyclical view of the world, presenting us rather with a linear view of history. Indeed, Cahill believes that the biblical writers invented history. He says of them, 'we should not doubt that their intention was to write a chronicle of real events, essentially faithful to their sources.'[5] However well-intentioned, Cahill is somewhat confused about the cyclical view of history, equating it with something like Nietzsche's idea of eternal recurrence.[6] Furthermore, he seems to have discounted the various

4. On all of this see René Guénon, *The King of the World* (Hillsdale: Sophia Perennis, 2001), especially chap. 2, and 'Some Remarks on the Doctrine of Cosmic Cycles', in *Traditional Forms and Cosmic Cycles* (Hillsdale: Sophia Perennis, 2003). The only problem (if we can term it such) with the latter work is Guénon's basing the length of the present *manvantara* on the reign of the Sumerian king Ziusudra (Xisuthros) whom he equates with Manu Vaivasvata. Ziusudra, in Berossus' account of the Babylonian flood narrative, is the equivalent of Utnapishtim in the *Epic of Gilgamesh* and thus the man who survived the flood. Now Guénon sets his reign at 64,800 years, a figure on which he bases the length of our *manvantara*. However, Berossus and a second source give his reign as 36,000 years. On the other hand, Berossus gives 64,800 years as the reign of another Ante-Diluvian king named Enmalgalanna. Further, the Sumerian King List begins with the following: 'When the kingship was lowered from heaven the Kingship was in Eridu. [In] Eridu A-lulim [became] King and reigned 28,800 years; Alalbar reigned 36,000 years, 2 kings reigned its 64,800 years.' (Thorkeld Jacobsen, *The Sumerian King List* [Chicago: Univ. of Chicago Press, 1939], p71. See also p76 fn. 34.)

5. *The Gifts of the Jews* (New York: Doubleday, 1998), p129. In his book *Abraham* (New York: William Morrow, 2002), p60, Bruce Feiler is much nearer the truth when he states: 'The Bible would fail as history; it disappoints as reportage. But this may be exactly why it succeeds as narrative—and scripture.'

6. René Guénon warns against this idea, stating that it implies 'the existence of a repetition that is impossible and clearly contrary to the true traditional notion of cycles, according to which there is only correspondence and not identity' (*Traditional Forms and Cosmic Cycles*, p9). Perhaps influenced by Seneca, St Augustine

purposes of the biblical writers which we mentioned in chapter 1. And as scholars throw doubt on the historicity of more and more of the Bible, it becomes harder to take Cahill's pronouncement seriously. As I will show presently, reading the Bible from end to end gives us just the kind of cyclical picture that Cahill believes has been superseded. With this in mind, let us turn to some comparisons in order to make our point.

Of particular interest to us are the correspondences between Manu Vaivasvata and Adam, Noah and Moses. Like Manu, Adam is pictured as ruler of the world and as the Prototype of man. Besides this, both Adam and Manu had their wives produced from their ribs. The most obvious correspondence is between Manu[7] and Noah, since both are warned of a flood which they survive. Manu's connection with Moses might at first seem more tenuous since the latter is not presented as the Primal or First Man. But Moses functions as legislator, and, while the royal and priestly functions are split between him and Aaron, we must keep in mind that Aaron is his brother and functions as his alter-ego. And it was Moses to whom God appeared in the theophanies of the bush and mountain. We must also take into consideration that just as Noah escaped drowning in the ark, Moses escaped drowning in the basket which floated on the Nile, and the same Hebrew word, *tebah*, is used for both ark and basket. Further, we must not forget the drowning of the Egyptians after the Israelites had crossed through the Red Sea. While none of these matches are exact, they are close enough to be significant, and would seem to indicate a primordial spiritual tradition showing itself in different guises in different places.

---

takes the cyclic view of history to mean that everything will be 'repeated, in the same form' (*The City of God*, bk XII, chap. 14) and that 'the same events happen repeatedly' (chap. 18). This makes it easier for him to poke fun at the cyclical view, but he is only knocking down a 'straw man'. Certainly, Plato (*Timaeus* 22 and *Laws* 677), in discussing the various periodic destructions, never suggests such a thing, nor do most ancient sources.

7. In his role as survivor of the flood Manu's name is Satyavrata. For more on the story see René Guénon's article 'Some Aspects of the Symbolism of the Fish' in *Symbols of the Sacred Science* (Hillsdale, NY: Sophia Perennis, 2004), chap. 22.

Not only are there parallels between Manu and biblical personages, but also between the doctrine of ages and early biblical history. The state before the separation of Eve from Adam (Genesis 2:4B–17) represents a condition beyond or prior to any age. It is deathless because it is beyond time. Even after the separation (2:21–23), people live in a state which is beyond distinctions such as good and evil, a more perfect state than one in which people feel constrained by moral rules. They do good naturally and not out of feelings of obligation. They act from spirituality rather than morality. Food is readily available in the form or fruit and seeds, and in general there is no struggle to maintain life. But then comes the fall (3:1–7) when Eve and Adam eat of the Tree of Knowledge of Good and Evil, of duality, and the 'death sentence' is pronounced while they are still in the Garden of Eden (3:17). Nevertheless, we learn that Adam lived 930 years (5:3).

The fall of Adam and Eve can be said to usher in the first true age—the Adamic or Ante-Diluvian Age. It would include their being cast out of the Garden of Eden (3:23) and end with the flood. Alternatively, the Adamic age could be seen as beginning with the casting out, and ending with the flood. But this may be one of those cases of a distinction without a difference.[8] Even in this age certain conditions continue. Everyone speaks one tongue, lives without laws, and is capable of a direct relationship with God. People keep flocks, but it is not clear that they eat meat. They live for many hundreds of years, and though they have to till the soil and raise animals to survive, we are given a picture of unity with God and with each other.[9] But there are also indications of a progressive degeneration, such as the murdering of Abel by Cain. And by the time of Lamech, several generations after Adam, life has become very tough indeed. 'When

8. There are several plausible ways of dividing the early biblical narratives into ages, and the present one differs from that of the first edition of *Adam and Eve* by following more closely the pattern of destructions.

9. Likewise, Plato, in several places (*Statesman* 271–2, *Laws* 713), describes the Age of Cronos, the Golden Age, as one where God ruled the earth through demigods, i.e., had a much closer relationship to humans. Plato describes this age as one of leisure where obtaining food is concerned, but otherwise it is comparable to the Golden Age of the Bible. It is followed by the Age of Zeus, god of law and justice.

Lamech has lived 182 years, he begot a son. And he named him Noah, saying, "This one will provide us relief from our work and from the toil of our hands, out of the very soil which the Lord placed under a curse"' (Gen. 5:28–29). Finally, 'The Lord saw how great was man's wickedness on earth, and how every plan devised by his mind was nothing but evil all the time.' (6:5). He decided to blot out all the men and beasts He had created, and hence the flood. It is immaterial whether we are to view this as the end of a whole cycle or just the end of the Ante-Diluvian Age, for it is not our contention that an exact copy of the Hindu system is to be found in Genesis.

The flood ushers in the Post-Diluvian or Noahide Age in which people live only about half as long as previously (e.g., Abraham lives to only 175 years, as Genesis 25:7 relates), eat other creatures (thus introducing a new relationship between humans and beasts, and perhaps between beasts themselves) and are given some few laws to live by (9:1–5). The direct relationship with God has been shattered, but a connection between the heavenly and earthly realms is established by a covenant whose sign is the rainbow (9:8-17). The planting of the vine by Noah (9:20) is another indication of a connection between God and man (wine symbolizing Divine blessing or influence), but not as direct a connection as before.

Unfortunately, the regenerated human race degenerates once more and people say to each other, 'Come, let us build us a city, and a tower with its top in the sky, to make a name for ourselves; else we shall be scattered all over the world' (11:4). The end result of this, and the hallmark of the Noahide Age is the appearance of many languages. Here again we see the movement from unity to disunity, order to disorder. The degeneration continues and we meet with the first report of idolatry (11:31). The Noahide Age culminates with destruction of the wicked people of Sodom and Gomorrah (19:24-28), which is just the flood story on a small scale, complete with its one surviving family.[10] Thus begins the Abrahamic Age.

10. It is interesting to note in connection with this last remark that just as Noah gets drunk after the flood (Gen. 9:21), Lot gets drunk after the destruction of Sodom and Gomorrah (19:33). Furthermore, the results are somewhat similar. We will have more to say about this in chapters 7 and 8.

The new age includes the slavery of the Hebrew people in Egypt. Here too we meet with a picture of the depravity of the human race, especially in Pharaoh's call for the murder of every newly born male Hebrew child (Exod. 1:15–16). This is followed by a partial destruction, viz. the various plagues and the drowning in the Red Sea (Exod. 7–15), and the ushering in of the Mosaic Age. The Mosaic Age, by virtue of the great number of laws deemed necessary, should be understood as lower or worse than the others. It is in this age that God's decision to limit people's lives to 120 years (mentioned in Genesis 6:3) seems to take hold.[11] Although the advent of Moses brings with it a regeneration, the Israelites are pictured as backsliding almost from the moment of the Exodus. In any case, the beginning of the Mosaic Age should be seen as paralleling the beginning of the Noahide Age, the basket of Moses on the Nile being a miniature of the ark of Noah on the flood-waters.[12]

We are not claiming that the ages we have identified in the Bible correspond exactly to the Golden, Silver, Bronze, and Iron Ages. But it is clear that underlying the biblical narratives is a plan according to which the generation of the world is followed by a degeneration, and then successive eras of regeneration and degeneration which are pictured in a multitude of different ways. In each case, there is a saved remnant, an idea which becomes more pronounced in later Judaism, especially among the Essenes. Although members of the Judeo-Christian tradition tend to view history as having one beginning and end, certain of their beliefs run counter to this notion. As the Essenes did, most religious Jews and Christians believe in a Judgment Day with a great destruction which will be followed by God's rule on a renewed earth. Thus we have Revelation 20–22, and also many prophetic passages such as Isaiah 13:9 which refer to the 'Day of Yahweh'. That day will bring destruction and darkness, but it will be followed by a great renewal such as that mentioned in Isaiah

11. That Job is said to live for 140 years (Job 42:16) is not inconsistent with this, for Job is understood to have lived in pre-patriarchal times (cf. Ezek. 14:14).

12. For the Kabbalistic interpretation of the doctrine of cycles see the 'Doctrine of Shemittot' in Gershom Scholem's article 'Kabbalah' in the *Encyclopaedia Judaica* (Jerusalem: Keter, 1972), vol. 10, pp579–583.

61–62. And in Isaiah 65 we find the most famous passage describing that renewal.[13] It begins:

> For behold! I am creating
> A new heaven and a new earth;
> The former things shall not be remembered,
> They shall never come to mind.
> Be glad then and rejoice forever
> In what I am creating. (65:17–18)

And it ends:

> The wolf and the lamb shall graze together,
> And the lion shall eat straw like the ox,
> And the serpent's food shall be earth.
> In all My Sacred mount
> Nothing evil or vile shall be done. (65:25)

People will have to work for their food (65:21), and there will be death (65:20), but they will seem young at a hundred years and live as long as trees (65:22). This period can easily be viewed as a new Golden Age.[14]

In fact the book of Daniel, which is admittedly late, contains a full-blown doctrine of ages. Daniel, while interpreting a dream of King Nebuchadnezzer, details four kingdoms which rule the whole earth in succession—of gold, of silver (implied), of bronze, and of iron (Daniel 2:36–40). He states further:

13. For a full discussion of all the 'Day of Yahweh' passages cf. *The Day of Yahweh and Some Relevant Problems* by Ladislav Cerny (Prague: Karlovy University, 1948).

14. Should it be surprising that the pseudo-religion of communism contains a similar view? According to communist theory, early humans lived in classless societies and thus were examples of primitive communism. Somehow or other the people of these societies became 'differentiated into separate and finally antagonistic classes.' But in the end, after a bloody revolution, communism will be restored in the world, bringing about a paradisiacal age. In effect, both the Bible and Marxist writings speak of a great battle before the installation of a new Golden Age. But whereas the Bible states the battle will take place in heaven as well as on earth, according to Marxism the battle will take place only on earth. (Cf. Karl Marx and Frederick Engels, *Selected Works* [Moscow, 1958] 1, p34 [p109 in the 1969–70 edition] on primitive communism.)

> And in the time of those kings, the God of heaven will establish a kingdom that shall never be destroyed, a kingdom that shall not be transferred to another people. It will crush and wipe out all these kingdoms, but shall itself last forever—just as you saw how a stone was hewn from the mountain, not by hands, and crushed the iron, bronze, clay, silver, and gold. (2:44–45)

It is true that the passages we have mentioned seem to point to a never-ending Golden Age to come, yet there is both an implied and an explicitly stated doctrine of ages in the Bible, and this would point to a cyclical view of history.

The history of the human race presented in the narrative from the beginning of Genesis to the time of Moses reads like a description of a child growing into adulthood. We begin with orders and punishments and end with a group of laws. There is certainly a symbolism in the notion of childhood, most especially in that it represents primordial purity and innocence. And just as a child can be said to degenerate into an adult (or in Kant's words, a beautiful butterfly turns into an ugly worm), civilization degenerates down through the ages. Again, in youth we have no cares and time seems to move slowly. As we age our cares multiply and the days seem to slip by unnoticed. Should we conclude that the cycle of ages is no more than the human life cycle writ large?[15] There is a parallel here, but it only shows the analogies between all levels of Existence—the great and the small, the life cycle of the world and that of a human being. Besides, we are, after all, microcosms or little worlds, a matter that will be discussed in chapter 4. But there is a much deeper

15. See Arthur Herman, *The Idea of Decline in Western History* (New York: The Free Press, 1997), chap. 1. Besides those who have suggested that the idea of ages is dependent on some obvious facts of life rather than on any real evidence, there are others who just make fun of the idea. Perhaps Cervantes falls into this latter category, as in *Don Quixote* he has the protagonist give an account of the Golden Age which degenerates into a description of lovely maidens roaming around without fear covered only with vines and leaves (pt. 1, chap. 11). It is, of course, difficult to tell just what Cervantes is trying to convey to his readers. His general idea seems to be to contrast the ideal with the imperfections of life. But in doing so he recognizes the ideal which is unattainable in this world but which is to be kept in mind lest we fall into a sub-human state.

symbolism to the early historical narratives, and to bring this out we will combine a doctrine of Maimonides with some views of René Guénon.

According to Maimonides[16] the genealogies presented in Genesis are to be seen as spiritual rather than natural.The idea of spiritual genealogies, while not very well known in the West, is commonplace in the East. Thus in the Hindu Upanishads we read in various places that a doctrine or higher knowledge was handed down over the centuries from one person to another. And the annals of Ch'an Buddhism contain at least three different genealogies tracing the teaching of Buddha down to the Ch'an patriarchs in China. This reading of the biblical narrative is supported by the beginning of Genesis 5. In the first few verses it is said that Adam was created in the image of God, and that Adam begot Seth in his own image. As Maimonides points out, this is said only of Seth, and it is through Seth that the lineage of Noah and the patriarchs is traced. Further support for the idea of spiritual genealogies is found in the practice of blessing. Noah blesses his son Japheth, the progenitor of Abraham. Abraham blesses Isaac, Isaac blesses Jacob, and Jacob blesses Joseph. Indeed, when God tells Abraham to leave his country and go to another land, He says, 'And I will bless you; I will make your name great, and you shall be a blessing.... and the families of the earth shall bless themselves by you' (Gen. 12:1–3). This blessing (*berakhah*)[17] is the imparting of spiritual influence. What we have then is a narrative about an unbroken primordial spiritual tradition—Divine wisdom and influence handed down from generation to generation.[18]

It is here that we bring to bear Guénon's interpretation of the

16. *The Guide of the Perplexed*, pt. 1, chap. 7.

17. The Arabic equivalent is *barakah*.

18. The use of the production of generations of people by sexual union as a symbol of the transmission of spiritual wisdom down through the ages should not be surprising. As we shall see in chapter 5, the production of Eve from the rib of Adam symbolizes a loss of completeness. Thus the union of male and female symbolizes a return to primordial wholeness. It is interesting that at the point of sexual fulfillment one loses one's sense of separateness and incompleteness and attains a sense of unity and non-purposiveness. One has the experience of dwelling at the

symbolism of the ark.[19] In his view the ark serves as the conservator of the tradition in the period between two cycles of ages during which the great deluge takes place. It is at one and the same time the center of creation and the supreme spiritual center which cannot be destroyed and which serves to regenerate the world. We may add to this that the same role is played by the basket of Moses, for it is Moses who is pictured as bringing the law of God to humanity after the Exodus.

It is with respect to the Israelites serving as custodians of this tradition, an ark as it were, that they are called 'a light of nations' (Isa. 42:6). Their custodianship is shown on the tangible level by their carrying around the Ark of the Covenant, the seat of God on earth, i.e., the center of His spiritual influence or Presence on earth.

If our analysis is correct, the picture presented by the early historical narratives of the Bible is of one primordial spiritual tradition serving as a conduit for Divine influence into the world. This influence is personified in the figure of Adam, the Prototype of man. Whether the Adamic tradition goes back to the very beginning of our cycle of ages or represents a subsidiary development, as Guénon insists, is not an important issue as far as we are concerned. And this especially in light of Guénon's claim that the Adamic tradition joined with the main tradition at the time of Abraham.[20] What is important is that it embodies the primordial spiritual tradition.

The complete doctrine of ages presents us with a true picture of where we stand today. Our position, in the latter part of the Iron Age, is marked by the ubiquity of popular culture in which the lowest tendencies in people set the standard and in which otherwise

center or middle point of the Wheel of Existence—the point of non-action (*wu-wei* in Taoism), which is one of the aims of spiritual practice. Thus it is that the carrying-on of a spiritual tradition can be symbolized by a history of people produced through sexual union.

19. *The King of the World*, chap. 11.

20. See *The King of the World*, chap. 6. According to Guénon the central primordial tradition entered and thereby legitimated the Adamic tradition in the person of Melchizedek (Gen. 14) whom he equates with Manu Vaivasvata. We will say here only that his views are problematic on a number of accounts but worth consideration nevertheless.

hollow people are famous for being famous; by economic considerations overriding all others (to the extent that the whole of past history is explained on an economic basis as if the primordial spiritual tradition did not exist); by religion being reduced in one part of the world to either moralism or 'social justice' or mere entertainment, and in another part to a harsh intolerant reaction to modernism; by the reduction of spirituality to 'New Age' pabulum; and by an increasingly materialistic mode of thought in which only the physical world is recognized and people are seen as mere hunks of flesh which are thereby expendable for the 'common good.'

What passes for the intellectual elite in our day comprises mostly partisan individuals. Intellectuals today do not even concern themselves with general principles, much less the universal. When they use generalizations it is always in bad faith, namely when it is convenient to make a point—a kind of special pleading.

Intellectuals were and should be concerned with the intellect or spirit, i.e., with the supra-individual level where all oppositions are reconciled. But at the very least, intellectuals should operate from an impartial or objective position beyond nationalism, political ideology, party politics, and causes of one sort or another. The exact opposite has been the case, leading to predictable results.[21] In his own way, George Orwell summed up the present situation of humanity in the opening line of a book review: 'Modern man is rather like a bisected wasp which goes on sucking jam and pretends that the loss of its abdomen does not matter.'[22]

21. In a very prescient book written by Julian Benda in the 1920s, namely *The Treason Of The Intellectuals—Clercs* in the French edition (NY: W.W. Norton, 1969), the author examines the failure of intellectuals to remain neutral or unbiased, with special emphasis on their embrace of nationalism. One exception to this trend in the twentieth century was the playwright Eugene Ionesco who explained in his *Fragments of a Journal* (NY: Grove Press, 1969) that he wanted to portray humanity in a way stripped of any partisan mentality. Indeed, his plays depict the human condition.

22. *An Age Like This*, ed. by S. Orwell and I. Angus (New York: Harcourt, Brace, Jovanovich, 1968), p154. Just how much we have lost is detailed in C. S. Lewis's 1940s book *The Abolition of Man* (San Francisco: Harper Collins, 2001).

3

In the Beginning

When God began to create the heaven and the earth—the earth being unformed and void, with darkness over the surface of the deep and a wind from God sweeping over the water—God said, 'Let there be light'; and there was light. (Gen. 1:1–3)

Most English translations of Genesis commence with the words 'In the beginning'. This is not quite correct and has led to some misunderstandings. A better translation, and certainly less misleading, would be, 'When God began to create,' for Genesis does not start at the beginning but at some point along the way: the point of universal manifestation.

The stages of creation are described differently in the various spiritual traditions, but they have one thing in common: they distinguish between God as He is in Himself, God as He reveals Himself (the Personal or Theistic God of most believers), and God as the Maker of the universe. The latter two are often run together with the second seen as an aspect of the first. The Gnostics, who viewed matter as evil, looked upon the God of Genesis (who they styled the Demiurge, following Plato) as the evil entrapper of the Spirit in matter and thus as completely separate from the true God. This misunderstanding was no doubt due to a failure to view the creation as part of a larger process stemming from possibilities inherent in God (which He made actual by His Will) and completely impelled and infused by Him. It is as if they took one aspect of God, as seen from the human perspective, and considered it as a separate being. But it is impossible to malign the Maker of the universe without at the same time maligning the true God.

God as He is in Himself has been referred to as the Supreme Principle or the Unmanifest (Guénon), *Nirguna Brahman* (*Brahman* without *gunas* or unqualified) or *Purusha* (Hinduism), the *Tao* (the Way, Taoism), *Sunyata* (Emptiness, or *Dharmadhatu* (the Ground, or Basic Space of Phenomena) or Buddha-nature (Buddhism), *Ein Sof* (Without End or Infinite, Kabbalism), the *Ungrund* (Boehme), and the Ground of Being (Tillich).[1] God as He reveals Himself (and as He is generally understood in the West) has been called Being (Parmenides, St Gregory, Al-Arabi, Guénon), the Godhead or God the Father (Christianity), *Saguna Brahman* (Brahman with qualities) or *Ishvara* or *Purusha*[2] or *Atman* (the Self, Hinduism), and *T'ai-i* (the Great or Supreme One, Taoism). Actually, the *Tao Te Ching* mentions the nameless *Tao* and the *Tao* that can be named. The first corresponds to *Nirguna Brahman* and the second to *Saguna Brahman*. Similarly in Hinduism we have references to *Purushottama* and *Purusha*, *Paramatman* and *Atman*, *Parabrahman*, and *Aparabrahman*.[3] Being, the first manifestation or determination of God, has been designated the Spiritual Sun in many spiritual traditions.

Generally speaking, what corresponds to Being in Kabbalism is *Adam Kadmon*—The Primordial or Principial or Universal Man. In Sufism the equivalent name is *Al-Insanul-Kamil*. *Adam Kadmon* is constituted by the ten *Sefirot* or aspects of *Ein Sof* which form the Archetypal World taken as a whole.[4] The *Sefirot* are thus comparable to the Forms of Plato which compose the realm of Being and which are the pattern for the cosmos. But according to the *Zohar* (1.16B), it is *Ḥokhmah* or Wisdom—the second of the *Sefirot*, which

1. St John Damascene (in *De fide orthodoxa*, 1.4) refers to God as 'above Being itself.'

2. Especially in the *Rig Veda*, x.90.

3. Sometimes it is Being which is said to have the two aspects which correspond to those we have just mentioned. On this, cf. *Fakhruddin Iraqi*: *Divine Flashes*, trs. W.C. Chittick and P.L. Wilson (New York: Paulist Press, 1982), pp 6–17.

4. The *Sefirot* are literally the primordial numbers or enumerations. Fortunately or unfortunately the various Kabbalists had different ways of expressing the same truths. In Lurianic Kabbalism *Adam Kadmon* is the first production within *Ein Sof*, and the *Sefirot* are His attributes.

corresponds to Being. It is said to proceed from the first *Sefirah*—*Keter* or the Crown, which is considered the Primordial Ether or the infinite possibilities inherent in *Ein Sof*.[5] It turns out that the Form of the Good plays the same role in the archetypal realm of the Forms as *Keter* plays in the realm of the *Sefirot*. *Keter* is one of the *Sefirot*, yet as the chief *Sefirah* from which all the others derive, it is all but equivalent to God as He is in Himself. The Form of the Good is classed together with the other Forms, yet Plato indicates that all of these Forms depend on it for their being and that it is 'beyond Being' or it 'transcends Being' (*Republic*, 509B).

God as Creator, we have said, is often seen as an aspect of God as He reveals Himself. But in this particular capacity we find Him referred to as the Demiurge (Plato—*Timaeus* 29A), as The Great Architect (Masonry), and as *Visvakarman*—the All-maker, or *Prajapati*—the Lord of Creatures, or *Narayana*—the dweller on the waters, or *Brahma*—the Creator (Hinduism).

We can picture the process of creation, which can be considered temporally only from our point of view, as moving from the Infinite or Ground to Oneness of Being to the Unity of Existence from which the universe proceeds.[6] Or we can refer to the Unity of Being and the Unicity of Existence, but the signification remains the same. In passing we might note that the Oneness of Being is sometimes pictured as a point which contains all the possibilities of manifestation, e.g., in the case of *Ḥokhmah*. It is said that all of creation is the *Zohar* or Radiance of this point (*Zohar*, 1.15A). Similarly, Tibetan Buddhists speak of the Primordial Purity (*ka-dag*) and its Luminosity.

No doubt there are other ways of describing the process by which the universe is manifested by God, but this one has the virtue of stressing that creation does not take place outside of God. We might say that it represents a certain development within God as long as

5. As the *Zohar* is very difficult to understand, a translation like that of Daniel C. Matt's of Part 1 with its multitude of notes is indispensable. Cf. *The Zohar: Pritzker Edition* (Stanford: Stanford Univ. Press, 2004).

6. Some writers, in discussing the stages of creation, use the term 'Being' where we use the term 'Existence'. For an example of this cf. Toshihiko Izutsu, *Sufism and Taoism: A Comparative Study of Key Philosophical Concepts* (Berkeley: Univ. of California Press, 1984).

we do not push that notion too far, for there is no *essential* change in God with the manifestation of the world, and He remains full and perfect. Perhaps Lurianic Kabbalism captures this idea by holding there is a *tzimtzum* or contraction within God, and in that 'space' creation proceeds.

We have used the words 'creation' and manifestation' interchangeably, but the two have somewhat different connotations. The esoteric term 'manifestation' does not imply separateness from God, whereas the exoteric or religious term 'creation' does carry this implication. In the one case we say that God (as Being) manifests Himself as the world, and in the other case that God creates the world. The first implies that the world has no reality apart from God. One of the best images of God's relationship to creation, although it is just an image, is given in the Upanishads. The picture is of a spider spinning and withdrawing its threads (*Mundaka Upanishad* I.1.7). First, the spider does not become any 'less' in spinning its web. Second it can spin and withdraw its threads. Third, it inhabits its web.

In order for creation to proceed the original source of creation must bifurcate or polarize, for the distinctive feature of creation is plurality or multiplicity. Thus Being, which is one, must project a second, and these will form a unity of two which we have termed Existence: the active principle and the primordial constituents of the universe.[7] Here is how Meister Eckhart explicates Genesis 1:1:

> ... recognize that the entire universe created by God is distinguished into two principles, the active and the passive....

7. In connection with the stages of creation ending with the polarization of Being we must call the reader's attention to the first two lines of chapter 42 of the *Tao Te Ching*: 'The Tao bore the One and the One bore the Two'.The One corresponds to Being (referred to as 'The Uncarved Block' in chapters 19, 28, 32, and 37) and the Two—Heaven (*T'ien*) and Earth (*T'i*)—correspond to *Purusha* and *Prakriti* in Hinduism, which we will explain presently. The phrase 'Mother Earth' refers even more profoundly to the Earth as a symbol of *Prakriti* understood as the substance of the world. *Te* (virtue, uprightness, or power) in the *Tao Te Ching*, which is what all things possess of the *Tao* and by virtue of which they exist and are what they are, seems to correspond to what we have called the Divine influence, although it may also be called the influence of Heaven.

> 'Heaven' is the active, 'the first unchangeable thing that changes others'; 'earth' is the passive inasmuch as it is especially material.[8]

We are presented with this unity of the active and passive poles of creation at the very beginning of Genesis.

In Genesis 1:2 we are told that at the beginning of creation the earth was unformed, 'with darkness over the surface of the deep and a wind from God sweeping over it.' Many have recognized that we are here given a description of the primordial chaos, but we must be clear about the meaning of 'chaos' in this context. Like many other words of ancient lineage the meaning of this one has become corrupted in modern times. It does not refer to the kind of frenetic and mutually destructive activity observed in such events as riots. Rather, it has the opposite sense: a cessation of activity, a dissolution into sameness, complete formlessness. Chaos in one's inner life would involve an all-encompassing lethargy and a dissolving of consciousness into oblivion. In short, chaos resembles death rather than life, as strange as this may seem to modern ears. Returning to our subject, we can say that the waters shrouded in darkness are the primordial constituents of the universe in perfect equilibrium. The darkness symbolizes the undifferentiated state of the constituents of the world and signifies that the total of the constituents has no definite qualities.

In searching through ancient Western doctrines we find something similar in the *apeiron* theory of Anaximander. The *apeiron* has none of the qualities of the four constituents of the world—coolness, wetness, hotness, and dryness—because it contains them in equilibrium.[9] We have no information from Anaximander on what it is that

8. *The Essential Sermons*, p101.

9. Alternatively, we could understand Anaximander's *apeiron* as the equivalent of the Hindu *akasha* (ether, *quinta essentia*), the fifth element from which are derived fire, earth, air, and water. However, the first interpretation seems preferable. Whether Anaximander's *apeiron* theory was really given in opposition to Thales' postulation of water as the origin and substratum of all things depends on whether Thales was talking about physical water or only using water in the traditional way as a metaphor for the passive pole of creation. Even if he was talking about physical water, we should keep in mind that he meant it as the substance of the whole cosmos, and not just the physical world.

stirs up the *apeiron* to produce the cosmos, as he evidently felt it was sufficient unto itself for the task, a mistake on his part. But we are given this information in Genesis 1:1—a wind (*ruaḥ*) from God. This wind is Being functioning as the active principle which throws the waters into disequilibrium with the resultant creation of the universe. But for the process to begin there must be a Divine Impulse from within Being, the Spiritual Sun, and this Impulse is the Word (Gen. 1:3): 'Let there be light.'[10] From this Impulse comes the Celestial Ray which shines on the waters bringing form out of formlessness. Guénon very perceptively points out that the waters in their chaotic or dark state refer as well to the inner state of a would-be initiate before it has been touched by the spiritual influence of the initiator.[11] Thus each rebirth of the initiate is an inner playing-out of the external drama of creation.[12]

The unity of two that precedes creation, which is described as wind and waters in Genesis and *T'ai-chi* in Taoism, is called in Hinduism *Purusha-Prakriti*. Here *Purusha* corresponds to the wind and *Prakriti* to the waters. The name *Purusha* is seemingly used to refer to three different things in Hinduism: the Unmanifest, Being, and one of the poles of Existence. However, we are really speaking of different aspects of one subject. The highest signification of *Purusha* is the Supreme Principle. Yet the word *Purusha* means Person, and we find in the *Rig Veda* X.90 that the world is created from a part of the body of the Primordial Person.[13] Thus *Purusha* is also the Principle of Existence. Finally, as *Purusha* polarizes Itself in order that creation proceed, it is only fitting that It be identified with the active pole of manifestation. As we said before, in the 'process' of creation God plays all the parts, and hence all the meanings of *Purusha*

10. This impulse is the Logos or Word mentioned in the beginning of John, which should not be confused with he Logos of Heraclitus or the Alexandrian Logos of Philo, Clement, and Origen. It issues from the heart of Being, and in the *Zohar* is said to actually originate within *Ein Sof* (1.15A).

11. *Perspectives on Initiation* (Hillsdale, NY: Sophia Perennis, 2004), chap. 4.

12. On the comparison between individual regeneration and cosmic generation, cf. Philo's *Questions and Answers on Exodus*, tr. Ralph Marcus (Cambridge: Harvard Univ. Press, 1970), bk 1, sect. 23.

13. This story indicates particularly the sacrificial character of creation.

merge in the end. In addition to these three meanings of *Purusha* we find that when broken down it signifies the dweller in the city (*puri*) and as such refers to the Divine Presence inhabiting the body and indeed the world. But this is really only the Unmanifest understood in terms of its relationship with the manifested world.

We have already mentioned that Being must polarize for creation to proceed and we can re-express this by saying that *Purusha* must project *Prakriti*, the passive pole of manifestation. In Kabbalistic terms *Ḥokhmah* projects the Third *Sefirah*, *Binah*—which is called the Mother of the other *Sefirot* and the rest of creation. Similarly, Plato, in the *Timaeus* (49–50), describes the passive pole as the receptacle, the nurse of all generation, that in which generation takes place, and the natural recipient of all impressions. It bears mentioning that the word *Prakriti* should not, as is often done, be translated by the word 'Nature'. Our concern is not so much that 'Nature' implies a formed world which equates more with the Hindu *Maya* who is worshipped as the Mother, since after all *Prakriti* (or *natura naturans* in scholastic terminology) is transformed into the world (or *natura naturata*). Rather, the problem is that today, most people understand the term 'nature' to mean the physical world, while *Prakriti* is not merely the 'mother' of the physical world, but of the subtle and formless as well.

The *Zohar* actually describes a rather complicated process which involves two pairs of active and passive poles and is not altogether consistent. We are told (1.15A) that the second *Sefirah*, *Ḥokhmah*, weaves itself a palace, *Binah*, the way a silkworm spins a cocoon of silk. (Note that nothing essential is lost from *Ḥokhmah*.) The other seven *Sefirot*, and by necessity all of creation, are said to emerge from *Binah* (1.15A–1.16A) beginning with the 'Let there be light.' However, the fourth *Sefirah*, *Ḥesed* or Wisdom, is said in one place to emerge directly from *Ḥokhmah* (1.16B) and in another place from *Binah* (1.18A). More importantly, the sixth *Sefirah*, *Tif'eret* or Beauty, seems to emerge directly from *Ḥokhmah* according to one account (1.16B), but both *Tif'eret* and the tenth *Sefirah*, *Shekhinah* (also called *Malkhut* or Kingdom), emerge from *Binah* according to other accounts (1.15B–1.16B). *Tif'eret* and *Shekhinah* constitute the second pair of active and passive poles and are referred to as heaven and earth (1.16B). The action of *Tif'eret* on *Shekhinah*, through the ninth *Sefirah, Yesod* or Foundation, which as it were joins them, brings form out of formlessness (1.15B–1.16B). While it is true that the *Shekhinah* is usually understood as the Presence of God in the world, here it is the equivalent of *Malkhut* which functions as the substance of creation. So we seem to have two different complete sets of active and passive poles, and the question arises: how shall we understand this? There is one other factor which may shed light on this problem. *Binah* is understood as the higher waters and *Shekhinah* as the lower waters (1.18A), the two being separated at the time of creation (Gen. 1:7). In chapter 7 we are going to discuss the significance of these two waters in our account of the flood. For now, let us say that if we think of *Tif'eret* as coming from *Ḥokhmah* and thus being a stand-in for it, and if we think of *Shekhinah* as emerging from *Binah* and thus being an extension of it, then some of the inconsistency, or if you will, some of the duplication dissolves.

The projection of *Prakriti* is sometimes described as *Purusha* making Himself into a pair of beings embracing (*Brihadaranyaka Upanishad* I.IV). But as a way of emphasizing that *Purusha* remains full and perfect through this projection, the creation of *Prakriti* is sometimes described as coming about by a process of sweating (as in the *Brihadaranyaka Upanishad* I.2.1 and in the *Chandogya Upanishad*, VI.II).[14] Perhaps the clearest and most complete version of

14. There seems to be an allusion to this process in Hymn x.129 of the *Rig Veda* where we start out with the One who breathed windless and who by *tapas* (austerity, heat) produced the world. An interesting Mordvinian variant of these stories which employs the symbolism of friends is mentioned by Mircea Eliade:

> God was alone on a rock. 'If only I had a brother, I would make the World!' he said, and he spat on the Waters. From his spittle a mountain was born. God split it with his sword, and out of the mountain came the Devil (Satan). As soon as he appeared the Devil proposed to God that they should be brothers and create the world together. 'We will not be brothers, but companions,' answered God. And together they proceeded to the creation of the World. [*The Two and the One*, tr. J.M. Cohen (New York: Harper & Row, 1965), pp 85-86.]

Eliade relates that in other stories the creators of the world are understood as brothers (ibid. pp 82–85). He also mentions a Bulgarian legend according to which God and His shadow combine to create the world (ibid.), and we find a similar story told about the Egyptian god Ra and his shadow.

the whole process is given in the *Laws of Manu* (I.5–13). There the Self-existent Lord produced water from Himself, deposited semen therein, and the semen became a Golden egg in which He resided. After a year He divided the egg in half and from the halves produced sky, earth and the atmosphere between.[15]

We have dwelt at length on the projection of *Prakriti* from *Purusha* because it is not mentioned in Genesis, but rather presupposed as something already accomplished. At any rate, it is time we said more about *Prakriti*—the waters—and the relationship of *Purusha* to *Prakriti*. *Prakriti* is constituted by the three *gunas* or tendencies—*sattva*, *rajas*, and *tamas* (which we will explain more fully in chapter 7)—in complete equilibrium. As such it is the passive principle of Existence which must be stirred into disequilibrium by the active principle *Purusha*—the wind of God sweeping over the water in Genesis 1:2—in order for the formation of the world to take place.

These two—*Purusha* and *Prakriti*—are in no way opposites, but rather complements. *Purusha*, although active, is said to be unmoving. It works as a magnet would work in drawing iron filings to itself. In fact, an alternative translation of the Hebrew word for 'sweeping over' (*rakhefet*) is 'hovering over', the later implying no motion. And here we can see the reason for Aristotle's designation of the active principle as the Unmoved Mover.[16] On the complementarity of *Prakriti* and *Purusha* we would allude once again to the passage in the *Brihadaranyaka Upanishad* in which *Purusha* becomes 'a woman and a man in close embrace' (I.IV.3), a unity perfectly pictured in the well-known Chinese *yin-yang* symbol. In this case the *yin* (dark) or passive aspect is equivalent to Earth and is comparable to *Prakriti*, while the *yang* (light) or active aspect is equivalent to Heaven and is comparable to *Purusha*.[17] The image of the woman and man in close embrace is a reminder that we can

15. *The Laws of Manu*, tr. Wendy Donniger with Brian K. Smith (New York: Penguin Books, 1991), p4.

16. This phrase can also be used as a description of the World Spirit since the Spirit is the locus of the Activity of Heaven (cf. chap. 5).

17. This particular symbol goes back only to the ninth century, but the terms and what they designate go back to ancient times. Guénon has pointed out that we

describe the Unity of Existence from which creation proceeds as the Primordial Androgyne. The importance of this description will become more evident in the following two chapters.

There are stories in which a being symbolizing the active pole slays another being symbolizing the passive pole in order to bring about creation. A well-known Hindu example involves Indra slaying the serpent Vritra, of which the story of St George and the dragon is a distant echo. Serpents and serpentine creatures like dragons are used as symbols of the substance of the cosmos for two reasons. They resemble both rope with its coils and twists and also the sea with its waves. Rope is a symbol of the passive pole of Existence in that it is ordinarily made up of different strands, just as the substance of the cosmos is generally described as a mixture, though one which is completely homogenized. For instance, in Hinduism it is conceived as a mixture of tendencies: the three *gunas*.[18] The sea is such a symbol because it consists of the plastic element water and because it surrounds land and thus appears all-encompassing. And anything living in the sea, whether serpentine or not, can also serve as a symbol of the passive pole. Thus we read in the Psalm 74 account of the creation:

> Oh, God, my king from of old,
> Who brings deliverance throughout the land;
> It was You who drove back the sea with Your might,
> Who smashed the heads of the monsters in the waters;
> It was You who crushed the heads of Leviathan,
> Who left him as food for the denizens of the desert;
> It was You who released springs and torrents,
> Who made mighty rivers run dry;
> The day is Yours, the night also;
> It was You who set in place the orb of the sun;
> You fixed all the boundaries of the earth;
> Summer and winter—You made them. (vv. 12–17)

---

can find symbols of Heaven and Earth in masonry. This pair of principles is symbolized by the plumb-line and level, the compass and try-square, and the try-square itself considered in a different way. Cf. *The Great Triad* (Hillsdale, NY: Sophia Perennis, 2004), chaps. 3 and 15.

And, we have in Job 26:

> He drew a boundary on the surfaces of the waters,
> At the extreme where light and darkness meet.
> The pillars of heaven tremble,
> Astounded at His blast.
> By His power He stilled the sea;
> By His skill He struck down Rahab.
> By His wind the heavens were calmed,
> His hand pierced the Elusive Serpent. (vv. 10–13)

Finally there is Isaiah 27, which on its usual interpretation refers to the vanquishing of evil in the world. But why not the vanquishing of evil by a great destruction prior to a new creation?

> In that day the Lord will punish
> With His great, cruel, mighty sword
> Leviathan the Elusive Serpent.

18. On the matter of the rope, when braided or twisted it becomes a symbol of the cosmos. Many of the *torii* or entrance gates of Shinto shrines in Japan (namely those is the so-called Churen style, which may well be the oldest) consist of two wooden poles with a braided rope stretched between them on which five tufts of rope hang. The gates would seem to symbolize the cosmos stretched between the active and passive poles of creation. The tufts would stand for the five basic elements (cf. fn 9). The braiding of the rope would also symbolize the constant flow or change in the cosmos. Of special interest is the extremely thick sacred rope hung in front of the worship hall of the Grand Shrine of Izumo. It is coiled rather than braided, and three tufts of rope (rather than the usual five) hang from it. This may be mere coincidence, but the three tufts could symbolize the three worlds. The rope, since it is only coiled and not braided may be an intermediate symbol and thus stand for the substance of the world as well. In that case the tufts would stand for the three tendencies which are in it. The Shinto conception of Nature (understood in the inclusive sense of *natura naturata* which encompasses more than the physical world) as sacred is comparable, on a certain level, to the Hindu worship of Maya. Speaking of the *torii*, Sokyo Ono, in his short book *Shinto The Kami Way* (Rutland, VT: Charles E. Tuttle, 1962), notes apologetically that the literal meaning of the Japanese characters for *tori* being '"bird perch," need not detain us here. The origin is obscure and has no particular relevance to its present use' (28–29). But what better symbol for a shrine can there be than a bird perch—something which draws to it animals from the sky. Birds have always symbolized heavenly influences.

> Leviathan the Twisting Serpent;
> He will slay the dragon of the sea. (v.1)

In these quotations it is unclear whether God is somehow vanquishing the sea or a monster of the sea, or whether that monster is serpentine or not. But in the end it all comes to the same thing.

Earlier, mention was made of the Celestial Ray, coming from the active pole of creation. In various traditions it is called the Solar Ray, the Heavenly Ray, and the Intelligible Light. Being—the Universal Self, the Spiritual Sun—projects the primordial 'waters' and shines on them. Its reflected image on the surface of the waters is the World Spirit. Or we can say that the World Spirit is a reflection of the Ray from the Spiritual Sun. This Ray and its reflection are the trunks of the two trees mentioned in the *Zohar* (3.156B). The first is usually described as upright and the second as inverted since it is a reflection of the first.[19]

We realize that not much would be lost in passing over the distinction between the Solar Ray and its reflection, and just referring to both as that Ray. We have indeed done this in the past. But in the present context it is important to be as precise as the subject permits, especially as we are dealing with symbolism that presupposes the distinction.

The Spirit is the first production of the passive pole of creation and constitutes the supra-formal or formless realm of universal manifestation. It may also be called the World Intellect (or *Buddhi* in Hinduism). Under its influence the World Soul (the subtle realm which is properly thought of as demiurgic) is produced, and under the latter's influence is produced the World Body (the physical realm). In Hinduism these are termed *Mahat* (as well as *Buddhi*),

19. On the subject of the inverted tree see the *Svetasvatara Upanishad* I.iii.9, and the *Katha Upanishad* VI.1. See also Ananda Coomaraswamy, 'The Inverted Tree', in *Coomaraswamy: Selected Papers*, vol. 1 ed. Roger Lipsey (Princeton: Princeton Univ. Press, 1977). In canto XXII of his *Purgatorio* Dante describes a tree (an offshoot of the Tree of Life) which seems to be inverted. Guénon writes about upright and inverted trees in *Symbols of Sacred Science* (Hillsdale, NY: Sophia Perennis, 2004), chaps. 5 and 52. In a book dedicated to Coomaraswamy, *The Golden Germ* (The Hague: Mouton & Co., 1960), Frederick D.K. Bosch has a chapter titled 'The Two Trees'. We will discuss the matter further in chapter 5.

Hiranygharba, and *Viraj* respectively. Understanding the nature of the World Spirit is difficult because it is the boundary or mediator between God and the world, what Sufis call the *barzakh* or isthmus. As a reflection of the Heavenly Ray it is God in the World, 'the Word made flesh'.

Expressing himself in a somewhat different way, Titus Burckhardt explains these matters in terms of *ar-Ruḥ* (similar to the Hebrew *ruaḥ*)—the Spirit. He writes of the Universal Spirit, the Universal Soul, and the Universal Nature, which would correspond in our terms to the World Spirit, World Soul and World Body. However, he says that the Universal Spirit has a created and an uncreated aspect. The created Spirit, he says, is born of *al-Haba*, the Sufi equivalent of the Hindu *Prakriti*. The uncreated aspect which is its immutable essence corresponds to what we have called Being or the Universal Self or Spiritual Sun. Burckhardt mentions that some Sufi writers compare it to the Face of God. It is in this way that Burckhardt explains how the Spirit is 'the mediator between the Divine Being and the conditional universe.'[20] (Of course, any level of reality between two others can be described as a mediator between them, but the truth is that the Uncreated Spirit is at one remove from the universe.) This mode of expression is in agreement with that of René Guénon and Ananda Coomaraswamy who in various writings use the word 'Spirit' to refer to the Self, Guénon at times calling it the Universal Spirit. Guénon in one place says, 'while it is often affirmed that the spirit is not other than *Atma* [Self], there are nevertheless instances in which this same spirit seems to be identified only with *Buddhi*....'[21] But he concluded that this just reflects a correspondence between different levels of reality.

We feel that in order to avoid ambiguity it is best to reserve the word 'Spirit' and phrase 'World Spirit' for the *Buddhi* or highest part of the manifested or conditioned world, the Divine part of the

20. Titus Burckhardt, *An Introduction to Sufi Doctrine*, tr. D.M. Matheson (Lahore: Sh. Muhammad Ashraf, 1959), pt. 2, chap. v.

21. 'Spirit and Intellect', in *Miscellanea* (Hillsdale, NY: Sophia Perennis, 2004), chap. 3.

world as it were. As the center of Divine Influence in all the planes of Existence within the cosmos it also functions as the World Axis.[22]

Both Guénon and Coomaraswamy write as if the Self actually dwells with the person as its Spirit. Yet as Guénon states in various ways, it is only a reflection of the Self which dwells within a person.[23] Nevertheless, taking the World Spirit as the reflection of a Ray from the Spiritual Sun or Self, we can say that it meets that Ray at the surface of the waters. Thus the Spirit, which cuts through all people as their individual spirits, connects them with the Spiritual Sun and hence with the Unmanifest Itself. Maimonides refers to this connection when he writes of 'the intellect that overflows toward us and is the bond between us and Him, may He be exalted.'[24] This at least is how things look from the perspective of human individuality, which is the perspective from which we all start. But because of our connection with the Unmanifest we are able to attain a level of consciousness beyond that of ourselves as individuals. In fact, each stage on the spiritual path will match the stages of God's manifesting the world, only in reverse order. The goal of the spiritual path is to return, in consciousness, to our origin—the Unmanifest. In the first stage one goes beyond body consciousness, in the next beyond the mind to consciousness of oneself as the Universal Self—the Witness Self—the same in all. Finally one achieves a state of consciousness beyond even the distinction between witness and witnessed. At this point one realizes that God plays all the parts in the drama of world-manifestation and that there has never been anything other than God.

22. We have not mentioned the Holy Spirit of Judaism and Christianity in this context because the correlations appear to be different. Apart from Its later adoption as one of the Persons of the Trinity, the Holy Spirit is found to correspond either to the Presence of God or to the Divine influence or power. That is to say, the phrase 'Holy Spirit' has been used to denote both things, and thus we are faced with something which seems to fall between the usual categories. The same is true of *Te* in Taoism (cf. fn. 7) and there may be in this a point of correspondence between the traditions of East and West.

23. *Man and His Becoming According to Vedānta* (Hillsdale, NY: Sophia Perennis, 2004), chaps. 5–9.

24. *The Guide of the Perplexed*, pt. III, chap. 52, p629.

We would be remiss in discussing the creation of the universe as described in Genesis 1–2:4A, if we did not comment on the significance of the six days of activity and one of rest. We will begin by noting Philo's views on the significance of the number seven:

> So august is the dignity inherent by nature in the number 7, that it has a unique relation distinguishing it from all the other numbers in the decade: for of these some beget without being begotten, some are begotten but do not beget, some do both these, both beget and are begotten: 7 alone is found in no such category.[25]

The point is that within the decade (which is itself symbolically significant) 7 is the only number neither divisible by any (giving a whole other than itself) nor divisible into any. He goes on to say the following:

> It is the nature of 7 alone, as I have said, neither to beget nor to be begotten. For this reason other philosophers liken this number to the motherless and virgin Nike, who is said to have appeared out of the head of Zeus, while the Pythagoreans liken it to the chief of all things: for that which neither begets nor is begotten remains motionless; for creation takes place in movement, since there is movement both in that which begets and in that which is begotten, in the one that it may beget, in the other that it may be begotten. There is only one thing that neither causes motion nor experiences it, the original ruler and sovereign. Of Him 7 may be fitly said to be a symbol. Evidence of what I say is supplied by Philolaus in these words: 'There is, he says, a supreme Ruler of all things, God, ever one, abiding, without motion, Himself (alone) like unto Himself, different from all others.'[26]

The idea is that 7 is a perfect number to represent Being, that primal point from which the cosmos springs, the Principle of the active and passive poles of creation.

25. Philo, *On the Creation*, tr. G.H. Whitaker (Cambridge: Harvard Univ. Press, 1929), sect. XXXIII.

26. Ibid., sect. XXXIII.

On the basis of what we have just said we can understand that the first six days of the week represent the six directions in which God manifests the world—the four cardinal points plus above and below. The seventh day represents the center from which manifestation proceeds and thus eternity in the midst of temporality as well. We find a similar symbolism in the six colors of the spectrum which resolve into white light. The Seal of Solomon (or Shield of David), which is a six-pointed star composed of inverted triangles, is a perfect symbol of the six directions of creation represented two-dimensionally. The center of this symbol corresponds to the center of creation and hence to the seventh day.[27] And Judaism's traditional symbol, the seven-branched *menorah*, has a similar significance. The *vajra* (or *dorjē*) of Tibetan Buddhism is a comparable symbol. The middle of the *vajra*, called the *thigle*, corresponds to the center of the Seal of Solomon.[28]

Like Philo, St Augustine believes that the number 7 is the perfect one to stand for the Divine, but he explains it in a somewhat different way. He notes that,

> . . . seven often stands for an unlimited number, as in 'the righteous will fall seven times, and rise again' [Prov. 24:16], which means, 'However many times he falls, he will not perish'—which is to be understood as referring not to the falls of wickedness, but to tribulations, which lead to humility. Similarly, 'seven times a

27. The star formed of inverted triangles was originally a widespread symbol and was only adopted as a symbol of Judaism in the last two centuries. In India it is known as the *shatkona* and represents the two aspects of the god Shiva. The first is transcendent, quiescent—the masculine side symbolized by the upper triangle; and the second is active, the primordial power or energy called *Shakti* which is constantly involved in creation, preservation and destruction—the feminine side symbolized by the lower triangle. Gershom Scholem notes that, 'In the Second Temple period, the hexagram was often used by Jews and non-Jews alike alongside the pentagram (the five-pointed star), and in the Synagogue of Capernaum (second or third century CE) it is found side by side with the pentagram and the swastika on a frieze.' He unfortunately adds, 'There is no reason to assume that it was used for any purpose other than decorative' ('Magen David', *Encyclopedia Judaica* [Jerusalem: Keter, 1972], vol. 11, p687).

28. Chogyal Namkai Norbu, *Dzogchen: The Self-Perfected State* (Ithaca: Snow Lion Publications, 1996), pp42–43.

day I will praise you' [Ps. 119:164] expresses the same thought as 'His praise is always on my lips' [Ps. 34:2].[29]

Putting the matter as Guénon might do so, 7 indicates an indefinite number and is thus suited to symbolize the unlimited or infinite nature of God.

The point of observing the sabbath should be clear by this time. It involves a return to the central repose, a focusing inward in contrast to the outward expenditure of attention and energy which characterizes the rest of the week. It is a dip in the sea of eternity from which we can return with renewed vigor. Of course, all of this is what the observance of the sabbath should be, and not necessarily what it is for most people. Much the same can be said for making the sign of the cross, a gesture with the same symbolic meaning as observing the sabbath—viz., centering oneself. The vertical axis of the cross symbolizes the Spirit or World Axis and the horizontal axis symbolizes our particular state of Existence. Their point of intersection is the still point around which our world revolves. It is of interest that the *Zohar* (1:32A) connects *Shekhinah*, which is the last of the seven lower *Sefirot* and is sometimes understood as the Divine word, with the sabbath, which is the seventh day of the week. But as we mentioned earlier, the *Shekhinah* is also understood as the Presence of the Divine in the world, analogous to the notion of Divine Providence. And the sabbath is considered the holy day of the week, God's day in effect. So we can say the *Shekhinah* is, so to speak, the Divine Presence in space, while the sabbath is the Divine Presence in time. We observe the sabbath in order to touch the Presence which is centered in the Spirit.

All remembrance of God, whether it takes the form of a prayer before meals or sleep or some other form, involves the potential for centering oneself. But whether the potential is actualized in a person's life depends on his or her intentions and receptivity. While a discussion on this subject would take us too far afield, we can say, what is in any case very obvious, that very few people are the least bit affected by activities meant for the purpose of centering them in the Spirit, the reflection of the Celestial Ray of the Divine Sun.

29. *The City of God*, bk IX, chap. 31, p466.

4

In the Image of God

And God created man in His image, in the image of God He created him; male and female He created them. (Gen. 1:27)

The ancient Greek commentator Xenophanes wrote:

> The Ethiopians say that their gods are snub-nosed and black, the Thracians that theirs have light blue eyes and red hair. But if cattle and horses or lions had hands, or were able to draw with their hands and do the works that men can do, horses would draw the forms of the gods like horses, and cattle like cattle, and they would make their bodies such as they each had themselves.[1]

It is unfortunate that even today in our 'enlightened civilization' many people still do take literally the idea that we are made in God's image. The picture of God as an old man residing in the heavens has not yet disappeared from our consciousness. But it must be admitted that most people have outgrown this view, a leftover from childish religion. What then is the meaning of this 'in His image'? It is a truism that simple questions have complicated answers, and this case is no exception to the rule. In fact, it is an instance of the rule *par excellence.*

What complicates matters is that there are really two images of God. In the lesser sense we can say that the manifested world is such

1. G.S. Kirk, J.E. Raven, and M. Schofield, *The Presocratic Philosophers*, second edition (Cambridge: Cambridge Univ. Press, 1983), p169.

an image, while in the higher sense it is Being which is an image of God. Put differently we could say that both the mundane and archetypal worlds are images, although the former is really an image of the image.[2] What further compounds our problems is that it is Primal or First Man who is said to be made in the image of God, and thus the typical human of our times cannot claim this distinction, except as a potentiality.

Taking the lesser sense of 'image' first, we may recall that the atomist Democritus of ancient Greece called man a microcosm (or little world system) in contrast to the macrocosm (the great world system or cosmos).[3] Titus Burckhardt, extending the thought of Pascal, remarks that,

> ... the world or the macrocosm clearly contains man who is himself its integrating part. But man knows the world and, given the principial unity of Being and Knowledge, this means that all possibilities of the world are in a virtual and principial sense present in man. [And he adds] ... man is a qualitative 'abridgement' of the great cosmic 'book', all universal qualities being in

2. Plotinus, in the *Enneads* V.I–II, identifies three hypostases or levels of reality which he calls the One or the Supreme or God Himself (corresponding to God as He is in Himself), the Intellectual Principle or Being (corresponding to God as he reveals Himself) and the Great Soul (corresponding to the World Soul), from which the fourth level of reality—Nature or the physical world (corresponding to the World Body)—derives. But what is important here is that he says 'The Intellectual Principle stands as the image of the One'(V.I.7) and 'Soul, for all the worth we have shown to belong to it, is yet a secondary, an image of the Intellectual Principle'(V.I.3). Cf. *The Enneads*, tr. Stephen MacKenna (New York: Penguin, 1991). Plotinus seems to skip one level of reality, what we have called the World Spirit or Intellect, and sometimes refers to the first level as 'the One' which is properly a designation of the second. Yet we think our identifications are correct. Perhaps he sees the World Intellect as an aspect of the Intellectual Principle.

3. In Sufism the macrocosm is called *al-Insan al-kabir* (the Great Man), and Plato, in the *Timaeus* (30c and d), refers to it as 'a Living Creature'. Similar to the view of Democritus is Philo's notion of the cosmos as a great plant and man as a small, though special, plant within it. This is found in his book *Concerning Noah's Work as a Planter* trs. F.H. Colson and G.H. Whitaker (Cambridge: Harvard Univ. Press, 1968), sects. I–IV. In ancient times the macrocosm was considered by others to be equivalent to God. But this pantheistic view, besides being incorrect, does away with the notion of the cosmos as image of God.

one way or another expressed in his form. [And he quotes St Gregory Palamas as saying] Man, this greater world in little compass, is an epitome of all that exists in a unity and is the crown of Divine works.[4]

Speaking of the archetypal world or Being as the primary image of God, we may note that it is often described as three-in-one. The Trinity of Christianity and the *Trimurti* of Hinduism are obvious examples, although many more will be given in the chapter on Abraham. The secondary image of God, namely the macrocosm or cosmos, is also tripartite (as we mentioned in the previous chapter), being constituted of the World Spirit, World Soul, and World Body. We could of course analyze the World Body or gross physical part of the cosmos as having mineral, vegetable and animal aspects, as well as being constituted by protons, neutrons and electrons. But more to the point, a human being or microcosm is tripartite as well, being composed of a spirit (or intellect), a soul and a body, the spirit being in effect the World Spirit within. Thus we are made in the image of God, although in the secondary image. Only Primal Man, by his completeness, is made in the primary image. However, we have the potential for attaining this completeness, and thus the possibility of remaking ourselves in God's primary image. For while the World Spirit or Intellect pervades all of creation, it is present within man in a special way which enables him to grasp his true relationship to God and achieve the sense of eternity. It is perhaps with this in mind that Maimonides states the following about man's being created in God's image:

> Now man possesses as his proprium something in him that is very strange as it is not found in anything else that exists under the sphere of the moon, namely, intellectual apprehension. In the exercise of this, no sense, no part of the body, none of the extremities are used; and therefore this apprehension was likened unto the apprehension of the deity, which does not require an instrument, although in reality it is not like the latter

4. *An Introduction to Sufi Doctrine*, pp88–89.

> apprehension, but only appears so to the first strivings of opinion. It was because of this something, I mean because of the divine intellect conjoined with man, that it is said of the latter that he is *in the image of God and in His likeness*, not that God, may He be exalted, is a body and possesses a shape.[5]

Although this quotation takes us away from our comparison of microcosm to macrocosm, it serves to point out that besides containing something of what everything else in the universe has, man possesses as well something which no other being has, namely the capability of intellectual apprehension, and thus expresses the cosmos in the most complete way. In the face of the modern mentality, we must stress that the intellect is not to be confused with mere reason which may deal with generalizations about individual things. Rather, the intellect is what enables us to grasp the supra-individual or universal. It is the presence of the intellect which gives us the potential for spiritual perfection.

Turning to the higher sense of 'image', it is Being or the Archetypal world, the first revelation of God, which will concern us. Being is explicitly pictured as the Cosmic Person in both Hinduism, as *Purusha*, and Kabbalism, as *Adam Kadmon*—Primordial Man. It is perhaps in Kabbalism that we have the clearest indication of what the phrase 'image of God' means, for the *Sefirot*, which in a way constitute *Adam Kadmon*, serve as an integrated picture of the possibilities inherent in God which are actualized in creation. As to the other side of the comparison, it is Primal Man—Adam—who, as a perfect picture of the original Unity of Existence, can be thought of as made in the image of the Oneness of Being.

In order to understand the nature of Adam we will have to focus on the phrase 'male and female He created them' (Gen. 1:27). This is a clear reference to Adam as androgynous, and we must recall in this connection the story of the creation of the human race in Plato's *Symposium* (189D–E) where the original androgyne is split into male and female and thence propagates the human race. We find confirmation of the androgynous nature of Adam in Gen.

5. *The Guide of the Perplexed*, pt. 1, chap. 1, p23.

2:21–22 when Eve is produced from Adam's rib. As the *Zohar* (1.34B) puts it, God sawed the original Adam in two. It also alludes to *Tef'eret* and *Shekhinah* (which here signify the active and passive poles of Universal Existence) as a Primordial Androgyne which has to be split apart for creation to proceed (1.35A–B). Adam may be considered a complete human balancing the masculine and feminine aspects of Existence, and integrating all of the elements of our particular state of Existence. This is true by virtue of Adam's place in the Terrestrial Paradise, the center point of the manifestation of our state of Existence which in a sense contains all things within it. Al-Arabi goes even further than this in describing Adam as the Perfect Man:

> He has expressed this polarity of qualities [in the Qur'an] as being His Hands devoted to the creation of the Perfect Man who integrates in himself all Cosmic realities and their individual [manifestations]... he [man] unites [in himself] the two modes, the [originated] Cosmos and the [originating and original] Reality, which are His two hands.[6]

In this way Adam integrates within himself all of the levels of manifestation and can be considered God's 'Vice-Regent'.[7] Thus Adam is King of the World, and since God is considered the Ultimate King (or King of kings), we can see still another meaning of the phrase 'in His image'. Adam's role as King is shown in Gen. 1:28:

> God blessed them [the androgyne Adam-Eve] and said to them, 'Be fertile and increase, fill the earth and master it; rule the fish of the sea, the birds of the sky, and all the living things that creep on earth.'

Somewhat related to this is a further meaning of 'in His image' which is brought out in Gen. 2:20 when Adam, before the split into Adam and Eve, names all the animals. On the Divine level naming is tantamount to creating—'In the beginning was the Word' (John

6. *Ibn Al' Arabi: The Bezels of Wisdom*, tr. R.W.J. Austin (New York: Paulist Press, 1980), pp55–56.

7. Ibid., p51.

1:1)—and Adam's naming the animals is really a reflection of the Divine activity.

For Al-Arabi, Adam is what is often called in esoterism the Universal Man, and as such is the perfect image of the original Universal Man—Being. However, in order to avoid confusion it is best to use the term 'Perfect Man' or 'Transcendent Man' for Adam. Such a being, though the product of Heaven and Earth, through realizing his essential identity with God has been liberated from the cosmos. He resides not only at the center of our state of Existence, but of all states of Existence and thus is virtually identical to the World Spirit which, joined with the Divine Ray, connects all the states of Existence to their source. As such he can be considered the *barzakh* or mediator between the unmanifested and the manifested. It is in this regard that he is symbolized by the cross[8] and may be identified as the Way to God. Piercing through the center of the Divine Sun or Being (and thereby united with the Unmanifest beyond Being) he can even be considered as the Logos or Divine word. And this can be more easily understood if we remember that viewed as the World Spirit he separates Heaven and Earth, which allows creation to occur, and at the same time unites Heaven and Earth so that creation actually takes place. With these thoughts in mind we can more easily understand the following statement of Al-Arabi:

> For the Reality, he is as the pupil is for the eye through which the act of seeing takes place. Thus he is called *insan* [meaning both man and pupil], for it is by him that the Reality looks on His creation and bestows the mercy [of existence] on them. He is Man, the transient [in his form], the eternal [in his essence]; he is the perpetual, the everlasting, the [at once] discriminating and unifying Word. It is by his existence that the Cosmos subsists and he is, in relation to the Cosmos, as the seal is to the ring, the seal being that place whereon is engraved the token with which the king seals his treasure. So he is called the Vice-Regent, for by him God preserves His creation, as the seal preserves the king's

8. The horizontal bar indicates our particular state of Existence, with the others, which we may term the heavens and hells, above and below that line.

> treasure. So long as the king's seal is on it no one dares to open it except by his permission, the seal being [as it were] a regent in charge of the kingdom. Even so is the Cosmos preserved so long as the Perfect man remains in it.[9]

Following the comments in chapter 2, in the biblical account of creation it is best to view the figure of Adam, the Primal Man, as the Prototype of humanity rather than a human being. However, as such he represents what is possible for human beings, and any human who has realized his identity with the Unmanifest—that is to say, any Perfect Man—is for all intents and purposes identical with the original Adam.

Guénon, in various works, steadfastly refuses to identify Adam with the Perfect Man. Rather, he views Adam as the True Man who resides at the center of our state of being, but not all the other states. The True Man is one who has reached the end of the path initiated by the first rebirth but not as yet that of the second rebirth, and thus has not realized the Supreme Identity. We can perhaps reconcile these two descriptions of Adam by saying that on one level he represents the Prototype of humanity and on another level (or from a different point of view) he represents human beings of the Adamic or Golden Age. The normal person of that age was already centered in the Spirit and only had to undergo what we have called liberation from the human state. If Adam is viewed in this way, then we must say that the typical human of today is made in an image of the image of God. If Adam is viewed as the Prototype of humanity, then we must consider ourselves as made in the image twice removed.

9. Ibid., p51.

5

Adam and Eve

PERHAPS THE MOST WELL-KNOWN STORY in Genesis is that of the fall of Adam and Eve in the Garden of Eden. But as much as it is known, so much is it misunderstood. There have been no lack of interpretations of this story, and many of them have been symbolic. But because the people making these interpretations have approached the story in such wrong-headed ways, the results, as we might expect, have been less than edifying.

According to the literalistic view, every sentence in the story is to be taken historically and considered true. In opposition to this is the scientistic view: every sentence is to be taken historically and considered false. Some of this group, in an attempt to be charitable, find in the story of the fall the first recorded example of the theory of evolution: from the innocent ape to man.

Then we have the moralistic interpretation. According to this view, the story of the fall (like the rest of the stories in the Bible) is not literally true but serves as a backdrop for teaching certain moral lessons.

The structuralistic idea is that the story is not literally true but demonstrates the essentially binary nature of human thought. For example, the passage from naked to clothed represents the civilizing force of society exerted on life as it would be in a state of nature. According to another anthropological view the leaving of paradise symbolizes the passage from a foraging culture to a farming culture. Finally, the psychologistic views. According to one of these the expulsion from the Garden symbolizes birth and its attendant trauma. According to another the loss of innocence and subsequent expulsion from the Garden represent growing up (reaching puberty) and leaving home. About these last two views it must be said that the birth trauma is a modern invention and that in biblical times people lived for the most part in extended family units.

None of these approaches takes seriously the possibility that the creators of this and other stories to be found in the Bible were consciously attempting to transmit spiritual truths in a symbolic fashion. Some atheists view these stories as folktales and conclude that they are of entertainment value at best. This approach is half correct and half incorrect. These stories are at least akin to folktales, but the proper conclusion to draw from this is that they have great significance on a symbolic level.[1]

As we have already acknowledged, most Bible stories function on different levels, and the story of the fall is no exception to this rule. On the most superficial level it explains how snakes lost their legs and became enemies of mankind. On a somewhat more profound level it explains why life has to be so hard and why people have to die.[2] Of course, the explanation for our hard lot which is offered in Genesis is not satisfactory to many people. If someone who had never heard of Judaism or Christianity read the account of the disobedience and punishment of Adam and Eve described in chapter 3, he might well come away with a very negative opinion of God. On a literal level the whole episode reads like the story of a parent who told his children not to eat the fruit of a certain tree on his property and who punished their disobedience by running them out of his house and sentencing them to hard labor followed by execution. For all the fuss that is made over the biblical disobedience by literalists (most of whom do not understand the true meaning of 'obedience to God') it is hard to see the story as reflecting positively on

1. For more on this matter cf. Ananda Coomaraswamy's excellent article 'Primitive Mentality' in *Coomaraswamy: Selected Papers*, vol. 1 (Princeton: Princeton Univ. Press, 1977), pp 286–307.

2. There are stories all over the world which explain how mankind had a chance for an easy life or immortality and how some progenitor or culture hero let it slip away either by doing something forbidden or foolish, or by lack of care, or by not being in the right place at the right time, or by being asleep at the important moment. All of these tales have an air about them of lessons for children who are evidently supposed to draw the proper moral. That is not to say that none of them has a deeper meaning.

God. But it is precisely this bad taste left in our mouths that should alert us to the possibility that we are not approaching the story in the proper manner. If someone who had never heard of citrus fruits was given an orange with the information that it was a fruit, he might just bite right into it. The rind would taste quite bitter and he might conclude that this was one fruit which was not worth eating. But if he was then given a little more information about the orange he would most likely eat it properly and reverse his judgment. The literal meaning of the story of the fall is just its outside, and is not very palatable. But like the orange, it has an inside, a symbolic meaning which is full of spiritual nourishment.

Before getting to the 'inside' of the story we must clear up a humorous misunderstanding which has arisen in the minds of some people due to the connection between sexual awareness and death in the story of the fall. These people have drawn the conclusion that the way to long life is abstention from sexual activity. While sexual awareness is certainly a problem for the spiritual life, and while over-indulgence in any way can lead to an early death, the view we are considering cannot be taken seriously. For the general wellbeing and stability of life on this planet, it is imperative that animals which reproduce sexually be subject to death.

In order to begin a serious consideration of the story of the fall we must put aside completely the idea that it recounts an historical event. Its value lies in its being true for all times and persons, and it is in this respect that we all suffer the effects of 'original sin'. In being conceived, born and maturing, we all recapitulate God's manifestation of the world and its fall.[3]

The fall is prefigured in the splitting of the androgynous Adam into Adam and Eve. On the universal level it symbolizes the splitting of *Purusha* and *Prakriti* which necessarily precedes creation. And just as the splitting of Adam necessarily results in the imperfection of Adam and Eve which leads to their fall, the splitting of the Unity

3. W.L. Wilmshurst, in his book, *The Meaning of Masonry* (New York: Crown, 1980), takes a similar viewpoint in explaining the symbolism of this story. He goes on to compare the fall of Adam and Eve to the 'fall' of Persephone which was the subject of the Eleusinian Mysteries (pp193–194).

of Existence into the duality of *Purusha* and *Prakriti* (Heaven and Earth, the wind and the waters) necessarily results in the imperfection of the cosmos which leads to its fall. This imperfection of the cosmos is often referred to as the evil in the world, and it is hardly necessary to mention that much ink has been used in trying to account for its existence.

As Spinoza pointed out, much of what we call evil is merely what we do not happen to like. Thus we dignify as absolute something that is quite relative. However, this sort of self-centered attitude goes to the central nature of evil: it is the predation of one thing on another. If there was no multiplicity but only a unity, then there could be no evil. But if there was no multiplicity, if there was no separation of the poles of Existence, then there would be no cosmos. That there are even two things implies the possibility of what we call evil. Viewing this same subject from a somewhat higher perspective we may cite two very succinct comments by Frithjof Schuon:

> What people fail to understand is that the divine nature implies manifestation, creation, objectivation, and what is 'other-than-the-Self', and that this projection implies imperfection and therefore evil, since what is 'other-than-God' cannot be perfect, God alone being good.... The whole problem lies in that fact that the serpent was in Paradise. Had he not been there Paradise would have been God, or rather it could not have had any separate existence. To exist means not to be God, and so to be 'evil'.[4]

In connection with the first comment we should recall Jesus' statement, 'No one is good but God alone' (Mark 10:18). It is best to use the word 'perfect' in preference to 'good' when describing God, for using the latter term gives the impression that we are judging God in moral terms, and He is quite beyond such categories which can only have to do with the multiplicity of Universal Existence.

Returning to the splitting of the androgynous Adam, we can say that it results in two incomplete halves. Now this is, of course, the current human position, and it is of interest to examine the various

4. Frithjof Schuon, *Spiritual Perspectives and Human Facts*, tr. Macleod Matheson (London: Faber and Faber, 1954), pp50 and 52.

human responses to this loss of completeness, or as we might describe it, this loss of the balance between the active and passive poles of creation as objectified in us. One response is engaging in sexual intercourse. The problem here is that besides the fact that only the physical side of the person is involved, the effect of unification lasts a very short time. A much higher response is marriage which engages the emotional and mental sides of the person (and in general the soul) and is or should be a long-term matter. A much lower response is the orgy, although it has evidently not always been so viewed.

Here we must pause for a moment to correct a misconception found in the writing of Eliade and others having to do with the aim of recapturing the primordial completeness or unity.[5] According to these commentators, what people are aiming at in rituals designed to bring about such a unity is an experiential return to the primordial burbling soup, the original chaos in which all opposites are united. It may be that in certain degenerate societies this parody of a spiritual idea has provided a justification of orgiastic rituals. According to this way of thinking our great aim is to bring about a state of chaos internally and externally as a way of cancelling out internal and external division. It is said that the demonic apes the Divine, and this is a case in point, but we must never mistake this distortion of spirituality for the real thing.

In the first place the aim of regaining the androgynous state has to do not with a reunion of opposites but with a uniting of complements—the masculine and feminine poles of creation. The resultant condition is very far from chaos, the latter being the natural state of one of the two poles. In the second place, achieving the androgynous state is a spiritual rather than a physical matter and thus cannot be brought about by physical or external activities. If Tantric Buddhism and Hinduism seem like exceptions to this rule, it is because they are very poorly understood in the West.[6] In the

5. Cf. Mircea Eliade, *The Two and the One*, pt. II, especially pp 111–124.

6. For a proper perspective on this matter cf. Marco Pallis, 'Considerations on the Tantric Alchemy', in *A Buddhist Spectrum* (New York: Seabury Press, 1981), chap. 5, and René Guénon, 'The Fifth Veda', in *Studies in Hinduism* (Hillsdale, NY: Sophia Perennis, 2001). *Dzogchen*, the Tibetan extension of Tantric Buddhism, *means* Great Completion.

tantric path one takes seriously the view that everything in the world is essentially the Ultimate Reality, or to put it in more Western terms, that the true nature of everything is God. The implication of this view is that nothing in the world is abhorrent or impure. For instance, in the Tantric Buddhism of Tibet, often called Vajrayana Buddhism, practitioners do not deal with the five poisons or afflicting emotions (desire or craving, aversion or anger, ignorance, pride and envy) by avoiding them, or by substituting something else for them, but by realizing their true nature—using them for firewood, or even for food, as it is sometimes said. Thus anything, including the sexual act, can be a means of attaining enlightenment. However, this act was not originally part of tantric practice, and at least in Tibetan Buddhism it is not considered central or essential. Rather it is taken as one among many means to an end.

Obviously the sexual act can be taken as a symbol of the rejoining of the two poles of creation and thus invested with more than a physical significance. Indeed, in Hinduism (*Chandogya Upanishad*, V.VIII) it is given a sacrificial significance, and it can very easily be understood as symbolizing the creative activity of the masculine or active pole on the feminine pole. Further, in Tibetan Buddhism there are many *Yab-Yum* (Father-Mother) images of sexual embrace used for visualizations having to do with meditative practices. These images typically symbolize the union of compassion with wisdom, or skillful means with intelligence, or sometimes bliss with emptiness. But none of this implies that the act alone can bring about spiritual regeneration. Again we must say that the reintegration of the person is a spiritual one, and it is to this that the passages from the *Gospel According to Thomas* mentioned by Eliade refer. In Logion 22 we read:

> Jesus said to them: When you make the two one, and when you make the inner as the outer and the outer as the inner and the above as the below, and when you make the male and the female into a single one, so that the male will not be male and the female [not] be female... then you shall enter [the Kingdom].[7]

7. Guillaumont et. al., *The Gospel According to Thomas* (New York: Harper & Row, 1959), p17.

And in Logion 106 we read:

> Jesus said: when you make the two one, you shall become sons of man, and when you say: 'Mountain be moved,' it will be moved.[8]

These quotations, which would otherwise be puzzling, take on an obvious significance in light of our discussion. In order to enter the Kingdom of God, in order to become sons of Man (the androgynous Adam) we must reverse the process of the original splitting into Adam and Eve and become whole again. This reversal can be described as regaining Paradise or as regaining the fruits of the Tree of Life.

In the fourth century, there arose a group of Christians who called themselves the Adamites and referred to each other as Adam and Eve. They held church in underground vaults and in the nude. All who joined were supposed to be virgins. Evidently they regarded their underground meeting place as the Earthly Paradise and felt that they had regained the original standing of the biblical Adam and Eve by virtue of their sexual purity. In effect they had dispensed with their sexuality and thus had become complete in the way we have explained.[9]

The Terrestrial Paradise has been called by many names: the Garden of Eden, the Land of the Hyperboreans, the Isle of the Blessed, and Ultima Thule among others. In many cultures there are stories of such lands, pictured sometimes atop inaccessible mountains, sometimes on faraway islands as in the cases of the summit of Dante's Mount Purgatory and the abode of the Taoist immortals called Penglai by the Chinese and Mt Horai by the Japanese. Unfortunately, these lands, which survive all floods, have become invisible in our times, underground or hidden in the Adamite's case. They are symbols of the center of Divine influence on earth, and their indestructibility despite all the cataclysms and the degeneration of the world symbolizes the persistence of this influence. Their invisibility in our age symbolizes the spiritual blindness which is obvious

8. Ibid., p53.

9. Wilhelm Fraenger, *Hieronymous Bosch* (Amsterdam: Overseas Publishing Association, 1999), pp17–18. A similar group appeared in the fourteenth century.

throughout the world.[10] While we must understand these paradisiacal lands as symbolizing the center of Divine influence in our plane of Existence, we can admit that at all times there have existed physical spiritual centers which can be regarded as the focal points of spiritual influence in the world.

Truthfully, the two trees in the Garden of Eden are really different aspects of the World Tree, a symbol for the world in many different spiritual traditions. Daniel 4 contains a description of it in a dream of King Nebuchadnezzer:

> I saw a tree of great height in the midst of the earth;
> The tree grew and became mighty;
> Its top reached heaven,
> And it was visible to the ends of the earth.
> Its foliage was beautiful
> And its fruit abundant;
> There was food for all in it.
> Beneath it the beasts of the field found shade,
> And the birds of the sky dwelt on its branches;
> All the creatures fed on it. (4:7–9)[11]

10. 'The word of the Lord came to me: O mortal, you dwell among the rebellious breed. They have eyes to see but see not, ears to hear but hear not; for they are a rebellious breed' (Ezek. 12:1–2).

11. Geo Widengren, in his study *The King And The Tree Of Life In Ancient Near Eastern Tradition* (Uppsala: A-B Lundequistska Bokhandlen, 1945), seems to want to differentiate between the Cosmic Tree and the Tree of Life (p57), at least as far as Mesopotamian myth is concerned. He notes Sumerian literature in which the Tree of Life is growing in Paradise by the streams containing the Water of Life. In other literature the king is described as watering the Tree of Life in a temple grove symbolizing Paradise, functioning as a gardener (p15). Perhaps there is something similar in the folktale 'Aschenputel' (Cinderella), where after getting her father to bring her a twig from a hazel tree, Aschenputel plants it on her mother's grave and waters it with her tears. We must remember that from this tree come her beautiful clothes and everything else. Cf. Samuel D. Fohr, 'Cinderella And All-Kinds-Of Fur' in *Cinderella's Gold Slipper* (Hillsdale, NY: Sophia Perennis, 2004). Speaking of twigs, Widengren cites texts in which kings are called shoots from the Tree of Life, and compares this to biblical passages where future kings (possibly messianic) are described as shoots or branches, passages such as Isaiah 11:1, Jeremiah 23:5, and Zechariah 3:8 and 6:12 (pp50–52).

The Tree of Life is the trunk of the World Tree and constitutes the World Axis around which our realm and all others are manifested. The branches to either side of the trunk are parts of the Tree of Knowledge and can be understood as constituting the various realms of Existence. They also symbolize the dual activity of the World Axis, creative and destructive, depending on whether a cycle of ages is beginning or ending. In Taoism it is called the Middle Way (as the center of the various realms of Existence) and the Way of Heaven (since it is the path of the Influence or Will of Heaven). In the Bible it is sometimes symbolized as an undying fire (Exodus 3:1–2), and at others as a pillar of cloud, a pillar of fire (Exodus 13:21), a flaming sword (Genesis 3:23), and a mountain (or its spine, Exodus 17). It is along this Axis that we find the Divine Presence in the world.[12]

Mention was made in chapter 3 of a different set of two trees, one upright and one inverted. No doubt the inverted tree is really the World Tree with its roots above (*Katha Upanishad*, VI.1) since it symbolizes the world. The supernal upright tree is really the realm of Being conceived as a pattern for this world, the Sefirotic Tree of Kabbalism. As we mentioned earlier, the trunk of the upright tree is the Ray from the Spiritual Sun or Being which brings light out of darkness. When it hits the 'waters' or passive pole of Universal Existence it is reflected inversely, the trunk of that reflection being the World Axis. Or we can say that the whole supernal world of the *Sefirot* is reflected inversely in our world.

12. Ultimately we must say that the Divine Presence pervades the world, since the world is but a manifestation of God Who contains it. But from our point of view the Presence exists in a central place. The Hindu worship of *Maya* affirms the absolute point of view. *Maya* can be equated with the world or cosmos. But it can also be equated with *Prakriti*, as the latter is the source of the world. *Maya* is often described as Illusion in that it hides the true character of its underlying Reality—*Saguna Brahman* or Being. Being is one, but through ignorance we experience it as a plurality of entities in a state of becoming—i.e., as *Maya*. Thus *Maya* appears as the manifested world over and against *Saguna Brahman*. In truth it is but the *Shakti* or Power (constituting a Veil of Ignorance) of *Saguna Brahman* and as such is inseparable from It and worthy of worship.

Where the Celestial Ray hits the waters is the Sundoor of the cosmos, the Celestial Paradise.[13] The Ray's image, the World Spirit or Axis, goes down through the various planes of Existence forming the center of each, and as well it forms the spirit or center of every human being. Plato (*Republic* 616) describes it thus:

> ... extended from above throughout the heaven and earth, a straight light like a pillar, most nearly resembling the rainbow, but brighter and purer ... for this light was the girdle of the heavens ... holding together ... the entire revolving vault. And from its extremities was stretched the spindle of Necessity, through which all the orbits turned. It's staff and its hook were made of adamant.[14]

On its connection with humans Plato (*Laws* 644–45) has the following to say:

> May we not conceive each of us living beings to be a puppet of the Gods, either their plaything only, or created with a purpose? Which of the two we cannot certainly know—but we do know, that these affections in us are like cords and strings, which pull us different and opposite ways, and to opposite actions; and herein lies the difference between virtue and vice. According to the argument there is one among these cords which every man ought to grasp and never let go, but to pull with it against all the rest; and this is the sacred and golden cord of reason, called by us the common law of State....[15]

In this passage Plato applies the notion of the golden cord to both the reason within a person and to the law of the state. But it is the

13. Dante describes the Empyrean, the Celestial Paradise beyond the heavens, as a gigantic white rose (*Paradiso*, cantos XXX–XXXI) upon which shines 'the eternal Light', 'the exalted light', 'the living ray' (canto XXXIII). Dante Alighieri, *Paradiso*, tr. Robert and Jean Hollander (New York: Anchor Books, 2008). Plato describes the Heavenly Paradise in the *Phaedo* 110–11 as a world above our own.

14. Edith Hamilton and Huntington Cairns, eds., *The Collected Dialogues of Plato* (Princeton: Princeton Univ. Press), p840. The translation is by Paul Shorey.

15. *The Dialogues of Plato*, fourth edition, tr. Benjamin Jowett (Oxford: Oxford Univ. Press,1953), vol. IV, pp210–211.

first that occupies us here. Plato refers to what he calls the highest part of the soul in this way, and it is what we have termed the spirit. In the *Republic* (590) he calls it the 'divine ruler' within the person, and says, 'it is better for everyone to be ruled by divine reason, preferably within himself and his own, otherwise imposed from without,'[16] the latter no doubt by the 'common law of the state', assuming it is a properly run state.

The central position of the Tree of Life is shown by the four rivers which begin in Garden of Eden and flow out into the rest of the world (Gen. 2:10). These rivers symbolize the four directions of space and we can view them as dividing the earth into four quarters radiating out from the center of manifestation. It is worth noticing that the Land of the Garden is not watered from above 'but a flow would well up from the ground and water the whole surface of the earth' (2:6). Generally, God's inspiration, influence, and sustenance are thought of as coming from on high. As rain, which is sustaining and purifying, also comes from on high, it is a natural symbol for God's influence. However, in the Garden of Eden there is no rain but rather a flow of water from the ground. This flow also symbolizes God's influence, and as it comes from the ground rather than from on high, we can conclude that in some sense the Garden and the trees within it are in the midst of God. That is to say, when we are positioned at the Tree of Life in the midst of the Garden, God is not *up there* but *right here*.

We have already indicated that just as we can speak of the center of our plane of Existence, we can also speak of the center of the human being. We are all connected to the World Spirit by our own spirits, what St Thomas Aquinas calls our created intellects in his *Summa Theologiae*, and we can re-express this by saying that the World Spirit runs through all of us. It is for this reason that Philo locates the Terrestrial Paradise, as well as the Tree of Life and the Tree of Knowledge, within us.[17] Indeed, as far as spiritual growth is concerned it is necessary to think of them as within, and understand

16. *Plato/Republic*, tr. G.M.A. Grube, rev. by C.D.C. Reeve (Indianapolis: Hackett Publishing Company, 1992), p262.

17. Cf. *Concerning Noah's work as a Planter*, pt. IX.

the journey to them as an inner one. Androgynous Adam, the Perfect Man, resides in consciousness at the center of his being. There he experiences completeness and unity with all the other beings of the earth. This is shown in Gen. 1:29–30 where God gives the fruits and seeds of plants to man as food. One who discerns his unity with the rest of creation does not seek to harm any living thing as a means of feeding himself.

The experience of unity is shattered when Adam and Eve eat the fruit of the Tree of Knowledge of Good and Evil, and the change which comes over them is really the fall into dualistic consciousness. Once one experiences the world in terms of oneself and others, mine and thine, good and bad, the fall has occurred. Some commentators link eating the forbidden fruit to the fall into moral relativism or subjectivism. While there is some plausibility to this interpretation, we believe that the truth is better expressed by reordering these words: eating the forbidden fruit led to the fall into the relativism of morality, a matter we discussed in chapter 1 and will take up again in chapter 6.

It is not accidental that sexual awareness is linked with the fall, for it is at the time of puberty that humans lose the last vestige of the primordial world-view. Before it they had been complete (not needing a sexual partner) and balanced (containing male and female aspects in nearly equal amounts). Internally they were neuter and externally they treated others in this way. But with the dawning of sexual awareness they begin to see people first and foremost as males and females who are to be treated differently and viewed as objects for the fulfillment of desires. To sum up, puberty and the coming of sexual awareness is an example on a certain level of the division of androgynous man.

The serpent who tempts Adam and Eve to eat the fatal fruit[18] is, as we indicated in chapter 1, a dual symbol. The connection between

18. The identification of this fruit as an apple by the Roman Church in the fifth century seems to have been an attempt to discredit Celtic Christianity and in general the Celtic spiritual tradition. The Celts called their paradise 'Avalon' or the Isle of Apples, and they viewed apple cider much as Christians viewed wine made from grapes. As to the symbolism of drunkenness, see our discussion of Noah in chapter 7.

the snake and the tree (or suitable substitute) in spiritual symbolism is quite well known. One need think only of the Ancient Greek *caduceus* and the archetypal Hindu picture of the Devas and Asuras churning the ocean for its hidden treasure of *amrita* by pulling on either end of a serpent wrapped around the world mountain. In the first place, the snake, like the Tree of Life itself, is a symbol of immortality. We must remember that this Tree, which is a symbol of the World Axis, represents the center of the world as well as every human being. As such, it is the place of immortality or consciousness of the eternal.[19] Adam and Eve's portrayal as immortal before the fall symbolizes this state of consciousness which is that of the complete person. Now the snake, by virtue of shedding its skin every so often, seems thereby to be constantly renewing its life and thus immortal. This idea is found in the Babylonian *Epic of Gilgamesh* from the early second millennium B.C. In this epic, part of which we will compare to the story of Noah, the hero Gilgamesh loses his chance for immortality when a snake steals the herb of immortality from his boat, eats it, and sheds its skin (Tablet XI). In fact, the connection between the snake and the World Axis is so strong that there are African spiritual traditions in which the World Axis is considered a celestial serpent. In these traditions the rainbow is assimilated to a serpent. But as we shall see in the chapter on Noah, the rainbow is still another symbol of the World Axis.[20] Thus in the Yoruba language the word for rainbow, *osumarē*, contains the word for big snake, *erē*.[21] On the other hand, the shedding of the skin is also a symbol of death and rebirth. This connects the snake with the Tree of Knowledge since it has both positive (rebirth) and negative (death) aspects, or to use moralistic terms, good and evil aspects.

19. There is no better symbol of the place of immortality than the evergreen tree which is to be found in all Shinto shrines. Shinto priests conducting ceremonies outside of shrines bring along at least one branch of such a tree.

20. This is mentioned in René Guénon, *Symbols of Sacred Science* (Hillsdale, NY: Sophia Perennis, 2004), chap. 64, 'The Bridge and The Rainbow'. It seems the ancient Chinese and ancient Greeks may also have assimilated rainbows to serpents. On the various symbols of the World Axis cf. chaps. 51–65 of *Symbols of Sacred Science*. See also our discussion of Moses' staff in chapter 11.

21. This information was supplied by 'BioDun Ogundayo.

The snake as tempter and cause of the fall is a symbol of the world manifested around the World Axis. (Its various coils can be seen as symbolizing either past and future cycles of manifestation or planes of Existence higher and lower than the earthly.) The world, through its effects on the senses, draws us ever out and away from the center of our being. Just as a snake entraps a victim by coiling around it the world can be said to entrap us by envelopment. In leading us away from our center it causes us to feel incomplete and thus puts desire in the place of peace. Actually, desire is but one side of a coin whose other side is aversion, and together they lead us to divide the world into what is good and what is evil. The cherubim which God sets to guard the entrance of the Garden of Eden after He has exiled Adam and Eve can be seen as symbolizing this judgmental view of the world.

Speaking of the serpent, Meister Eckhart puts forth a different view of its symbolism when considered together with Eve and Adam. Following St Augustine's exposition of the matter in *On The Trinity*, Eckhart takes the triad serpent-Eve-Adam to symbolize 'the sensitive faculty that we share with the brute beasts,' 'the rational faculty that is directed to external things,' and 'the superior rational faculty that cleaves to God.' Or again, they are 'the sensitive faculty', 'the inferior reason', and 'the superior reason'.[22] In our terms these correspond roughly to the body, soul and spirit. And certainly this way of understanding the serpent is in complete agreement with what we have just said. However, there is a problem with this interpretation and it concerns Adam. Eckhart himself says that 'our highest faculty' is 'the image of God with God and God with it.'[23] This is a particularly felicitous way of putting the matter, since we have explained that the World Spirit is a reflection or image of the Celestial Ray from God understood as the Spiritual Sun on the waters or substance of creation, and thus the spirit within each of us, as a part of the World Spirit, is also an image of God. But then 'our highest faculty' or spirit is incorruptible, yet Adam ate of the fruit and fell along with Eve. There is still a further problem with

22. *The Essential Sermons*, p108.
23. Ibid., p110.

lumping the serpent in with Eve and Adam, namely that, besides being of a different species (which by itself is not disqualifying[24]), it is really added on to the other two in the story, thus forming a sort of cobbled-together triad rather than a natural one.

There is still another way of understanding the fall which is perfectly consistent with the first we presented. As a distancing from the Spirit it represents the development of the psycho-physical individuality and hence the ego. This development involves a sense of separateness from the rest of creation, and subsequently there arises a desire for certain things and an aversion to other things. As before, this leads to evaluation or seeing things as good and evil. The end result is a loss of joy or bliss and the beginning of suffering due to either not getting (or losing) what we desire or getting what we have an aversion to. In our lives, as we mature, it is our fate to be thus cast out of paradise. Our purpose in life is to consciously work to reverse this process. On this subject Frithjof Schuon writes:

> Man complains of his sufferings, such as separation and death; but has he not inflicted them *a priori* upon the Self, by his very egoity? Is not individuation a separation from the divine 'I' and is not the *ego* itself a death in respect of infinite Life? It will be objected that we are not responsible for our existence; but man ceaselessly recreates, in his actions, this responsibility which he thinks he does not have; in this, taken together with the foregoing considerations, lies the deeper meaning of original sin. Man suffers because he wishes to be 'self in opposition to 'Self'.[25]

The Buddhist Wheel of Existence is comparable as a symbol to a section or cut of the tree surrounded by the snake. In the wheel we observe a place of central repose or peace surrounded by the moving spokes and rim. Typically we find ourselves on the rim of that wheel as it spins around. Our proper goal is to slide down one of the spokes toward the center and thus reach a point where we have

24. Plato, in the *Republic* 588C-589B, compares the rational, spirited, and appetitive parts of the soul to a man, a lion, and a hydra-like beast.

25. Frithjof Schuon, *Gnosis: Divine Wisdom* (Hillsdale: Sophia Perennis, 1990), p84.

stopped spinning—the Terrestrial Paradise. Now we must envision an axle going through this wheel and joining it to another wheel through which it also passes. This axle is the World Axis, and our goal after reaching the Terrestrial Paradise should be to move up this Axis to the Celestial Paradise or Sundoor[26] at the 'top' of the cosmos where it joins the Celestial Ray, following this Ray to the Spiritual Sun and finally achieving what is often called union with God, but which is actually the realization of our already existing identity with God. This journey, which involves two deaths and rebirths, as we will explain in chapter 7, is an inner one, taking place in the consciousness of the human being.

26. The Celestial Paradise is in effect the doorway to the Spiritual Sun or God as He reveals Himself, and thus we must go through this door of the Sun—the summit of the cosmos—to reach God. On this see Ananda Coomaraswamy's 'The Symbolism of the Dome' in *Coomaraswamy: Selected Papers*, vol. 1, ed. Roger Lipsey (Princeton: Princeton Univ. Press, 1977).

6
Cain and Abel

IN GENESIS 4 we are faced with one of those stories which, when taken historically, is unacceptable.[1] The main theme of the story is God's preference for Abel's sacrifice. No reason is given for this preference, and commentators who have wrestled with this story have attempted to make up for this deficiency. The end result has been a rewriting of the story rather than an explanation of it. On the other hand, if we go below the surface of the literal meaning we find that the story makes perfect sense as it stands, and has great heuristic value even though it ends on a negative note. In our own analysis we do not claim to have exhausted its symbolic significance, but we have at least given indications as to the direction its interpretation should take.

Others have looked below the surface of the story of Cain and Abel, but they have not been interested in its spiritual significance. In this connection we must say that while this story may be a reflection of an older one dealing with the rivalry between smiths[2] and herders with a nod to the relatively more regular life of the herders over that of the itinerant smiths, and while the original story may have been used to explain the wandering nature of the smith's work, the story as it appears in Genesis has its own meaning. And it is this meaning we must respect and keep in mind as we interpret it symbolically.

1. On the outward absurdity of certain Bible stories see Frithjof Schuon's 'The Demiurge in North American Mythology', in *Logic and Transcendence* (Hillsdale: Sophia Perennis, 1984), chap. 8.

2. The name 'Cain' probably meant smith. This would help explain why the development of technology was attributed to Cain's descendants. In Gen. 4:1, the name is related to the word *kanah*, which means to get or acquire.

Maimonides cites a doctrine of the Sages

> according to which every man is accompanied by two angels, one to his right and the other to his left, angels identified with the '*good inclination*' [*yetzer ha tov*] and the '*evil inclination*' [*yetzer hara*]. They also say that *the evil inclination* is produced in the human individual at birth.... On the other hand, *good inclination* is only found in man when his intellect is perfected.[3]

Although Maimonides explains the two inclinations in exclusively moral terms, traditionally the so-called evil inclination is understood as the natural appetites or cravings within an individual. The good inclination develops later in life and acts as a control on these cravings.

We may refer to these inclinations as the higher and lower tendencies within us, which are recognized in all spiritual traditions, as in the Hindu tradition where they are designated as *sattvic* and *tamasic*. These tendencies, which are symbolized by Abel and Cain, stem from our very make-up. We are constituted of body (*soma*), soul (*psyche*, *anima*) and spirit (*pneuma*). The last is the Divine part of us and may be called the intellect (in the traditional and proper meaning of the word). As we have noted, it corresponds to the World Spirit on the cosmic level and thus constitutes the *barzakh* or boundary (cross-over point) between the Divine and human within us. In the *Republic* Plato calls it the *logistikon*, Aristotle refers to it as the *nous*,[4] Kabbalists designate it as the *neshamah*, and in Hindu doctrine it is called the *buddhi*. This is the part of us which Aristotle says determines our proper function which involves contemplation (*theoria*). It is our essence and is for this reason referred to as our heart.[5] As the supra-individual part of us it contrasts with our soul

3. *The Guide of the Perplexed*, bk III, chap. 22, pp489–90.

4. The Greek word *nous* is often translated as 'mind', as in Plutarch's *Moralia* (cf. next footnote), but it should be understood that this is something beyond what we usually call the mental. As we remarked in chapter 4, our reason deals with individual things through generalizations but never deals with the supra-individual or universal. If we wish to use the word 'mind' here it should be understood in much the way Buddhists and Hindus understand the word '*manas*'.

5. The biblical injunction to love the Lord 'with all thy heart, and with all thy soul and with all thy might' (Deut. 6:5) contains a reference to the three aspects of

(the seat of our ego-sense and mental functions) and body, which together constitute what has been called our 'psycho-physical personality' or individuality. The soul, 'caught' between the body and spirit can play the part of devil or angel depending on whether it follows the outward (or downward) pull of the senses or the inward (or upward) pull of the spirit.[6]

The Sufis call the soul under the spell of the lower tendencies the *nafs* or lower soul. It is compared to a mule which stubbornly wants to go its own way and must be disciplined to serve as a vehicle for spiritual advancement. But in the lives of most people this mule is never trained, as the story of Cain and Abel symbolizes.

We must note first of all that Cain is the older of the two brothers. Now while it is true that from the metaphysical point of view the spirit always takes precedence over the soul and body, it is also true that the lower tendencies are the first to develop in a human being and may therefore be termed the oldest. Second, Cain is described as a tiller of the soil, which again suggests the lower tendencies. The higher tendencies, being the last to develop, are aptly symbolized by the younger brother Abel. Besides, he is described as a shepherd, and this has many spiritual connotations including leader, guide and protector. In comparing Cain to Abel and discussing their symbolism, St Augustine puts the matter this way:

> Now Cain was the first son born to those two parents of mankind, and he belonged to the city of man; the later son, Abel,

a human being. Plato, in the *Republic*, identifies what we have called the spirit as a part of the soul, albeit the highest part. He calls it the rational part, which is a little misleading (cf. the previous footnote). In the *Timaeus* (69 C–D) he refers to it as the immortal part of the soul. In this connection we should say that it is often referred to as the higher soul or higher mind or higher reason or higher intellect. Plutarch comments on the error of including the *nous* (the spirit or higher mind) as a part of the soul in his dialogue 'Concerning the Face which Appears in the Orb of the Moon' tr. Harold Cherniss and William C. Hembold in *Moralia* vol. XII (Cambridge: Harvard Univ. Press, 1968), 943A. See also 'On the Sign of Socrates' tr. Phillip H. DeLacy and Benedict Einerson in *Moralia* vol. VII (Cambridge: Harvard Univ. Press, 1968), 591 D–F.

6. Frithjof Schuon (cf. *In the Tracks of Buddhism*, p99) describes the struggle between the higher and lower tendencies as the opposition between knowledge (in the sense of wisdom) and passion.

> belonged to the City of God. It is our own experience that in the individual man, to use the words of the Apostle [1 Cor. 5:46], 'it is not the spiritual element which comes first, but the animal; and afterwards the spiritual'.... For in the individual man, as I have said, the base condition comes first, and we have to start with that; but we are not bound to stop at that, and later comes the noble state towards which we may make progress, and in which we may abide, when we have arrived at it. Hence it is not the case that every bad man will become good, but no one will be good who was not bad originally.[7]

St Augustine expresses himself in narrowly moral terms at the end, but his overall view accords with our own. And we certainly agree that the higher tendencies do not always win out over the lower.

There is no doubt that the story tells of a preference for the herding over the farming life, but this too has a spiritual significance. A farmer, being sedentary, has a tendency to build up a store of material possessions which entrap him in the lower life. A herder, who must pasture his flocks in different places, cannot afford the luxury of piling up possessions. Further, the spiritual view of life entails seeing ourselves as visitors on this earth, as travellers passing through, and not as sedentary owners of property. Similarly it is said that we must view ourselves as actors on a stage rather than take our worldly doings too seriously. And again, that we must take the part of the guest rather than the host.[8] Only as sojourners can we develop the non-attachment necessary to escape the worldly life and pursue the spiritual life.

While the story shows a preference for the nomadic life, it also, as Guénon points out, symbolizes the swallowing up of the nomadic by the sedentary life, for this is one of the meanings of the slaying of Abel by Cain. 'Solidification', to use Guénon's term, is one of the marks of the passage of ages, and it reaches a peak in the last age of the cycle. One aspect of this solidification is the tendency of the sedentary way of life to take over completely so that there is no more

7. *The City of God*, bk xv, chap. 1, p596.
8. *Tao Te Ching*, chap. 69.

room for the nomadic way of life, i.e., life on this earth becomes fixed.[9] It might be thought that in the current century there has been a change to a more nomadic existence in that employees are constantly shifted from one locality to another due to the practices of national and international corporations; but appearances are misleading. What we observe is a constant shifting from one fixed location to another. This shadow of the nomadic life carries with it all of the worst aspects of the sedentary life and none of its best aspects. It is another sign of the degenerate nature of our times.

Returning to the central theme of our interpretation we can easily see why God prefers Abel's sacrifice to Cain's. The product of the lower tendencies is worldliness, while that of the higher tendencies is spirituality. But as all those who have pursued the spiritual path know, the lower tendencies are jealous of their prerogatives. Taking the path of worldliness is akin to rowing downstream while taking the path of spirituality is analogous to rowing upstream against the current. The first is the path of least resistance and the second of greatest resistance. The pull of the current is constant, and if we are not careful we will be swept downstream. This is indeed the point made by the story of Cain and Abel. The murder of Abel by Cain symbolizes the killing off of the higher tendencies by the lower.

If the lower tendencies prevail within a person he will be condemned to become a 'restless wanderer' (Gen. 4:14), cast out like Adam and Eve from Eden. Life teaches us that in the pursuit of the lower or worldly things enjoyment fades quickly and the search must be taken up for new forms of pleasure. It is a never-ending quest and accounts for the peculiar frenzied activity that marks our own worldly age. Having persuaded ourselves that 'getting there is half the fun,' we have embarked on the project of convincing ourselves that there is really no goal and the journey counts for everything. It can be said of us, as it is said of Cain (4:16), that we have settled in the land of Nod—the land of Wandering.[10]

9. *The Reign of Quantity* (Hillsdale, NY: Sophia Perennis, 2001), chap. 21. Temporal space has been eliminated by our obsession with scheduling.

10. The restless wandering of Cain is to be distinguished from the life led by the herder. Cain represents the 'driven' human being, constantly seeking solace in the

The full verse from which we have just quoted reads: 'Since You have banished me this day from the soil, and I must avoid Your presence and become a restless wanderer on earth—anyone who meets me may kill me.' On a superficial level the story, as we have said, accounts for the wandering nature of the smith's work: his ancestor was banished from the land for polluting it. But we are interested in the profound meaning of the story, and we thus offer the following interpretation. Anyone who has eschewed the spiritual life has decided to avoid the Presence of God, which amounts to rejecting the Divine Indwelling, for it is the inner presence to which reference is being made. Such a person, estranged from the center of his being, sees himself as subject to harm and death. It is only in his individuality that he is subject to harm and death, but since he tends to identify himself with his body (or at best his psycho-physical individuality) he is naturally fearful.

Contrasting with the Cain orientation is the Abel orientation, in which the person identifies himself correctly with the spirit, his true center, which is supra-individual or universal. It is not that he loses his human individuality while on the earthly plane, nor even his sense of individuality, although the latter may be interrupted for brief periods. Rather he is no longer attached to his individuality. Such a person 'leaves no tracks' on his way through life. He is like a clear window through which the Spirit of God shines. Unconcerned with his safety, what harm can befall him? In the *Tao Te Ching* we read the following description of the sage, the man of *Tao*:

> I have heard that one who is a good preserver of life does not meet tigers or wild buffaloes, And in fighting is untouched by weapons of war.There is nowhere for a buffalo to butt its horns, Nowhere for a tiger to fasten its claws, And nowhere for weapons to lodge their blades. How is this? Because in him there is no room for death.[11]

---

external world. Abel represents the purposeful human being, moving through the external world where necessary, but understanding that his true home is not to be found there

11. Chapter 50. This English version is based mostly on the translation of Wing-tsit Chan (Indianapolis: Bobbs-Merrill, 1963).

Where there is no ego, or better, where the ego has been surpassed, there is no room for death. Fearlessness and ease replace fear and anxiety.

In responding to Cain's desperate cry,

> The Lord said to him, 'I promise, if anyone kills Cain, sevenfold vengeance shall be taken on him.' And the Lord put a mark on Cain, lest anyone who met him should kill him' (Gen. 4:15).

In order to understand the symbolism of the mark of Cain we must keep in mind the differences between the two types of persons we just described. The Abel type, ruled by the higher tendencies, not only cannot be harmed, but also will not harm others since he views others as connected with himself through the Spirit. On the other hand, the Cain type, who is ruled by the lower tendencies, not only can be harmed, but also will be disposed to harm others since he views them only in their mode of individuality and thus as completely other than himself. The mark of Cain is supposed to be protective and so we must ask: what is it that protects Cain-like people from each other? The answer is at once obvious: morality—the legislation of human activity by God. Morality is what is given (or left) to human beings in their fallen state. As Jacques Ellul says, 'Morality is a product of those societies in which the sacred fades out and tends to disappear. It is a weak substitute for that which had been radical, ultimate, and established beyond dispute.'[12] Far from being the aim of the spiritual life it is merely a necessary condition of the worldly life if it is to be livable at all. We can view the mark of Cain as the moral sense or conscience from the inner point of view and as the Law of God from the outer point of view.[13] The mass of mankind must be considered the sons of Cain, as we shall see shortly, and thus they share Cain's mark. The few who are saintly or holy are quite beyond morality, the motivation for their actions springing

12. *The New Demons*, p54.

13. This view of the Law of God is, after all, not so very different from St Paul's notion of the Law as condemning mankind (Rom. 3–9) rather than providing a means of being saved. Unfortunately, while Paul was thinking esoterically, he has typically been interpreted exoterically.

from quite another source than the constraint of conscience or moral laws.

Following the mark narrative we find information about the descendants of Cain who are described as the bringers of technology to mankind (Gen. 4:21–22). Technology is another necessary concomitant of the fallen state, and it is to be noticed that in stories of almost all cultures the bringing of technology to mankind takes place after, and as if to make up for, some spiritual dislocation.[14] Our tremendous dependence on technology makes it difficult to imagine that there was an age when man was such, and his conditions such, that little or no technology was needed for his survival.

While some technology is harmful, much of it is relatively beneficial to mankind. Among other things, Cain's descendants brought us musical technology, and early instruments such as the lyre and pipe are mentioned explicitly (Gen. 4:21). These instruments have a certain spiritual symbolism[15] and, in truth, early technology was always spiritually symbolic in one way or another, thus showing that its introduction was due to Divine influence.[16] And it must be remembered that Cain, although pictured as opposing the Divine order of things, is still presented as being much closer to God (viz., direct contact) than the general run of humanity in our own age. The problem is that, as technology has developed in the musical realm and all others, the beneficial quality of its products has diminished greatly. Perhaps it would be clearer to say that its risks are beginning to outweigh its benefits, and that people themselves, as a result of working with technology, are becoming more machine-like. Yet every 'advance' has been embraced eagerly in the

14. It is certainly significant that, in many parts of the world, stories describing the transmission of technology to mankind involve the punishment of mankind as well as the 'culture hero', e.g., the story of Prometheus, and various trickster stories of the American Indians.

15. That of the pipe is brought out in Rumi's *Masnavi* and that of the lyre in the sayings of Heraclitus.

16. All ancient stories on the subject trace the original source of technology back to God. That people in our times have seen fit to ignore this is an example of the modern tendency to elevate man or human reason to the status of divinity. The dire results of the human direction of technology are becoming only too apparent.

West and the Western world-view is slowly but surely penetrating into the East. This is one of the reasons why we must hold that the mass of mankind are the sons of Cain, even though according to the Bible this cannot be literally true since all the descendants of Cain were killed in the flood.

The other reason is bound up with the most well known of all the passages from the story of Cain and Abel. We are referring to Cain's reply when God questions him concerning the whereabouts of Abel: 'I do not know. Am I my brother's keeper?' (Gen. 4:9). This question encapsulates the philosophy of life held by most humans, regardless of their political, religious, or economic posturing. And it cannot be otherwise for Cain-like people. If one sees only the individuality of oneself and others, then one cannot help but treat others in an inferior way, or at least this will be the general tendency.

But not all of humanity is subject to this tendency. The Bible records the birth of Seth (Gen. 5:3), who, as we mentioned previously, was born in the image of Adam.[17] Side by side with the majority of people who are Cain-like, there are beings who have not rejected the Spirit of God and who view themselves as their brothers' keepers. St Augustine describes these two sorts of people as those of the city of man (the earthly city) and those of the City of God (the Heavenly City). And he says, '... the earthly city was created by self-love reaching the point of contempt for God, the Heavenly City by the Love of God carried as far as contempt of self.'[18]

From another angle we can say that side by side with the development of civilization along Cainite lines, the primordial spiritual tradition has survived, even if it has been invisible to most people, and even if it has been subject to great pressures from the forces of 'progress'.

17. In his excellent article 'Seth' in *Symbols of Sacred Science* (Hillsdale, NY: Sophia Perennis, 2004), chap. 20, René Guénon expounds on the fact that the Egyptian Set (which is really equivalent as a name) has the negative qualities associated with Cain. Indeed, the genealogies given for Cain and Seth in the Bible have some names in common and many that are similar. The article deals with the dual nature of symbols, a matter we touched upon explaining the symbolism of the serpent in chap. 5.

18. *The City of God*, bk XIV, chap. 28, p593.

7

The Ark and the Tower

THE GREAT REGENERATORS OF THE EARTH, such as Noah and Moses, are symbols of the infusion of the Divine influence into the world in times of need. Reading the statement of Lamech about his son Noah (which we quoted in chapter 2), 'This one will provide us relief' (Gen. 5:25), we cannot help but think of the well-known statement found in the *Bhagavad Gita*. It is spoken by Krishna, who is considered to be one of the incarnations of Vishnu (who may be understood as God in this context):

> Whenever there is decay of righteousness and a rising up of unrighteousness, O Bharata, I send forth Myself. For the preservation of good, for the destruction of evil, for the establishment of righteousness, I come into being in age after age.[1]

This comparison takes on added weight when we remember that just before the story of the flood the human race is said to have sunk to a very low level (Gen. 6:5–6). We must also mention the Mahayana Buddhist description of the journey to spiritual realization as 'crossing over the ocean of birth and death,' 'Mahayana' meaning the great raft. And Buddha himself spoke of the enlightened person as one who has 'crossed over' the stream.

In order to better understand the symbolic significance of these bodies of water it will reward us to turn to the Babylonian *Epic of Gilgamesh*, which contains a prototype of the Noah story. In Tablet

1. Translation by Eliot Deutsch (New York: Holt, Rinehart and Winston, 1968), IV: 7–8, p55.

XI, lines 21–27, Utnapishtim, the equivalent of Noah, recounts that he was told the following:

> Man of Shuruppak, son of Ubar-Tutu, Tear down [this] house, build a ship! Give up possessions, seek thou life. Despise property and keep the soul alive! Aboard the ship take thou the seed of all living things.[2]

Utnapishtim is being told that for the life of the Spirit he must give up the worldly life, and it is no coincidence that Utnapishtim was subsequently granted immortality by the gods. We are to interpret this immortality in the spiritual sense, rather than the crude spatio-temporal sense.

The *Dhammapada*, a work of early Buddhism, contains a similar message:

> Give up what is before, give up what is behind, give up what is in the middle, passing to the farther shore of existence. When your mind is wholly freed, you will not again return to birth and old age (D.348).[3]

We seem here to have a reference to the near bank of *samsara* and the farther shore of *nirvana*, although the water itself would seem to be a part of *samsara*. 'Few amongst men are those who reach the other shore. The other people here run along this shore' (D.85). 'But those who, when the law [Buddha's teachings] has been preached to them, follow the law, will pass to the other shore, (beyond) the dominion of death which is difficult to overcome' (D.86). Again, 'Empty the boat, O mendicant' (D.369), and 'A mendicant who has freed himself from the five fetters [lust, hatred, doubt, pride, and false views] is called one who has crossed the flood' (D.370). The water or flood to be crossed is that of desire, anger, etc. Crossing it we are free from *samsara*, the cycle of birth and old age (i.e.,

2. Translation by E.A. Speiser from *Ancient Near Eastern Texts*, ed. James B. Pritchard, third edition (Princeton: Princeton Univ. Press, 1969), p93.

3. *The Dhammapada*, S. Radhakrishnan, tr. (Oxford: Oxford Univ. Press, 1969), p93. This translation also appears in *A Sourcebook In Indian Philosophy*, ed. Sarvepalli Radhakrishnan and Charles A. Moore (Princeton: Princeton Univ. Press, 1957).

change) and hence death. In other words, the ocean must be crossed if we are to attain the sense of eternity, *nirvana*, in this life. As we mentioned earlier, in certain traditions paradise is described as an island across the ocean, and now we can add that voyaging across the ocean to paradise symbolizes overcoming our lower tendencies and reaching the center of our being wherein resides the Divine Presence or Indwelling (the *Shekhinah*). To use a Buddhist mode of expression, it is to travel from the conditioned world to the unconditioned.

With these ideas in mind we can say that the water on which the ark floated may be understood as corresponding to 'the ocean of birth and death'. (The waters on which Jesus walked are the very same.) They are the waters of attachment to worldly things and the results of this attachment, which are twofold. On the one hand there are the desires to gain and keep the things to which we are attached. On the other there are the negative emotions which result from not being able to gain or keep these things. Thus we have a turbulent sea of attachments, desires, anger, and all the rest. Life—that is, immortal life in the spiritual sense—is gained only if we can keep from being drowned in this sea of ordinary life. With the raft of the correct view wedded to spiritual practice we can shed our sourness, feelings of disappointment, criticalness, discontent, jealousy, envy, negativity and harshness, in favor of cheerfulness, praise, contentment, trust, benevolence, positiveness, and kindness.

The ark functions as a symbol on at least three different levels. In the context of the present discussion it symbolizes that by which we can escape being drowned in the lower tendencies. In Buddhism, the raft to cross the ocean of birth and death is Buddha's *Dharma* or Teachings. But this is only one manifestation of the primordial spiritual tradition which shows itself in the Bible as well. It is this tradition which is the ark for all people at all times, and it is this tradition which we are presently endeavoring to explain.[4] This very same tradition is the vehicle for spiritual rebirth, and that brings us to the

4. In a secondary way a particular spiritual tradition may be considered an ark, and in a tertiary way a particular building, if properly constructed, may serve this purpose.

other two symbolic meanings of the ark. The ark is at once the seed or egg of the regenerated world and the regenerated person.

Scholars long ago noted that the flood story is really a creation story (although perhaps it would be better to call it a re-creation story). The idea of the world coming from a cosmic egg floating on the waters is found in many cultures, and in contemporary times this sort of picture is derided because it represents the cosmos as an organism which develops in the way all living beings develop. It is thus considered a reflection of times when people did not know any better. Such views are based on too literal an interpretation of what is essentially symbolic in nature, and they completely miss its significance.

Before we discuss the ark as cosmic egg it will be helpful to talk of the waters on which it floated, for in this context the waters serve to symbolize something different from what was just mentioned. They are the lower waters which were separated from the upper or heavenly waters according to Gen. 1. The word *mabbul*, which is translated as 'flood' in 7:10, actually refers to the heavenly waters. In Hinduism, the two waters taken together are called *Prakriti*, which is one of the two poles of Universal manifestation. It is the passive or plastic principle in contrast to the active principle which is called *Purusha*. In Aristotelian terms they correspond to the pairs Substance (*hyle*) and Essence (*eidos*), pure potentiality and pure act, prime matter and the Unmoved Mover.[5] *Prakriti* is often thought of as made up of two parts—the higher part containing the possibilities of formless manifestation and the lower part containing the possibilities of formal manifestation.[6] In the Babylonian *Enuma Elish* they are referred to as the god Apsu—the sweet water—and the goddess Tiamat—the bitter water—who lie together before creation. In the flood narrative, the two, as it were, come together once again, the heavenly waters serving to spiritually regenerate the world.

5. In Taoism they are represented by the *yin-yang* symbol. In Christianity the active and passive poles are signified by the pair Holy Ghost (or Spirit)/Virgin Mother.

6. Cf. René Guénon, *Man and His Becoming according to Vedānta* (Hillsdale, NY: Sophia Perennis, 2001), chap. 5, n8.

In chapter 2 we mentioned Guénon's view according to which the ark served as the conservator of the spiritual tradition as well as the center of creation in the period between two cosmic cycles. It is the latter function which concerns us at present. As the story relates, it contains at least two of every animal, i.e. the seeds of creation. The ark is also a symbol of the Unity of Existence before the creation of the plurality which is our world, although we must say that it is a unity poised on the brink of multiplicity. This can be seen from its shape, which is greater in one direction than another (Gen. 6:15), and it is for this reason that it can be compared to an egg. The unevenness in shape as compared to a sphere indicates that the central point has been split into two foci. This split in the primordial egg is also represented by the Chinese *yin-yang* symbol, which, though circular, is divided into two parts which, *in this context*, correspond to the duality of earth and sky which we find in the myths of Greece and the Middle East. In order for creation to proceed, the sky and earth (which symbolize the formless and gross physical worlds) must be separated (or propped apart) to allow room for the atmosphere or subtle realm.[7] In the *Enuma Elish* this is accomplished by Marduk, and in the Hindu *Rig Veda* (x.121) it is brought about by Brahman in the role of Creator who 'inhabits' the cosmic

7. The three realms or worlds—gross physical, subtle, and formless—are called in Hinduism the *Tribhuvana—bhu* (earth), *bhuva* (atmosphere or intermediate region), and *svah* (heaven). In Buddhism there is the *Triloka—Kamaloka* (realm or world of desire), *rupaloka* (realm of form), and *arupaloka* (formless realm). These correspond to *Olam ha Asiyyah* (the world of making or achieving), *Olam ha Yetsirah* (the world of formation), and *Olam ha Beriah* (the world of creation) according to some schools of Kabbalism. Maimonides seems to refer to these worlds in pt. II, chap. 30 of *The Guide of the Perplexed* as the seas, the firmament and what is above the firmament, all of which, he says, come from the primordial 'water'. The midrashic literature contains many comparisons of the three sections of the tabernacle (described in Exod. 25–27) to the three realms (cf. *Exodus Rabbah*). These views are admirably summarized by Rabbi Manasseh ben Israel in Question 100 of his *Conciliator* (tr. E.H. Lindo, New York: Hermon Press, 1972). In his discussion he mentions that the cherubim on the ark which was placed in the holiest part of the tabernacle are often understood as male and female and are taken to symbolize causes and effects. But this is just another way of referring to them as the active and passive poles of creation. Thus the cherubim represented the primordial duality of which we have spoken.

egg (*Brahmanda*) in the person of the Golden Embryo (*Hiranyagharba*—whose realm is properly the subtle.) While this is not the method actually described in the biblical story (which we will get to shortly), it is possible to view Noah in the role of separator, but only with the proviso that we consider him as a personification of Divine influence and not as a human being.

We have been concentrating on the shape of the ark, but something must be said about its structure. This will entail looking at its symbolism from a somewhat different perspective. It is described as having three decks and an opening for daylight near the top (Gen. 6:16). If the ark is really the egg of the world then all of these details must have significance. We must not be lulled into thinking that this is just a typical way of building a sea-going vessel, for no ship that ever sailed the seas was built like the ark.

In order to understand its structure we must note that *Prakriti* is said to be constituted of three strands (qualities or tendencies) in perfect equilibrium. They are the three *gunas*—*sattva* (illumination, the upward tendency), *rajas* (activity, the expansive tendency), and *tamas* (darkness or inertia, the downward tendency). *Prakriti* is completely passive, but under the vivifying influence of *Purusha* the *gunas* are thrown into a state of disequilibrium which results in the formation of the world. Now as the waters on which the ark floated are really *Prakriti* or the feminine pole of creation, we can view the ark or cosmic egg as a production of *Prakriti*, and its three decks will then correspond to the three gunas. The sunlight shining on the top of the ark after the flood corresponds to the Solar Ray proceeding from *Purusha*.[8] Thus, as creation is said to take place due to the influence of *Purusha* on *Prakriti*, in the biblical story it is the result of the influence of sunlight on the contents of the ark.[9]

8. As we explained in chapter 3, this Solar Ray can be seen as proceeding from *Purusha* taken as Being—the Principle or source of both *Purusha* and *Prakriti*. Its reflection is the World Spirit or Intellect (*Buddhi*) which is the first production of *Prakriti*.

9. An architectural representation of the ark with its opening near the top is the Gothic cathedral with its rose window. The word for the central portion of the cathedral, 'nave', derives from the Latin *navis* (ship) and is related to the old German *naba* (hub). It is from the latter that we derive the word 'navel' for the place

With this in mind we can comprehend the significance of the two birds which Noah releases from the ark after it lands but before it discharges its contents. They are, of course, the raven and the dove (Gen. 8:6–8). Much has been made of the personality and habits of these birds, but as far as their spiritual symbolism is concerned the only thing that matters is their colors—black and white. Here again we have the symbolism of the Spiritual Ray—white—and undifferentiated or prime matter—black. It is worth noting that in the corresponding section of the *Epic Of Gilgamesh* three birds are released—a dove, a swallow and a raven. Now each of the gunas has a color associated with it: *sattva*—white; *rajas*—red; and *tamas*—black. Swallows come in different colors, but a common type is brown and orange, and this is close enough to red. Thus the three birds would seem to correspond to the three *gunas*. Whichever version of the story we choose, the important thing is that the birds are released just before the ark lands and the world is repopulated, i.e., just before creation takes place. In the biblical version stress is being put on the idea that creation proceeds from the action of *Purusha* on *Prakriti*. In the version from the *Epic of Gilgamesh* stress is being put on the idea that the world is made up of the three gunas. It may seem that we are straining credulity in making these comparisons between spiritual traditions. But we believe there is a correspondence between all true spiritual traditions, and that this was more apparent in ancient times.[10]

As we indicated previously, the ark is also the seed or egg of the regenerated person. This is shown by the use of the number forty in describing the length in days of the flood in the J version of the story. A whole book has been written on the significance of the age

---

where the umbilical cord is attached. Thus the nave, like the ark, is at one and the same time the ship to get us across the lower waters, the hub of creation, and that point from which creation proceeds.

10. In the Preface we stated that all authentic spiritual traditions are inspired by the same reality, so we should expect to find similarities in them. But there is also the matter of borrowing or diffusion from one spiritual tradition to another. A perfect example of this is the Christian saint Josaphat (a version of the word 'Bodhisattva') who is really the Buddha in Christian garb.

of forty as well as the number itself.[11] But while it is affirmed that it represents 'a new beginning, or rebirth' we are never told why it should be so. Many biblical examples are given, such as the Israelites wandering forty years in the wilderness, but we are not told why the number forty occurs so frequently. There is an old Jewish tradition that it takes forty days for an embryo to be completed,[12] and this may have influenced the Catholic view that it takes forty days for an embryo to be ensouled. But why forty rather than some other number? Our answer begins with the fact that the peoples of the ancient Near East divided the days of the year into seven-day weeks, probably based on the lunar month. Now there is something which takes forty weeks (and not nine months as we usually say today) that is very important to humanity, namely the normal period from conception to birth of a child, a matter easily ascertainable even in ancient times. Thus the number forty symbolizes a new beginning and it is not surprising that forty years was considered the length of a generation. But a new beginning also fits very well with the idea of spiritual generation.[13]

The significance of rebirth in spiritual advancement has been noted earlier and in this connection we can regard the outside of the ark as a kind of womb from which the regenerated person will be born. The tripartite division of the ark corresponds on one level to the physical, emotional and mental aspects of a person. These are related to the part of the body below the waist, the torso, and the head. However, it also refers to the three modalities of human existence which we mentioned in the last chapter: the gross physical

11. Stanley Brandes, *Forty The Age And The Symbol* (Knoxville: Univ. of Tennessee Press, 1985). See especially chap. 4.

12. Ibid., p70.

13. The symbolism of rebirth is discussed in great detail by Guénon in chapters 32, 33, and 41 of *Symbols of Sacred Science*. There is also a great deal of information on the two rebirths in his book *Perspectives on Initiation* (Hillsdale, NY: Sophia Perennis, 2004). Every spiritual initiation involves leaving behind one's old way of life and taking up a new way of life. Put differently, it is dying to one way of life and being born into another. From this we can understand the Gospel saying, 'those who lose their lives for my sake will find it' (Matt. 16:25). Having died to the old life at the time of initiation one receives a new name. The important thing to note about initiatic rebirth is that it marks the beginning of a process, not the end.

(body), the subtle (soul) and the formless or universal (spirit). The first interpretation, which is the one most natural in our own age, shows a preoccupation with the physical modality. And it must be said that in Western society the emotional and mental life of people is generally focused on the body, and the other modalities are in effect not admitted. But as we pointed out in our discussion of esoterism, in spiritual advancement there are really two deaths and rebirths, and they correspond precisely to the two higher modalities of human existence. These deaths and rebirths were the concerns of the initiations into the 'Lesser Mysteries' and 'Greater Mysteries' at Eleusis in ancient Greece. Plutarch (*Moralia* 943A–B) comments that 'one death reduces man from three factors to two and another reduces him from two to one.' He adds that Demeter 'disassociates the soul [and presumably the *nous* or spirit] from the body' and Persephone 'detaches' the *nous* from the soul.[14] Although it is perhaps and oversimplification, we could describe the first death as an overcoming of the body and the second as an overcoming of the soul, and we can say that in the *Divine Comedy* Dante accomplishes these tasks by working his way through hell and purgatory.[15]

The ray of sunlight shining on the top of the ark is, as we have said, the Divine Ray. The light which reaches the inside of the ark is equivalent to the reflection of the Solar Ray on the 'waters' of creation and is thus the World Spirit or Axis which functions as the center of the person. Restating something we described at the end of chapter 5 we can say that the first rebirth initiates a movement toward the Axis and the second begins a movement up the Axis to

14. *Moralia* 943A–B, 'Concerning the Face Which Appears on the Orb of the Moon', p199.

15. The soul is the seat of the mind, and in his famous *Shobogenzo*, the great Zen Master Dogen writes: 'I, Dogen, made a prostration before my late master, the ancient Buddha Tendo, for the first time on May 1, [1225]. The direct face to face transmission was given to me, one who has mastered a small part of the vast Buddhist Teaching. I attained a certain degree of dropping off body and mind and brought the transmission to Japan.' *Shobogenzo*, trs. Nishiyama and Stevens (Tokyo: Nakayama Shobo, 1977), 'Menju', p141. The phrase 'dropping off body and mind' was used often by Dogen's Chinese teacher Ju-Ching (Rujing). In Japanese it is '*shinjin datsuraku*' and Dogen used this phrase in his own teachings.

its source which is the Divine Ray, whose own source is Being—the Spiritual Sun, the latter constituting the 'face' (or first determination or appearance) of the Ultimate Reality which is the true goal. The first involves the engagement of the subtle modality and the second involves working through this modality to engage the formless modality. We could also describe this situation by saying that the Spirit lies dormant or hidden within a person, and his function is to uncover it and trace its path back to God. It involves a winding up of what has been unwound in creation, a retracing in consciousness of the steps of God's manifestation of the world. In doing this, a person will break through his individuality (which comprises the first two modalities), and this 'liberation' (or 'exaltation') of the spirit is described in Hinduism as its upward penetration through the crown of the head (the *brahma-randhra*), which corresponds to the window near the top of the ark. It is a movement from the manifested world to the domain of the Unmanifest and thus a movement out of the cosmos symbolized by the head.[16]

Returning to the topic of the regeneration of the world, the completion of this process is signified by the covenant of the rainbow (Gen. 9:8–17). We can look upon this story as merely a folktale explanation of the existence of rainbows, but its inner meaning is quite profound. The six colors of the rainbow which come out of the white light of the sun are another symbol of creation, comparable to

16. Charles Luk describes a Tibetan tantric practice called *Pho-wa* for opening the Aperture of Brahma on the crown of the head. It involves the repetition of a special mantra as well as visualization. Cf. *Secrets of Chinese Meditation* (London: Rider & Co., 1964), pp198–201. In his book *Bardo Teachings* (Ithaca, NY: Snow Lion, 1982), pp10–11, Lama Lodo warns against doing this practice before one is near death, as it may lead to one's premature demise. For those who have not been initiated beforehand, the practice can be done by a Lama for someone who is on the point of death. Either way its purpose is to ensure the transference of consciousness through the crown of one's head. 'There are nine different openings through which the consciousness can escape.... If the consciousness escapes through the crown of the head (the Opening of Brahma) the being will be reborn in *Dewachen*, the western paradise of Amitabha.' Giuseppi Tucci in his book *The Religion of Tibet* (Berkeley: Univ. of California Press, 1980), pp100–101, also describes this practice which should be done before death is immanent as long as one has adequate instruction and supervision.

the animals which come out of the ark when the earth has dried. Furthermore, reaching from the sky to the earth, the rainbow is a symbol of the World Axis from which the influence of God radiates into the world. The covenant is one of peace between God and creation, and we must try to understand what is involved in this peace.

After regeneration, the world is in proper alignment with God, or as we might say, the world is centered in the Divine Presence. Necessarily, human beings are also in their proper relationship with God. This results in an external and internal peace. External in that, when the elements of creation are in their proper relationship to God, they are also in their proper relationship to each other, and this state of affairs may be described as peace; internal in that persons who are in their proper relationship to God are filled with the inner peace of spiritual attainment. It is perhaps not accidental that viewing a rainbow tends to cause us to forget our cares and become more peaceful. And, in light of our interpretation, we can see that there is something after all to the old tale of the pot of gold at the end of the rainbow. That elusive point where the rainbow touches the earth is really the point of intersection of the Spirit or World Axis with our particular state of Existence. There, indeed, is a pot of gold, but it is not to be found by any earthly route. Reaching this point, which is really the Earthly Paradise we have described previously, we are content. Desiring nothing, we are, as it were, wealthy beyond all dreams.[17]

According to Gen. 9:20, Noah is said to have planted a vineyard. Symbolically, this is a reference to a spiritual center. The wine which comes from the grapes is a symbol of the elixir of immortality, which is really the Divine influence, and the story of Noah's drunkenness (9:21–23) must be understood in this light. Noah is pictured as a man who has absorbed the Divine influence and is in a state of realization. In this state, which superficially resembles drunkenness, one has risen above the plurality of the manifested world, and views things from 'the standpoint of eternity'.

There are two passages in the *Brihadaranyaka Upanishad* which

17. It is no coincidence that Iris, the goddess of the rainbow, happens to be Juno's messenger and thus comparable to Mercury. Like Mercury she serves to connect the gods to mankind.

bear on this matter. The first provides a basis for understanding the second.

> For where there is duality as it were, there one smells another, there one sees another, there one hears another, there one speaks to another, there one thinks of another, there one understands another. Where, verily, everything has become the Self [*Atman*], then by what and whom should one smell, then by what and whom should one see, then by what and whom should one hear, then by what and to whom should one speak, then by what and on whom should one think, then by what and whom should one understand? (II.iv.14)

> As a man, when in the embrace of his loving wife, knows nothing without or within, so the person, when in the embrace of the intelligent [*prajna*] self [*Atman*] knows nothing without or within. That, verily, is his form in which his desire is fulfilled, in which the self is his desire, in which he is without desire, free from any sorrow. (IV.iii.21)[18]

There is also a short section of the *Chuang Tzu* about the renowned Emperor Yao which is comparable to the section of the Noah story we are discussing:

> Yao brought order to the people of the world and directed the government of all within the seas. But he went to see the Four Masters of the far away Ku-she Mountain, [and when he got home] north of the Fen River, he was dazed and had forgotten his kingdom there.[19]

Ku-she mountain, the land to the north, is none other than the Terrestrial Paradise, which, as we have mentioned, is the center of our world. To visit it is to taste the nectar of immortality, to reach a state of consciousness beyond individuality and duality. It is no wonder that somebody having this realization would appear dazed or

18. *The Principal Upanishads*, tr. S. Radhakrishnan (London: George Allen & Unwin, 1974), pp201 and 262.

19. *Chuang Tzu*, tr. Burton Watson (NY: Columbia Univ. Press, 1968), p34.

drunk, and this whether he has realized his essential unity with God or he has stopped somewhat short of that.

Ham's breaking in on Noah while the latter is drunk and naked symbolizes the worldly breaking in on the spiritual. Perhaps we should say it represents the disrespect of the worldly for the spiritual. The punishment Noah meets out for this offense is that Ham, through his son Canaan, 'shall be a slave to his [Ham's] brothers' (Gen. 9:25). The worldly person, symbolized by Ham or Canaan, is always a slave, a slave to his own desires. But there is still another inner meaning of Noah's curse. From the spiritual point of view it is proper than Canaan, who symbolizes the body or lower tendencies, should be a slave to the other brothers who symbolize the soul and the spirit, or in general, the higher tendencies.

If we do not accept Noah's drunkenness as a symbol of a spiritual state, what then can we make of the whole story of Noah? Taken literally, it seems that the one man God considered righteous (Gen. 6:9) turned out to be a drunkard. Here is one more case where a biblical story calls out to be interpreted symbolically.

Before leaving the subject of Noah and his sons we should indicate a peculiarity in the story, at least from the viewpoint of traditional symbolism. In traditional stories involving siblings, it is the youngest who is the hero and the oldest who is the villain, or at least the older ones are of lesser quality than the youngest. But in the story of Noah, Ham, who is identified as the youngest son in Gen. 9:24, is the villain. The answer to this seeming exception to the rule is that the story is corrupt, and in fact problematic in a number of ways.[20] First, in all the listings of Noah's sons leading up to 9:24, Ham is placed in the middle and Japheth at the end, making Japheth the youngest son. Second, it is not Ham who is punished but his son Canaan. Third, in 9:25 Canaan, not Ham, is identified as one of the three sons. So it is unclear from the Biblical account whether or not Ham is one of Noah's sons, much less his youngest son. Speaking of Ham, he is said to have a son named Cush (10:6), a name that has been linked with the Ethiopians and inhabitants of Northeast Africa

20. Rabbinic commentaries on the anomalies of the story have not been helpful, to say the least. There is a possibility that two sources have been conflated.

in general. People who wish to blame the enslaving of blacks by whites on the Bible, or on Judaism, claim the Bible justifies such slavery by Noah's curse. However, this seems to be a willful misreading of the text. According to Gen. 9:25, Noah does not curse Ham (and thereby all this sons) or Cush. He curses only Canaan. The final twist on this matter is that the supposedly cursed Canaanites were probably not conquered but rather converted to the Israelite religion.

If Noah's ark is a symbol of regeneration, the Tower of Babel is a symbol of degeneration. 'Babylon' means gate of the god, and the tower referred to in Gen. 11 was probably the ziggurat connected with the Temple of Marduk. It was called 'Etemenanki', which means house of the foundations of heaven and earth, and was destroyed around 1550 BC by the Hittites.

The names 'Babylon' and 'Etemenanki' are certainly suggestive of a spiritual center, and it would seem that there was at one time such a center in Babylon which subsequently degenerated. This view is compatible with the story in Genesis as long as we date the decay of the center before the building of the tower.[21] The name of the tower indicates that it was considered to be a symbol of the Axis of the world, connecting Heaven with Earth. As we have said, this Axis is really the World Spirit around which the world is manifested, and

21. A major theme of the Torah and the rest of the Old Testament is the combatting of spiritual degeneration in the form of idolatry. It may well be that Judaism was meant to fill a spiritual void in its part of the world attendant on the decay of a previous spiritual tradition centered in the Sumerian culture. We should not make the mistake of assuming that before the rise of the major Western religions there was just ignorance and superstition. This view, typical of the modern mentality, is actually very far off the mark. It has engendered the notion that the ancients, in their ignorance, worshipped the sun and various divine couples. That the sun may have symbolized God (and not a sun-god) or that certain of these couples may have symbolized the two-fold nature of *Prakriti* (and not physical waters) hardly enters anyone's mind. *A propos* of this we can remark that the ancient mysteries are bound to seem like a lot of magical claptrap to those who do not grasp the traditional ideas which provided their basis. If we understand ancient myths and rituals in their lowest possible way, as was already being done 2,000 years ago in the Roman Empire, it is not surprising that we should dismiss them as earlier primitive forms of worship that we have outgrown. The biblical prophets, too, may have underestimated the spirituality of the surrounding cults and overestimated the amount of idolatry. But the despicable practices associated with many of the cults certainly point to degeneration.

thus it is the gateway to God. The problematic aspect of the tower is spelled out very clearly in Gen. 11:3:

> They said to one another, 'Come, let us make bricks and burn them hard.'—Brick served them as stone, and bitumen served them as mortar.

People in different cultures have used many naturally occurring objects as symbols for the World Axis, including trees, mountains, meteorites, and large rocks. But the Tower of Babel was not a natural object, and as the biblical story clearly states, it was not constructed of natural objects.

In Gen. 11:5–6 we read:

> The Lord came down to look at the city and tower which man had built, and the Lord said, 'If, as one people with one language for all, this is how they have begun to act, then nothing that they may propose to do will be out of their reach.'

He then confounds their speech and stops them from building the city (11:7–8). On a superficial level we can view this as an explanation for the existence of many languages. Also on this level it would seem that God was jealous of what the people of Babylon were doing. If we reject this hypothesis, we will have to look deeper for the significance of this story.

Essentially it involves a reversal of roles. The builders of the tower had taken upon themselves the prerogatives of God. The world axis comes down from God to earth, and thus it is improper for it to be viewed as going in the opposite direction. Any natural object can serve as a symbol for the axis because, as part of God's creation, it can be said to come from God. But as we have already made clear, not only was the tower not a natural object, it was not even constructed of such objects. In short, it was the product of human technology.

The point of the story is that spiritual realization comes from above, or, as we like to say, by the grace of God, and not from below. It is not a product of man's physical or mental activity but something that occurs when man has gone beyond such activity. And here one recalls Matt. 11:12: 'From the days of John the Baptist until now the kingdom of heaven has suffered violence, and the violent take it by force.' This is probably a reference to the activities of the Zealots, and as such it expresses the idea that God's reign on earth is not brought about by man, but by God.

When people, following their lower tendencies, turn from their center (which is Divine) to what makes up their individuality (their egos), the result is not only inner disharmony but outer disharmony as well, for the unity of the human race is a unity through God, and cannot be achieved through any kind of human technique such as world government. Thus God's 'punishment' is really the only possible outcome of the actions of the tower builders. Our own time supplies a peculiar twist on this result. As technology advances with its 'towers' humanity is becoming more and more tribalized.

This story also contains a reference to the splitting of the primordial tradition and its universal symbolic language. The result is not so much a loss of the tradition as its being expressed in multifarious ways in such a manner as to hide its unity and prevent different aspects of it from being understood in various places. One might also say that it marks the period when the tradition has become hidden or covered, both as a sign of the age and as a means of protection.

There is no doubt that technology has made our lives easier and more pleasant. In any case, the population density of the earth in our epoch does not permit a return to simpler days. However, we should recognize that technology's effect on communication has been mixed. We can instantly connect with people on the other side of the earth, but the quality of our communications has diminished. It is another case of quantity driving out quality. Messages are becoming shorter, partially due to the decrease of our attention spans which is another effect of technology. And we often avoid voice communication with those nearby. The speed of technology has made us impatient with even the slightest delay in communicating or doing anything else in life. Running is in, walking is out.

We are spending more and more time in and with our technological marvels, whether at work or leisure or on the way from one to the other. They can become addictive and dehumanizing, turning us into machines. As we are social animals, a preoccupation with technology will be psychologically debilitating, keeping us apart rather than bringing us together.

8

Abraham and Isaac

THERE ARE TWO GREAT STORIES OF YEARNING in Genesis and both involve the father-son relationship. In one case the son is not yet born and in the other the son is 'lost'. The first concerns Abraham's wish for a son, and this theme is the subject of many stories which contain spiritual symbolism. Often these stories involve a test of the father and this one is no exception. But in the midst of the Abraham-Isaac story is another—that of Lot and the destruction of Sodom and Gomorrah, and it is to this other story that we will turn our attention first.

Sodom and Gomorrah are, of course, individual towns, but they represent in capsule form the degeneration of the human race. Only Lot was able to escape this downward tendency, much as Noah was the only one to escape this general tendency of his time. The treatment the Sodomites wished to accord the angels who visited Lot is another symbol of the disrespect of the worldly for the spiritual.

Gen. 19 contains a rather remarkable story which sheds much light on the symbolism of the whole episode. Lot has invited the angels into his house:

> They had not yet lain down, when the townspeople, the men of Sodom, young and old—all the people to the last man— gathered about the house. And they shouted to Lot and said to him, 'Where are the men who came to you tonight? Bring them out to us, that we may be intimate with them.' So Lot went out to them to the entrance, shut the door behind him, and said, 'I beg you my friends, do not commit such a wrong. Look, I have two daughters who have not known a man. Let me bring them out to you, and you may do to them as you please; but do not do anything to these

> men, since they have come under the shelter of my roof.' But they said, 'Stand back! The fellow,' they said, came here as an alien, and already he acts the ruler! Now we will deal worse with you than with them.' And they pressed hard against the person of Lot, and moved forward to break the door. But the men stretched out their hands and pulled Lot into the house with them, and shut the door. And the people who were at the entrance of the house, young and old, they were struck with blinding light, so that they were helpless to find the entrance. (vv. 4–11)

We must view this scene as taking place within a person. The townspeople of Sodom are the lower tendencies of the individual, especially the various desires which press in around a person. Lot symbolizes the soul under the influence of the spirit, and the presence of the angels in Lot's house symbolizes the presence of the World Spirit or Intellect. It might be thought that the Spirit is always present in a person and thus cannot be symbolized as a guest. However, while the World Spirit is always present, it is not always paid heed.[1] Inviting the angels into his house symbolizes turning to the Spirit.[2]

Lot's readiness to sacrifice his unmarried daughters symbolizes the willingness to throw a bone to one's desires. While still under their sway one cannot disregard them altogether. But neither can one give in to them altogether by turning away from the Spirit, which in this case would be symbolized by delivering the angels to the crowd. Freeing oneself from the lower tendencies often involves treading a fine line between indulgence and denial. Too much denial at a particular time may lead to a reaction in the opposite direction and one may end up being swamped by a flood of desires.

1. One recalls here Meister Eckhart's rather striking comment, 'Mark that anyone who wishes to hear God speaking must become deaf and inattentive to others.' He adds, 'God's speaking to us is nothing else but God's becoming known to us through his gifts ... that raise us up and irradiate our minds by his light.' *The Essential Sermons*, pp 114–15. The end result of this irradiation is absorption in the Real, or what we might call spiritual relaxation.

2. In reality the ego is the guest of the Spirit, but from the perspective of the ego it appears the other way around.

The crowd wants to be intimate with the angels, and on a literal level, it is of course sexual intimacy that is meant. But on the symbolic level it is intimacy between the flesh and the spirit that is meant, or better, subjecting the fruits of the higher tendencies to the lower tendencies.[3] We must also notice the portrayal of a reversal of proper roles. The flesh wants to take a masculine or active role with respect to the spirit, whereas in reality the spirit plays this role in relation to the soul and body.

The townspeople call Lot an alien who is acting like a ruler. As a newcomer he symbolizes the soul under the influence of the higher tendencies which develop later. The men of the town, symbolizing the various desires, are obviously old residents, and to them the higher tendencies are very much alien. These higher tendencies deserve to rule, but, as we mentioned in the case of Cain and Abel, the lower tendencies have had their way too long to give up easily.

The angels, pulling Lot into the house and blinding the crowd symbolizes the truth that as a person turns to the Spirit within, It will help him fend off his lower tendencies. To put the matter differently, if a person can give his higher tendencies some rulership over his lower tendencies, the Spirit will add to this rulership. The light that blinds the townspeople is the light of the Spirit whose ultimate source is God as he reveals Himself, the Spiritual Sun.

In the conclusion of the Lot episode, the angels manage to persuade only a reluctant Lot, his wife, and his unmarried daughters (i.e., that in him which is still untouched by worldliness) to flee Sodom (Gen. 19:14–16). This contrasts with the case of Noah in which the whole family was saved before the destruction. It is of note that Lot refuses to flee to the hills, but instead insists on moving to another town named Zoar (19:17–22). The reluctance to flee, and the wish to move to another town has its own significance. Lot symbolizes a soul for whom the spiritual tendency is not very strong. What we have is a picture of an indecisive person loathe to give up his former life, and we will find this same picture presented

3. Similarly in Matthew: 'When you give alms, do not let your left hand know what your right hand is doing' (Matt. 6:3). Egoism is always ready to spring out and destroy every higher accomplishment.

on a larger scale in the story of the fleeing Israelites in Exodus. It seems that no matter how difficult is the life of inner slavery to one's desires and how glorious the spiritual life, most people would rather cling to their old ways. Lot's decision to move to another town is really a decision in favor of what town-life symbolizes—the life of materiality.

The family is told not to look back at the destruction of Sodom and Gomorrah (Gen. 19:17), but, in the most well-known part of the story, Lot's wife does look back and is turned into a pillar of salt (19:26). The theme of not looking back when on the spiritual quest and of the attendant effects of looking back is common in spiritual stories, e.g., Orpheus and Eurydice. Often the protagonist is turned into a stone, and we find in folktales that it is a chief trick of the devil to turn his charges into stones. In order to fully understand this we must keep in mind Guénon's comments about the solidification of the world in the Iron Age.[4] The picture of the typical human being as a stone is difficult to accept, especially in light of the mania for activity and emotionalism which characterizes our age. Nevertheless, if we consider the main character of inanimate objects and take a closer look at the life of the typical person, we will find that the analogy is not so far-fetched. An inanimate object cannot bring about any change in itself, although it is subject to change as a result of outside forces, and this is exactly the predicament of the typical individual. Sunken in worldliness, taken up with vanity, and subject to his various desires, he is caught in a mechanical, habitual mode of life. The ego-centered life is indeed the life of a stone or pillar of salt. Those living this sort of existence have achieved death in the midst of life. We can describe this state as death with respect to the Spirit, or spiritual death. The destruction of Sodom and Gomorrah is no less than the destruction of the lower tendencies. If we are attached to them, if we must look behind us when fleeing them, then we are incapable of spiritual progress.

The parallel of the destruction of Sodom and Gomorrah with the flood in Noah's time is shown most clearly in Gen. 19:30–35. Lot's daughters are pictured as thinking that the rest of the human race

4. See chap. 6.

has been destroyed, thus feeling the need for cohabitation with their father. That Lot's drunkenness must not be taken in the same way as Noah's is shown by the fact that, while Noah drinks of his own accord from the produce of his vineyard, Lot is tricked into drunkenness by his daughters.

Turning our attention to the story of Abraham, we find that it shows many similarities to the story of Noah. Just as it is said of Noah, 'This one will provide us with relief' (Gen. 5:29), so it is said of Abraham, 'And all the families of the earth / Shall bless themselves by you' (Gen. 12:3). Noah is the one man of his generation called to be the progenitor of a spiritually renewed world; Abraham is the one man of his generation called upon to remake the world spiritually, to practically begin the world anew. Noah is connected with a general destruction; Abraham is connected with the destruction of Sodom and Gomorrah. The only difference is that Abraham protests the coming destruction (Gen. 18) whereas Noah does not. Noah is ordered to make a journey over water; Abraham is ordered to make a journey over land. Just as Noah's journey can be interpreted spiritually, there is a long tradition in Judaism, Christianity and Islam of interpreting Abraham's journey as a spiritual one.

The story of Abraham begins with God telling Abram (for that was his original name), 'Go forth from your native land and from your father's house to the land that I will show you' (Gen. 12:1). Ordinarily 'father's house' would refer to the Divine Realm, but here it is the equivalent of 'native land'. In the present case, 'native land' refers to the manifested world, and 'the land that I will show you' to the Terrestrial Paradise, the center of the manifested world. In short, Abram is being asked to make a spiritual journey.[5]

5. One's native land may be a symbol of the manifested world or of one's ultimate source, depending on the point of view. From the stance of individuality, which involves ignorance of our true nature, one's native land is the world. But from the enlightened point of view, which involves the realization of our essential identity with God, one's native land is what Buddhists call the 'Pure Land'. In essence this is God Himself. There is a Zen koan which illustrates the second point of view. It is the eighth in a collection of one hundred koans titled *The Iron Flute*, tr. Nyogen Senzaki and Ruth Strout McCandless (Tokyo: Charles E. Tuttle Company, 1961) (see continuation, next page):

The Lord goes on to say, as we mentioned in verse 2, 'I will make of you a great nation, and I will bless you; I will make your name great, and you shall be a blessing.... And all the families of the earth shall bless themselves by you' (Gen. 12:2–3). This would seem to indicate that not only is Abram to achieve the Terrestrial Paradise but the Celestial Paradise as well, thus joining Heaven and Earth and acting as a conduit for the Divine influence.

Meister Eckhart, in the characteristic way he has of explicating the spiritual symbolism of Scripture, analyzes Gen. 12: 1–3 somewhat differently, although it comes to the same thing in the end. After stating, 'Rise up then to the intellect; to be attached to it is to be united to God,' he adds:

> Act and potency are divisions of the existence of all created being. Existence is the first act, the first division; but in the intellect in God, there is no division. This is why Scripture always exhorts us to go out of this world, to go out of ourselves, to forget our house and the house of our origin, to go forth from our land and our relations so that we may grow into a great people, so that all nations may be blessed in such a person (see Gen. 12:1–3). This best takes place in the region of the intellect where without doubt all things, insofar as they are intellect and not other, are in all things.[6]

> Yun-chu, a Soto master of Chinese Zen, had many disciples. One monk, who came from Korea, said to him, 'I have realized something within me which I cannot describe at all.' 'Why is that so?' asked Yun-chu, 'it cannot be difficult.' 'Then you most do it for me,' the monk replied. Yun-chu said, 'Korea, Korea!' and closed the dialogue. Later a teacher of the Oryu school of Zen criticized the incident, 'Yun-chu could not understand the monk at all. There was a great sea between them, even though they lived in the same monastery.

The last comment is no doubt ironic. But of particular significance is the use of the monk's native land, Korea, to symbolize his ultimate source.

6. *Teacher and Preacher*, p226. In order to understand the end of this quotation, it will be best to give another: 'Here note that when we say that all things are in God [that means that] just as he is indistinct in his nature and nevertheless most distinct from all things, so in him all things in a most distinct way are also at the same time indistinct' (p209). Things lose their individuality or become indistinct in God. To repose in God we must reach a state of consciousness beyond the usual ego state.

We must travel then from our psycho-physical individualities to the supra-individual part of us. To put it in another way, we have to vacate our egos.

In Gen. 15 we find the first mention of God's promise of a son to Abram. The difficulty in understanding the symbolism of Isaac is that he stands for two different things. To begin with, as the fulfillment of God's promise he symbolizes the Divine Presence, and later on he symbolizes the most prized possession as well.[7]

But much happens before Isaac's birth. Chapter 15, besides recording God's promise, also describes a theophany. We are told that Abram divided up some animals, and then at sunset he fell into a sort of trance in which he had a vision of the Lord passing between the parts of the animals. In this vision the Lord repeats His promise and makes a covenant to fulfill His promise. Scholars have pointed out that the action parallels the typical way in which rulers entered into covenants in that age. The weaker would stand between split animals and declare that if he broke the covenant then this, the splitting, should happen to himself. In a reversal of roles, God takes the part of the weaker party, but all of this concerns the literal level of the story. What is of interest in the vision is that 'a flaming torch' passes between the parts of the animals. This flaming torch is really the World Spirit and signifies Abram's initiation into the higher life or spiritual way.

Gen. 17 recounts how God reminds Abram of the covenant, changes his name to 'Abraham', and changes his wife Sarai's name to 'Sarah'. He also orders Abraham to fulfill his side of the covenant by

7. Philo devoted a whole book, *Who Is the Heir of Divine Things*, to a discussion of Gen. 15, although it must be said that much of it is taken up with other matters such as his symbolic understanding of Rachel and Leah, the beloved and unloved wives of Jacob. Our views on the symbolism of Isaac are for the most part in agreement with his, for to him Isaac represents the fruits of the higher life: spiritual inspiration and the blessings of heaven. See especially sections 34–89. His beautiful description of Abraham's state, based on verse 5, deserves to be quoted:

> For he [Moses, the presumptive author] wished to picture the soul of the Sage as the counterpart of heaven, or rather, if we may so say, transcending it, a heaven on earth having within it, as the ether has, pure forms of being, movements ordered, rhythmic, harmonious, revolving as God directs, rays of virtues, supremely starlike and dazzling (tr. F.H. Colson [Cambridge: Harvard Univ. Press, 1967], sect. 88).

circumcising himself and all of the males in his group. Circumcision on the eighth day after birth is to be a sign of this covenant forever more. It might be thought that all of this should have taken place in chapter 15, for it is there that Abraham's spiritual rebirth had occurred. However, it happens that chapter 15 is from the J source and chapter 17 from the P source. Thus the story in chapter 17 is really another version of the story in chapter 15. In the earlier story stress is put on Abram's vision; in the later one stress is put on the symbols of rebirth. The most obvious symbol is the change of name, but circumcision also has this connotation. Besides the fact that it involves the organ of generation, it implies a stripping away of worldliness (the body) by way of getting back to the primordial purity.

In his remarks on Deuteronomy 30:6, 'Then the Lord your God will open up [others: circumcise] your heart and the hearts of your offspring to love the Lord your God with all your heart and soul, in order that you may live,' Nachmanides (Rabbi Moshe ben Nachman) relates circumcision to the 'days of the Messiah' which are effectively the beginning of the new Golden Age we mentioned in chapter 2.

> But in the days of the Messiah, the choice of their [genuine] good will be natural; the heart will not desire the improper and it will have no craving whatsoever for it. This is the 'circumcision' mentioned here, for lust and desire are the foreskin of the heart, and circumcision of the heart means that it will not covet or desire evil. Man will return at that time to what he was before the sin of Adam, when by his nature he did what properly should be done, and there were no conflicting desires of the will. . . .[8]

This description tallies with our description of the Abel type of person, the saintly type, given toward the end of chapter 6. Such a person will do good naturally, not out of a sense of moral obligation. Such is the spiritually reborn.

In between the two versions of God's covenant with Abraham

8. Rambam (Nachmanides), *Commentary of the Torah: Deuteronomy* (New York: Shilo Publishing House, 1971), p341.

mentioned above, we are told of the birth of Ishmael. Sarah, being childless, advises Abraham to take her slave Hagar as a second wife and perhaps beget a child. Hagar indeed becomes pregnant and gives birth to Ishmael. An angel of the Lord tells Hagar that her son will be 'a wild ass of a man; / His hand against everyone, / And everyone's hand against him' (Gen. 16:12).

Chapter 18 of Genesis details the announcement to Abraham and Sarah of the future birth of a son. We find such an announcement given by an angel of the Lord to another barren woman, namely the future mother of Samson (Judges 13:2–5). And of course there are the famous announcements by Gabriel to the barren but future mother of John the Baptist (Luke 1:5–25) and to Mary the future mother of Jesus (vv 26–35). But what is particularly interesting about the announcement to Abraham and Sarah is that the Lord visits them in the form of three men (Gen. 18:1–2). It seems that in revealing Himself to humanity God does so in a tripartite way. We have the well-known Trinity in Christianity: the Father, the Son and the Holy Spirit. But there is also the *Trimurti* of Hinduism: Brahma (the Creator), Vishnu (the Preserver) and Shiva (the Destroyer or Transformer).[9] And Hinduism also describes the Godhead as *Satchitananda* (Being-consciousness-bliss). In fact, Brahman is one of the Hindu names for the Ultimate Reality, which can be viewed without or without *gunas* or qualities. As we mentioned earlier, the *gunas* are three in number. Thus Saguna Brahman, or Brahman qualified, is really three-in-one. In Buddhism we have the *Trikaya* or Three Bodies of Buddha: *Dharmakaya* (the Reality Body), *Sambhogakaya* (the Heavenly or Bliss Body), and *Nirmanakaya* (the Earthly or Emanational Body). In Judaism, the *Musaf* or Additional Service for Rosh Hashannah (which is a substitute for the additional sacrifice that used to be offered at the Temple during the High Holy days) contains three sets of benedictions known as the *Malkhyot* (Kingdoms), *Zikhronot* (Remembrances) and *Shofarot* (Ram's horn Blasts) which refer to God as the King, the Rememberer and Recorder (of our

9. There is a curious similarity between the three members of the *Trimurti* and the Three Fates of Greek mythology. Clotho spins the thread of life, Lachesis measures it, and Atropos cuts it.

deeds), and the Revealer or Manifestor (of Himself) symbolized by the horn blasts. It is as if when we try to describe God we are driven to doing so in threefold terms.[10]

Chapter 21 records the birth of Isaac when Abraham is one hundred years old. Starting his second century is also a sign of rebirth, and we may view the birth of Isaac as both the fruit of Abraham's first rebirth and the occasion of his second rebirth. Abraham's yearning for a son is really a symbol of the yearning of a person for the realization of the Divine Presence. In the birth of Isaac he has realized this, or to use other words, he has touched base with the center of his being and has experienced the Terrestrial Paradise. And here we must repeat something we said in another connection. The Divine Presence is constant, but, from the perspective of the ego, it may seem present or absent.

Chapter 21 also records that one day Sarah finds Ishmael playing with (or possibly mocking) Isaac, and tells Abraham to 'cast out' Hagar and Ishmael (v. 10). God instructs Abraham to do Sarah's bidding, 'for it is through Isaac that offspring shall be continued for you' (v. 12), but assures Abraham that 'I will make a nation for him [Ishmael] too' (v. 13). And both Jews and Muslims agree that Ishmael is the ancestor of the Arab people, with the Qur'an (Sura 19) describing him in more positive terms.

While the Bible gives no description of Isaac comparable to the one of Ishmael, from the story of Issac's life we can see that he is meek and accepting of what comes his way. In other words, he is exactly the opposite of Ishmael. And he is the son who is picked by God to hand on Abraham's spiritual blessing to posterity. Thus he takes his place with Abel before him and Jacob after him as the younger son preferred by God. On the other hand, Ishmael takes his place with Cain before him and Esau after him as the older son not preferred by God. The very natures of Isaac and Ishmael are almost identical to those of Jacob and Esau, as we will see in the next chapter. What is important is that the older sons all stand for the lower

10. The triads just mentioned should not be thought of as all equivalent to one another. Let us say they are different ways of describing the threefold nature of God. And *Dharmakaya Buddha* is often understood as the equivalent of Buddha-nature.

tendencies which are the first to develop while the younger sons symbolize the higher tendencies which are the last to develop. As we said in our discussion of Cain and Abel, God naturally prefers the higher tendencies.

Abraham's spiritual struggle does not end with the birth of Isaac. In the second phase of the story Isaac becomes a symbol of the most prized possession, be it spiritual or worldly. More exactly, we should say he becomes a dual symbol. Abraham has already achieved a great deal on the spiritual path, but the question is whether he is willing to settle for the lesser when he has the possibility of achieving the greater. He has touched base with the World Spirit, but it is now up to him to pursue it to its source. God's asking Abraham to give up his son is symbolic of the need to give up the fruit of the first and lesser death and rebirth in order to gain the fruit of the second and greater death and rebirth. Thus, in the story of the proposed sacrifice of Isaac, God asks Abraham to make still another journey, this time to the land of Moriah where he is to 'offer him [Isaac] there as a burnt offering on one of the heights' (Gen. 22:2).

In chapter 22 we read about God's 'test' of Abraham, of which much has been written in an emotional vein. We must admit that the story has great emotional impact, and it is meant to deeply affect the hearer. Nevertheless, we must not be carried away by its literal meaning wherein at the last minute God gives Abraham a ram to substitute as offering, with the implication that human sacrifice is wrong. Rather, the power of the story should serve to reinforce its inner meaning for our lives. On the worldly level the question is whether we are willing to give up our attachment to even our most prized possessions in order to realize God. And we must understand 'possessions' in a wide sense to include fame and power as well as the more obvious things. We must note too that it is the attachment which must be given up. Abraham gets to keep his son, but he has demonstrated his lack of attachment. On the spiritual level the question is whether we are willing to settle for second best.[11]

11. There is an ancient Chinese story on a similar theme which is seemingly about filial piety but may have a deeper significance. When his wealthy father dies, eldest son Guo Ju gives his inheritance to his two younger brothers and, though he

The outcome of Abraham's test is summarized beautifully in Gen. 22:15–18:

> The angel of the Lord called to Abraham a second time from heaven, and said, 'By myself I swear, the Lord declares: because you have done this and have not withheld your son, your favored one, I will bestow My blessing upon you and make your descendants as numerous as the stars of heaven and the sands on the seashore; and your descendants shall seize the gates of their foes. All the nations of the earth shall bless themselves by your descendants, because you have obeyed My command.'

Much could be said about this quotation, but most importantly it shows that Abraham has reached the goal of the second rebirth and so has achieved the Celestial Paradise. By realizing God he has joined Heaven to Earth and become a source of blessing to the world.[12]

There is one more aspect of Abraham's story which bears discussion. If there is a theme running through his life it is sacrifice. In allowing his first son to be cast out he is making a sacrifice. In binding his second son to be used as an offering he is at least prepared to make still another sacrifice. As we mentioned earlier on, God's manifestation of the world is essentially sacrificial. In order to reverse that manifestation in consciousness we too must sacrifice. All sacrifices come down in the end to sacrificing our egos, crucifying them as it were.[13]

is married, undertakes to devote himself to looking after his mother. When his wife gives birth to a son, Guo Ju feels that he lacks the wherewithal to feed another mouth and so decides to bury his son. On digging a hole in the ground he discovers a pot of gold and a plaque which reads, 'For Guo Ju, The Filially Pious Son.' Cf. James Watt and Prudence Harper, *China: Dawn Of A Golden Age* (New Haven: Yale Univ. Press, 2004), p215.

12. According to the *Zohar* (1.119B), Abraham, through his test, successfully balanced in himself the attributes of rigor and mercy which are represented by the left and right sides of the Sefirotic Tree. This is not the place to go into a detailed explanation of these matters. But in chapter 5 we described the importance of regaining completeness in order to achieve even the first goal of the spiritual life.

13. Although he comes at the story of Abraham from a different perspective than ours, Bruce Feiler's book *Abraham*, which we noted previously, is very much worth reading.

9

Esau and Jacob

THE STORY OF ESAU AND JACOB is, in a sense, the obverse of the story of Cain and Abel, since the symbolic structure is the same but the outcome is different.

We are told in Gen. 25 that Esau and Jacob were twins, with Esau the older one. As is well known, in many cultures there are stories of twin culture heroes, and in some of these the twins oppose each other. But we must say first of all that neither Esau nor Jacob is represented as a culture hero, and second that the symbolic meaning of the story has nothing whatever to do with the culture-hero motif.

Gen. 25:27 informs us that 'Esau became a skillful hunter, a man of the outdoors; but Jacob was a mild man, who stayed in camp.' Isaac may have favored Esau (25:28) but God obviously favored Jacob. On a literal level it is difficult to understand why Jacob should be so favored, especially considering the fact that he takes advantage of Esau on two different occasions. But on a symbolic level the story makes perfect sense.

On one level Esau, the man of the outdoors, symbolizes the man of the senses or the man with his attention turned outwards. Jacob, who stayed in camp, symbolizes the man of spirituality or the man with his attention turned inwards. On another level, as we said in the last chapter, Esau represents the lower tendencies of a human being and Jacob the higher tendencies. One's higher tendencies keep one focused on the center of one's being, symbolized by the camp. We would expect Isaac, who symbolized the higher tendencies in contrast to Ishmael, to personify the active pole of the cosmos and favor Jacob. As well, we would expect his wife Rebecca, who as female would generally be connected with the passive pole or substance of the cosmos and hence the formed world itself, to favor

Esau. But instead there is a curious reversal of roles: Isaac favors Esau and Rebecca favors Jacob. There may be a parallel here with Sarah's favoring Isaac over the older Ishmael, and certainly Abraham complains when she tells him to cast out Hagar and Ishmael, but then Sarah was the biological mother of Isaac and not of Ishmael. It seems that if Isaac represents the active pole and thus, in a way, the World Spirit, it is in Its negative or testing aspect. And if Rebecca represents the world, it is in its positive or teaching aspect.

We have to remember that the world, as a manifestation of God, is divine. Thus the world is worshipped as Kali or the Mother by Hindus, although it would be more precise to say that the *Shakti* or energy of God which is responsible for the world is the true object of worship, also referred to as *Maya* or the power of illusion. The world, or the energy behind it, can pull a person down or be a source of blessing. While our birth can be the beginning of a descent into hell, it can also be a chance to ascend to the heavens.[1] It is a matter of what we choose to do in the situation in which we find ourselves. The world teaches us ambition and fills us with desire, but it does not specify the object of that ambition or the nature of that desire. It is like an equation containing variables for which we may substitute whatever constants we choose. In Hinduism the dual aspect of the world is expressed by the terms *avidya-maya* and *vidya-maya*, that which leads to ignorance of Brahman (the Ultimate Reality) and that which leads to knowledge. After all, as we pointed out in chapter 7, there is a *sattvic* basis to the world as well as a *rajasic/ tamasic* basis.

As we explained earlier, in Kabbalism, the tenth and last *Sefirah* or aspect of *Ein-Sof* (the Infinite) is alternatively called *Malkhut* (Kingdom or Sovereignty) or *Shekhinah* (the Divine Presence). It is typically understood as the female principle of the world—that from which the world issues. Yet Gershom Scholem makes the following point about it:

1. Cf. Al-Ghazali, *The Niche For Lights*, tr. W.H.T. Gairdner (Lahore: Sh. Muhammad Ashraf, 1952), p125, '... the visible world is, as we have said, the point of departure up to the world of the realm supernal.'

> From its source at 'the beginning of thought' in *Ḥokhmah* ('wisdom') [the second *Sefirah*], the thought of creation pursues its task through all the worlds, following the laws of the process of the *Sefirot* themselves.... Appearing from above as 'the end of thought,' the last *Sefirah* is for man the door or gate through which he can begin the ascent up the ladder of perception of the Divine Mystery.[2]

Thus in Kabbalism as well, the source of the world, and by implication the world itself, can serve as a vehicle for spiritual growth. In fact, there is nothing else which can serve as the vehicle so long as we are embodied. All the great spiritual teachers as well as the teachings they leave behind are parts of this world.

The first example of Jacob's taking advantage of Esau is found in the episode of the bread and lentil stew (25:29–34). One day Esau comes into camp famished and demands some of the stew Jacob is cooking. Jacob gives him the stew in exchange for his birthright. Now the birthright involves precedence, and there is no doubt that the world favors the lower tendencies and gives them precedence in human life. Everything is designed to foster and entrap people in these tendencies, and this is more true in our own time than ever before. Esau's 'hunger' is merely a symbol of all the lower tendencies. Jacob feeds Esau, giving Caesar his due as it were, but not before exacting an oath which gives precedence to himself. The lesson of this story is that the higher tendencies can take precedence over the lower, not by fighting the latter, but by giving them only what is necessary with the understanding that this is all they will get. We have here a similar situation to the one in which Lot offered his daughters to the townspeople of Sodom.

On another level the birthright symbolizes our rights as children of God. We are all royalty in that we are part of the family of the King of kings. That is to say, we have the eternal within us if only we would recognize its presence and not go through life as beggars. When the lower tendencies have precedence, we live as Esau—a beggar of food; we have, as it were, sold our birthright for some stew.

2. *Kabbalah* (New York: Meridian, 1978), p112.

But when the higher tendencies have precedence, we are on our way to claiming our birthright—the complete satisfaction and joy which comes of realizing our essential identity with God.

In chapter 27 we find the story of the final victory of Jacob over Esau. It is the well-known incident of Jacob and Rebecca's trickery whereby the blind Isaac mistakes Jacob for Esau and gives his blessing to the former. In this episode, Isaac functions as the transmitter of the spiritual influence he received from Abraham. The most important parts of the blessing are given in 27:29: 'Be master over your brothers' and 'Blessed they who bless you.' Thus the higher tendencies are given final rulership over the lower, and Jacob has become a source of spiritual influence in the world.

What is most important is not the particular kind of trickery used, but that it is used at all. The devil is full of tricks, but the devil can also be outsmarted by tricks. It is often the case that one must 'fight fire with fire', and this phrase has important implications for the spiritual life which would take us too far afield to discuss in this context. But on the matter of trickery, which can be viewed as one species of fighting fire with fire, we can say the following. The world must somehow be made to loosen its hold upon us. We can try to flee the world, but we will most often find that we have taken the world along. It is easy to be outwardly saintly in a cave, but one's inward life may not have changed at all. A better solution, and one which will ultimately have to be tried in any case, is to turn the world against itself.

The world teaches us that if we want to attain anything we must have a great deal of discipline or self-control. There is nothing to stop us from applying this teaching to the realm of spiritual advancement. It is a matter of transmuting lower aspirations into higher and then applying the same method, which in the latter case will take the form of fasting in all of its aspects.[3]

While most people substitute worldly constants into the equation of life, there is certainly no constraint in this regard. The deciding factor is always which tendencies have the upper hand. In this story,

3. Cf. Al-Ghazali, *The Mysteries of Fasting*, tr. N.A. Faris (Lahore: Sh. Muhammad Ashraf, 1968).

as opposed to the one about Cain and Abel, the higher tendencies are stronger and prevail. The spiritual nature of the present story is also shown by the method of trickery which Jacob uses—putting on an animal skin. Putting on such a skin is part of a ritual of rebirth in many cultures.[4] Of course, in the present context we are dealing with spiritual rebirth, and the signs of this rebirth are recorded in Gen. 28.

According to Gen. 28, Jacob flees Esau's wrath after obtaining Isaac's first blessing. He does this on the advice of his mother Rebecca (27:41–45), and here too we can discern a symbolic meaning. Once one is settled on the spiritual path one must be careful not to be pulled back to the worldly path. This is what is symbolized by Jacob putting some distance between himself and Esau. At one point in his travels he stops for the night and dreams of a stairway (the Hebrew *sulam* is very close to *shalom*, or peace) reaching up to the sky upon which 'angels of God were going up and down,' and he also beholds the Lord blessing him (28:10–15). This episode is really the indication that he has achieved the goal of rebirth. The stairway connecting the sky and the earth is the World Spirit or Axis connecting the Celestial and Terrestrial Paradises, and the angels symbolize the higher influences in their ascending and descending modes. Jacob has achieved the first stage on the spiritual journey in that he has travelled horizontally to his own true center. He must now travel vertically up the stairway, whose steps indicate higher states of Existence, to the abode of God.[5] It is also recorded (28:16–19) that Jacob, after describing the place as 'the gateway to heaven', took the stone he had put under his head before he went to sleep and set it up as a pillar which he anointed with oil. The stone is another symbol of the connecting link between Heaven and Earth.

In Verse 19 we are told that Jacob named the place of his vision '*Bethel*' or House of God, but it had previously had the name 'Luz'. Rabbinical tradition held that Luz was the city of immortality in

4. Cf. sect. 63 of *Myth, Legend and Custom in the Old Testament*, vol. 1, by Theodor H. Gaster (New York: Harper & Row, 1975).

5. If the stairway is understood as spiral then each sweep of it will symbolize a higher state of Existence.

that no one inhabiting the city could die. The spiritual meaning of this is that Luz was considered an intersecting point of the World Spirit and the world, a place where one could achieve a sense of eternity. We might add that the rabbis also held that there was a bone at the base of the spine which was not part of the gross physical body. They called the bone 'luz' and believed that it was from this bone that the person was recreated at the resurrection. On the spiritual level it is obvious that this bone of immortality is none other than the center of the person or that point in which the Spirit intersects man.[6]

The final chapter of Jacob's spiritual quest occurs when he is on his way to make peace with his brother Esau. At night and alone he wrestles with an angel until the break of day. He will not let the angel go until he receives its blessing. As a sign of his second and final rebirth the angel says, 'Your name shall no longer be Jacob, but Israel,[7] for you have striven with beings divine and human, and have prevailed' (Gen. 32:29).[8] This verse indicates that Jacob has indeed traced the World Axis to its source and has become a link between Heaven and Earth, a source of Divine influence.[9] It is noteworthy that after this incident Jacob is able to enter into a peaceful

6. As to why the spiritual center is pictured at the base of the spine and how this doctrine fits in with that of other traditions, see René Guénon, *The King of the World*, chap. 7, and *Symbols of Sacred Science*, chap. 32, 'The Heart and the World Egg'.

7. The name 'Jacob' probably means 'may God protect' and signifies the protection against the lower tendencies God offers to those on the spiritual path. The name 'Israel' originally meant 'may El persist (or persevere or prevail)'. In this passage the name is reinterpreted to refer to the persistence or prevailing of Jacob. In the present context the two meanings are not opposed since the goal of Jacob with respect to God is the exact correlative of the goal of God with respect to Jacob.

8. He has 'striven' with the higher and lower, with Heaven and Earth, in different ways. While fighting the lower tendencies he has held fast to the Spirit. 'Can you discipline your physical soul (*p'o*, anima in the triad *anima, animus, spiritus*) and embrace the one (the *Tao*) and never let go?' (*Tao Te Ching*, chap. 10).

9. Cf. Joseph ibn Aknin's view of the symbolism of the wrestling match as mentioned in A.S. Halkin's article 'Yedaiah Bedershi's Apology', in *Jewish Medieval and Renaissance Studies*, ed. Alexander Altmann (Cambridge: Harvard Univ. Press, 1967), p170. Ibn Aknin, like Maimonides, uses the term 'Active Intellect' to refer to the World Spirit.

relationship with Esau. This reconciliation symbolizes the reconciliation of the higher and lower tendencies. After one has realized one's essential identity with God, the lower tendencies are no longer enemies, or better, they cease to be able to cause harm. They have, so to speak, been put in their place.

Much has been written on the subject of spiritual wrestling, and, in a way, it is the topic of this whole study. However, there are two important points to be made about his particular case. As the story indicates, a great deal of determination and perseverance are necessary to achieve the final goal. Further, the injury to Jacob's 'thigh' and the dislocation of his hip (Gen. 32:26), besides hinting at the subject of generation, signify that like any birth, this one involves pain. It is the pain involved in total dis-location, i.e., a wrenching of the person out of and beyond the cosmos.

10

Jacob and Joseph

THE SECOND GREAT STORY OF YEARNING in Genesis centers around Jacob and Joseph.[1] As in the case of Abraham and Isaac it is the father who yearns for the son, and in one respect the symbolism is the same. But we must add that the Jacob-Joseph story goes into detail about things only hinted at in the former story. We can also view the Jacob-Joseph story as a combination of the Cain-Abel and Esau-Jacob stories as it contains elements of both. But again we must add that although the ideas are similar they are expressed in different ways or from a different perspective. That certain themes seem to be repeated in the stories we are discussing is one more reason for accepting the interpretations being offered.

Anyone knowledgeable in spiritual matters will perceive readily that the story of Joseph is really the story of the vicissitudes of the Spirit in the world. It might seem as if Joseph is first represented in a bad light in that he is full of pride and thus cannot possibly symbolize the World Spirit. But this view goes against the whole flow of the story. In actuality, Joseph is represented from the first as pure of heart, and this characterization follows him throughout the story. He does not *claim* to be superior to his parents and brothers but merely *dreams* these things. And all through the story he is put upon by designing persons.

We are told in Gen. 37 that Jacob gave Joseph a special coat or tunic (37:3). The translation 'a coat of many colors' is a guess at the meaning of the Hebrew words. They could also be translated 'a coat

1. For a discussion of the symbolism of Jacob's problems in marrying Rachel, the mother of Joseph, see my discussion of substitute-bride tales in *Cinderella's Gold Slipper*, chap. 5, 'The Great Thirst'.

of many parts', and this does not contradict the first meaning. It is possible that similar garments were used to clothe statues of gods in other cultures, and it is also possible (taking into consideration 2 Sam. 13:18–19 and Ps. 45:13–14) that they were used by royalty. Indeed, another possible translation is 'ornamented tunic'. It matters little which of these translations we accept since they all point to the same thing. However, 'coat of many colors' is the most interesting if we view Joseph as symbolizing the Spirit. As we mentioned in the chapter on Noah and elsewhere, the World Spirit is often described as a reflection of the Solar Ray coming from the Spiritual Sun or Being. By necessity It will be a white light which, in the case of the rainbow, is divided into six colors. Joseph's robe and the rainbow are to be seen as comparable.

The other possible translations point to royalty and divinity, and it is in this light that we must understand Joseph's second dream: 'this time, the sun, the moon, and eleven stars were bowing down to me' (Gen. 37:9). Besides the Psalms, spiritual writings from around the world testify that everything in the universe 'bows down' before God. So again we must conclude that Joseph is a symbol of the Spirit which may be 'imprisoned' but never killed.

If we view Joseph in this way then we must view Jacob as symbolizing the soul under the influence of the spirit and Joseph's brothers as the lower tendencies. As usual the lower tendencies are quick to defend their influence and oppose anything having to do with the Spirit within man.

In the story, Jacob makes the mistake of sending Joseph out to where his brothers are pasturing their flocks (Gen. 37:12–14). This exposing of the Spirit to the lower tendencies symbolizes, among other things, putting the Spirit on the same level as the lower tendencies. In other words, Jacob's action indicates a kind of spiritual backsliding on the part of the soul in which the life of the Spirit is held to be of no more importance than the life of the senses. The result in the story is that Joseph is stripped of his tunic and thrown into a pit by his brothers who then dip the tunic in animal blood and present it to Jacob as proof that his son has been killed by a wild beast (37:18–33). That there are many parallels to these events in other well-known stories is beside the point. What is crucial is the spiritual significance of Joseph's being thrown into the pit. If the pursuit of the Spirit is put on the same level as the pursuit of the objects of desire, there is little doubt that the latter will swamp the former. The result will be to effectively cut one off from the influence of the Spirit. Thus, as far as Jacob is concerned, Joseph might as well be dead.

As the story continues, Joseph is sold to some slave-traders (chapter 37) and resold to Potiphar in Egypt (chapter 39). There he meets with a similar fate as befell him with his brothers, as we learn from a story based on the Egyptian *Tale of Two Brothers*[2] (the unmarried one living in the house of the married one). According to chapter 39, Potiphar's wife becomes enamoured of Joseph and when he repulses her advances she complains to her husband that Joseph has made advances, and Potiphar has him imprisoned. The story is really a duplicate of the first one with Potiphar substituting for Jacob and Potiphar's wife for Joseph's brothers. We may even conjecture that the same motive of jealously is operative since just as Joseph was his father's favorite he has also become the favorite of Potiphar. The only difference is that the reference to the lower tendencies is more explicit in the case of Potiphar's wife, and here we may bring out another aspect of both stories.

The worldly side of a person works to pull everything down to its own level, and thus it attempts to mix with the spiritual side in order to dilute and debase it. The external effects of this tendency can easily be seen in our own time. We have witnessed the debasing of religion until it has become a commodity to be hawked by salesmen as entertainers in mammoth churches. In this manner more and more people are enabled to 'get religion', but the religion they get is hardly worthy of the name. We can describe the situation more explicitly as the desire of the material to encompass and possess the spiritual, an absolute reversal of how things actually stand.

As we have already mentioned, the Spirit cannot really be harmed, and we find that Joseph suffers no ill effects from his imprisonment. Through his ability to interpret the meanings of

2. James B. Pritchard, *Ancient Near Eastern Texts* (Princeton: Princeton Univ. Press, 1969), pp23–25.

dreams he is eventually made a regent in Egypt, and we can see in this story the eventual triumph of the Spirit. Pharaoh's dreams about the cattle and the grain and Joseph's interpretations of these dreams (Gen. 41) actually relate to previous episodes in the story. In place of Joseph's brothers and Potiphar's wife we have the seven emaciated cows and seven shrivelled ears of grain, and in place of Joseph we have the seven healthy cows and seven healthy ears of grain. In Pharaoh's dreams the malformed cattle eat the healthy cattle and the malformed ears of grain eat the healthy ears of grain (41:17–21). Once again we have the theme of the worldly swallowing up the spiritual. Joseph's advice is to store up the Spirit against the predations of the lower tendencies (41:33–36). The executor of this plan is the Pharaoh who in this part of the story replaces Jacob and Potiphar. The storing of the grain symbolizes the pursuit of the spiritual life, and is quite comparable to the idea of keeping the lamps full of oil in the Parable of the Ten Bridesmaids found in Matt. 25. The emaciated cattle and shrivelled grain which eat and yet remain in their original states are perfect symbols of the lower tendencies, and especially of the desires which are never satisfied.[3] The ascendancy of Joseph to power in Egypt is a symbol of the ascendancy of the Spirit. Of course, it is only from the ego's limited point of view that the Spirit can appear to be a prisoner. From God's point of view, the Spirit is always in ascendancy.

Once Joseph has become the Pharaoh's chief vizier, the stage is set for the great reunion of Jacob and Joseph. First his brothers are put in a position of bowing down before him (chapter 42), signifying the lower tendencies bowing down before the Spirit. (Here we can recall the story in chapter 7 of Luke in which the prostitute washes the feet of Jesus with her tears and then anoints them with oil. While

3. Pharaoh's dreams of seven emaciated cows devouring seven healthy cows and seven shriveled ears of grain devouring seven healthy ears, and the interpretation of this dream by Joseph as meaning there will be seven years of abundance followed by seven years of famine, seem to reflect a section of the Epic of Gilgamesh. Tablet VI contains the story of Ishtar threatening to break open the door of the underworld and allowing the dead to rise and eat as the living, thus causing a shortage of food for seven years. Cf. Alexander Heidel, *The Gilgamesh Epic And Old Testament Parallels* (Chicago: Phoenix Books, 1963), p53 and pp121–22, for the relevant translations.

the two stories are not completely analogous, the main point is the same.) Finally Jacob is reunited with Joseph in Egypt (chapter 46) but not before he is asked to give up his other favorite son Benjamin (chapter 43). In this section of the story Jacob takes the part of Abraham and Benjamin the part of Isaac. The question is quite the same as before: are you ready to give up your most prized possession to reach God? In this case, Jacob must give up his child to obtain Joseph's food—the non-material sustenance of the Spirit. The emptiness felt by Jacob at the loss of Joseph, the numbness of heart when he hears that Joseph is alive (Gen. 45:26), and the joy at being reunited with Joseph (46:29–30) are all symbolic. The first signifies the emptiness of a life from which the Spirit, from the ego's point of view, has departed; the second signifies a return to the heart or spiritual center within a person; and the last signifies the spiritual realization of one's essential unity with God.[4]

4. The resemblance between the story of Jacob and Joseph on the one hand and the story of Demeter and Persephone or Kore (which formed the basis of the Eleusinian Mysteries) on the other is quite remarkable. We point this out not to imply that one was influenced by the other but only to show the worldwide nature of certain spiritual symbols. And we can take the opportunity to repeat that while stories such as that of Demeter and Persephone have an obvious natural symbolism (in this case relating to planting and harvesting), they also possess an underlying spiritual symbolism.

11

Moses and Aaron

As the goal of the esoteric path has been identified as liberation, and as the story of Moses and Pharaoh involves seeking freedom from slavery, it is important to identify the nature of that freedom and liberty. Isaiah Berlin wrote a well-known essay on the subject[1] which touches on many of the points we will discuss, but our views often diverge.

First of all there is what Berlin calls 'negative liberty', the freedom from constraint and coercion—what we usually call political liberty. There are citizens of democracies who, refusing to admit the obvious, claim that people in totalitarian states are approximately as free as those in democratic states. But they make this claim from the safety of their particular democratic state, and show no signs of being ready to emigrate to any totalitarian state.[2] Perhaps we are being unfair to such people... perhaps. It is possible they are thinking of some other kind of freedom which is lacking in democratic states, like economic freedom. The argument is that while there is freedom of choice in these states, a significant number of their citizens do not have many choices, and the ones they have are not appetizing. There is a kind of constraint here, although unless it is due to an intentional effort on the part of the government to hold some group down, it is not political constraint. In any case, the majority suffer from constricted choices in totalitarian states while only a

1. 'Two Concepts of Liberty' in *The Proper Study of Mankind* (New York: Farrar, Straus and Giroux, 1998). Berlin's point of view is basically atheistic.

2. Even Plato, no friend of democracy, preferred it to tyranny. Cf. *Republic* 566D–567 where he perfectly captures the modern totalitarian dictator in a description that is eerie to read considering how long ago it was written.

minority do in democratic ones. Still, the argument will be pressed, people are not really free even in democratic states because these states tend to be capitalistic, and citizens' choices are really determined for them by their exposure to the corporate-media complex which promotes rampant materialism. Here we begin to touch on what Berlin calls 'positive liberty'.

Instead of the rather opaque phrases 'negative liberty' and 'positive liberty', let us use the more transparent expressions 'outer freedom' and 'inner freedom'. Inner freedom, which concerns our choices, is more important than outer freedom as narrowly conceived by Berlin, although he does not think so. Besides the outer determinants of our choices mentioned above there are the inner determinants: 'irrational impulse, uncontrolled desires, my "lower" nature, the pursuit of immediate pleasures, my "empirical" or "heteronomous" self, swept by every gust of desire and passion,' to use some of Berlin's expressions.[3] Furthermore, we are each enslaved to a long list of habits and go through life in a generally mindless state, often unaware of influences on our choices and actions, and with our brains sometimes initiating actions a split second before we are aware of the fact. It would seem then that our choices are all determined by outer and inner factors and thus we are not free.

Many philosophers who have commented on what they call 'free will' instead of freedom, have claimed that if our choices are determined then we are not free. But others have pointed out that if our choices were not determined and thus uncaused events, then we would still not be free since we would be subject to these choices which could pop up at any time. Indeed, some philosophers have thought that our seeming experience of free will is an illusion, as if we could lift ourselves by our own bootstraps. Others have pulled back from this claim and held that as long as the determinants were internal, we could still be thought of as free, even though our choices had definite causes. However, the practitioners of esoteric traditions are unanimous in declaring that beings subject to the inner determinants listed above are not free. Their idea is that we must liberate ourselves from these impulses, and that the way to do

3. Ibid., p204.

this is to become detached from the things of the world. Gaining this inner freedom constitutes the first of the two main stages on the spiritual path, to be followed by gaining outer freedom or complete freedom from the effects of the cosmos.

In contrast to the self in the thrall of the passions, Berlin describes another self,

> variously identified with reason, with my 'higher nature', with the self which calculates and aims at what will satisfy it in the long run, with my 'real', or 'ideal', or 'autonomous' self, or with my self 'at its best....'[4] [And he comments that] ... the concept of the rational sage who has escaped into the inner fortress of the true self seems to arise when the external world has proved exceptionally arid, cruel and unjust.[5] [He adds], Ascetic self-denial may be a source of integrity and spiritual strength, but it is difficult to see how it can be called an enlargement of liberty.[6]

In other words, giving up on trying to get what we want may make us calmer, but it is also a tacit admission of the constraints on us. It must be said that he makes the same mistake Mary Douglas made in her comments on the ascetic approach which emphasizes inner development (chapter 1, 'The Esoteric and The Exoteric'). Yes, some people turn to this path because of poor outer conditions, but this is not why most people turn to it. The Buddha was not subject to an arid, cruel and unjust world when he decided to give up his worldly life, and neither was St Augustine when he decided to become a monk. These are just two people, but why should not they be our models rather than the unfortunate?

The real question is whether there is anything to this idea of inner freedom. Can our choices be conscious and free in the sense of spontaneous, not subject to inner or outer determinants but still reflecting our true nature and hence not things that just happen to us? The answer is that they can, provided they do not flow from our psycho-physical individualities or egos, but rather from our true

4. Ibid., p204.
5. Ibid., p210.
6. Ibid., p211.

self, the Universal Self—God, the same in all. For most people, caught in the web of their individualities, subject to overwhelming desires and emotions, defined by their mindless habits, and filled with thoughts over which they have no control, spontaneity seeps through rather rarely. For those who have gone some way on the esoteric path, spontaneity becomes more evident. It is the freedom of the Self of all of us which is subject to no outer constraint (since there is nothing outside to impinge on it) and no inner constraint (since desires, emotions, and habits do not control it). The Self, which acts through the spirit or Divine aspect of us, is beyond even the calculating self which Berlin describes, for a person ruled by the Self is not full of schemes and agendas, and is without purpose as it were. Achieving inner freedom, which is the subject of the Exodus, is really a matter of letting go of our egos, our individuality, and acting from the supra-individual part of us.

The symbolism of the Exodus is so obvious that it is quite well known. But few have discussed the implications of this symbolism or traced its ramifications. Then too, the only commentators to discuss the symbolic significance of the life of Moses in detail are Philo and Gregory of Nyssa.[7] That is not to deny that other commentators have written on one or another aspect of his life, but there remains much that can be said on this matter. We will begin with the overall picture and then get down to particulars. In keeping to our purpose in writing this book, we will dwell on the stories rather than on the laws handed down by Moses.

The flight of the Israelites from Egypt and their subsequent forty years wandering symbolizes a person's spiritual journey, with a whole people standing for an individual. The slavery in Egypt sym-

7. St Gregory's symbolic analysis is given in his book *The Life of Moses*. Philo's symbolic interpretations are not to be found in his book *The Life of Moses*, but rather in his *Questions and Answers on Exodus*. In his book *On Flight and Finding*, he discusses the episode of the burning bush, but his interpretation, if not far fetched, is at best superficial. Cf. the translation by F.H. Colson and G.H. Whitaker (Cambridge: Harvard Univ. Press, 1971). The *Zohar*, which we have referred to in connection with the creation story in Genesis, comments on the whole Torah. But we cannot learn much of an esoteric character from its sections which deal with Moses.

bolizes inner slavery to the lower tendencies or as we sometimes say, the flesh, although we should not construe this too narrowly. The forty years wandering represents the time of purification, for as the story shows, it is not all that easy to slough the lower tendencies. The promised land is the Land of God or the Celestial Paradise. Attaining it is equivalent to gaining outer freedom, in that one is no longer subject to the cosmos. When the story is viewed in this way, Moses becomes a symbol of the spirit and the higher tendencies within a person. Under the guidance of the spirit, the person reaches his ultimate goal. The death of Moses before his people enter the promised land symbolizes the truth that, at the last, all strivings must be given up. It could hardly be otherwise since all desires are burnt up in the heat of the Spiritual Sun.

Quite consistent with this view, though on another level, is the idea that the advent of Moses represents an infusion of Divine influence into the world, an idea to which we alluded in an earlier chapter. And we must admit that, at times, Moses symbolizes the World Spirit. Finally, we must also mention the view of Gregory of Nyssa according to which the life of Moses should be taken as a pattern for our own lives.[8] While a person is on the spiritual path and striving for the attainment of the spiritual goal he is in much the same state as the majority of mankind, but once he has attained the goal and has 'been elevated to divinity', he becomes 'an unapproachable sun', to use some phrases describing Moses from St Gregory's book *On the Canticle of Canticles*.[9] He becomes, in other words, a Perfect Man, and therefore a source of Divine light in the world. And this in turn ties in with the symbolism of Moses we mentioned at the beginning of this paragraph. Thus Moses can be seen as a person on the spiritual path, a symbol of the spirit within a person, and a symbol of the World Spirit. There is no inconsistency here since all of this symbolism is related.

The story of the Exodus begins with the Israelites in slavery to

8. *The Life of Moses*, tr. Abraham J. Malherbe and Everett Ferguson (New York: Paulist Press, 1978), bk 1, sects. 1–15. All subsequent quotations are from this edition of the book.

9. Ibid., p21.

Pharaoh (Exod. 1). As Pharaoh symbolizes the world, we are given a picture of the unavoidable and universal situation of all who are born. Pharaoh proceeds to order the death of all newborn Hebrew males. This favoring of the females over the males can be seen as the favoring of the lower tendencies over the higher or of the passive over the active.[10] The pull of the world is analogous to the pull of gravity in that it tends to keep human beings at the lowest possible level.

But the higher tendencies cannot be totally suppressed and they appear in the person of the baby Moses who is set out to float in the Nile (chapter 2). We could pause here and rehearse the many parallels to this story which exist, including the birth narrative of Sargon the Great, but this would not in any way lessen its spiritual significance. Mention has already been made of the meaning of floating on the waters in chapter 7. St Gregory's interpretation reads practically like a Buddhist exegesis (*The Life of Moses*, bk II, sects. 6–9). He refers to 'life as a stream made turbulent by the successive waves of passion, which plunge what is in the stream under the water and drown it.' The stream is but another symbol of the world. Moses is plucked out of the stream by Pharaoh's daughter, but while he is raised by his adoptive mother he is nourished by his true mother (Exod. 2:7–9). This signifies that our bodily needs are supplied by the world and our higher tendencies are nourished by God. In the end the higher tendencies exert themselves and Moses kills an Egyptian taskmaster. He flees Egypt and takes up the spiritually significant vocation of shepherd (3:1). This sets the stage for his first significant spiritual experience.

St Gregory is no doubt correct in attributing great importance to this fleeing of Egypt and embarking on the life of a shepherd (bk II, sects. 16–19). It symbolizes a flight from the outer life of the senses toward the inner life of the spirit. And it will perhaps not be assuming too much if we view Moses' father-in-law Jethro, a priest of the Midianites (Gen. 3:1), as taking the part of a spiritual master and initiator. Once one has turned one's attention inward the immutable Spirit within will show itself. In the story it takes the form of the

10. In this regard cf. Philo, *Questions and Answers on Exodus*, bk I, sect. 8.

bush which burns but is not consumed (3:2). Moses sees the bush on Mt Horeb (3:1), which indicates an elevated or spiritual state. A voice from the bush tells him to keep his distance and to take off his sandals since he is standing on holy ground (3:5). This particular verse has been the subject of many commentaries and the sandals have been taken to symbolize various things. These interpretations are by no means mutually exclusive but rather reveal different aspects of the symbolism of this wonderful story, much in the way polishing by different hands reveals the different facets of a beautiful gem.

In some passages that are quite Platonic, St Gregory relates the burning bush to Being (God) or that which is self-subsisting and unchanging, and the sandals to non-being (the world of the senses) which is changing and exists only by participation in Being. Truth, for him 'is the sure apprehension of real Being.'

> Sandaled feet cannot ascend the height where the light of truth is seen, but the dead and earthly covering of skins, which was placed around our nature at the beginning when we were found naked because of disobedience to the divine will, must be removed from the feet of the soul. When we do this, the knowledge of the truth will result and manifest itself.... In the same way that Moses on that occasion attained to this knowledge, so now does everyone who, like him, divests himself of the earthly covering and looks to the light shining from the bramble bush, that is, to the Radiance which shines upon us through this thorny flesh and which is (as the Gospel says) the true light and the truth itself. A person like this becomes able to help others to salvation, to destroy the tyranny which holds power wickedly, and to deliver to freedom everyone held in evil servitude. (bk II, sect. 22)

We might think at first that St Gregory is echoing the Platonic idea that we cannot completely apprehend the highest realities while in our bodies. But if we are to take the last part of the quotation seriously this cannot be his view, for we cannot help others from beyond the grave. By relating the sandals to the skins which were given to Adam and Eve after the fall he is at the same time relating them to those things associated with the giving of the skins: bodily cravings and human mortality. Thus one meaning of the order to remove the sandals is that sense-based desires must be put aside before the activity of the Spirit can be felt in one's life. Indeed, no approach to the Spirit within is possible if we are unwilling to discipline ourselves in this way. The other meaning of the order is that the sandals, as symbols of mortality, are totally incommensurate with the eternality of the Divine.

It is possible to go further along these lines without mentioning the skins. In the first place the sandals are products of human technology and are thus opposed to what occurs naturally—the works of God—and, as they are man-made, they are also worldly things. The message is that in approaching God we must put aside the things of the world. In the second place, as things created by man, they serve as a symbol for all created things and thus for the world itself. The message here is that in drawing near to the Divine we must put away the world.

A related but different interpretation is possible if we consider that there are two sandals. Recalling an earlier chapter we can say that Moses is being ordered to put away the dualistic view of reality. As one approaches the center of one's own existence and thus the center of creation all dualities disappear. If one is unwilling to let go of distinctions such as subject and object, mine and thine, good and bad, then it is impossible to fall under the Divine influence.

Still another interpretation of the verses in question is given by Al-Ghazali in several passages:[11]

> I assert . . . that Moses understood from the command *Put off thy shoes*, the Doffing of the Two Worlds, and obeyed the command *literally* by putting off his two sandals, and *spiritually* by putting off the Two Worlds.

In one passage he describes the 'Two Worlds' in three different ways:

11. *The Niche for Lights*, pp121–143.

> The world is Two Worlds, spiritual and material, or, if you will, a World Sensual and a world Intelligential; or again, if you will, a World Supernal and a world inferior.

He seems to be referring to the Archetypal world on the one hand and to the cosmos which is perceived in part by the senses on the other. While the one is higher than the other, they both proceed from God considered in His highest aspect. As he says,

> ...for this world and the world beyond [the senses] are correlatives and both are accidents of the human light substance, and can be doffed at one time and donned at another.

His comment is a reminder of the truism that anything other than God as He is in Himself, no matter how high it may be, is still something less than the Ultimate Reality.

We have yet to remark on the statement in Exod. 3:5, 'for the place on which you stand is holy ground.' This would indicate that Moses has reached the Terrestrial Paradise or the center of his being, and thus has reached the goal of his first rebirth. That he has not reached the ultimate spiritual goal is shown in what follows. He asks God for His name (3:13) and God replies *Ehyeh-Asher-Ehyeh* and tells Moses to say to the Israelites that *Ehyeh* sent him to them (3:14). Most scholars understand the name to mean I am that I am, or I will be what I will be. We are dealing here with the personal conception of God as Being, the same conception found in St Gregory's commentary. Thus when God tells Moses to say that *Ehyeh* has sent him He is really telling him to say that Being has sent him. But this is not the highest conception of God and Moses has not yet had his ultimate spiritual realization.

In his 'role' as Being, what more can God say in describing Himself than 'I am'? What then is the point of 'I am that I am'? Guénon, who presents the best modern commentary on these verses, feels that the 'most exact rendering' of the name is 'Being is Being'.[12] He first points out that any being 'confronting itself as it were in order

12. René Guénon, *Symbolism of the Cross* (Hillsdale, NY: Sophia Perennis, 2001), chap. 17, p93.

to know itself, duplicates itself into subject and object; but here again the two are one in reality.'[13] On the particular matter of God's name he says the following:

> In fact, Being having been postulated, what can be said of It (and, one must add, what cannot but be said of It) is first that It is, and then that It is Being; these necessary affirmations essentially constitute the whole of ontology in the proper sense of the word. The second way of envisaging the same formula is to postulate first of all the first *Eheieh*, then the second one as the reflection of the first in a mirror (image of the contemplation of Being by Itself).[14]

Thus God in describing Himself considers Himself as subject and object (or attribute) and says first 'I am' and then 'Being is what I am.' In this way we are given a picture of the inner life of God, if we may be permitted to use this expression, as Being contemplating Itself.[15] It must be kept in mind that while *we* may consider what is other than ourselves, there is no other than God, since 'all beings insofar as they are manifested in Existence' are 'really no more than "participations"' in Being.[16] Thus the description of God (as Being) contemplating Himself is a complete one which spells out very clearly the difference between God and man.

In speaking to Moses out of the burning bush, God orders him to lead his people out of Egypt. Moses demurs in various ways. According to the narrative of Exodus 4:1–5, Moses worries that the Israelites may not listen to him. The Lord's reply is to transform Moses' shepherd's staff or rod so that when he throws it on the ground it will turn into a snake and when he picks it up by its tail it will turn back into a rod. This will serve as a sign that Moses has indeed been sent by the Lord. We know from 7:8–13 that later on when Aaron threw down the rod in front of the Pharaoh it turned

13. Ibid., p91.
14. Ibid., p93.
15. Such a picture is analogous to Aristotle's description of the Divine Intellect (*Nous*) contemplating Itself—*Metaphysics*, bk XII, 1074B34.
16. *Symbolism of the Cross*, p92.

into a serpent, and when the Pharaoh had his magicians do the same with their rods, Moses' serpent ate their serpents. Once God has transformed the shepherd's staff of Moses (and the fact that it is a shepherd's staff is significant) it is no longer Moses' staff but God's. As such, like the Tree of Life, it is a symbol of the World Spirit or Axis. And let us recall from the discussion in chapter 5 that the serpent also stands for the World Axis and immortality, so the transformation of the rod to serpent makes no difference symbolically. There is in fact a Christian tradition according to which Adam, knowing that he was leaving the Garden of Eden forever, cut off a branch from the Tree of Knowledge and took it with him. He passed it down to Seth, and in time it came to Noah, Shem, Abraham, Isaac and Jacob.[17] It was at one point hidden in a cave by an angel, and was found there by the Midianite Priest Jethro who gave it to his son-in-law Moses. Thus, according to this story Moses' staff is really a branch from the Tree of Knowledge.[18] We have noted the basic identity of the two trees of the Garden of Eden, and certainly a branch can stand for a whole tree, so what we have here is a symbolic account equivalent to our own.

The Lord transforms another staff in the incident of Korah's rebellion narrated in Numbers 16–17. At one point He has Moses ask the leaders of each tribe to present a staff for placement in the tent of meeting (Num. 17:1–4). On the tribe of Levi's staff Moses puts the name of Aaron. God transforms this one staff so that 'it brings forth sprouts, produces blossoms, and bears ripe almonds' (17:8). The Spirit consumes or destroys but also creates. At the time of dissolution It pulls the rest of the cosmos into Itself, but at the time of manifestation or creation it gives forth the rest of the cosmos. As described, Aaron's staff is equivalent to the World Tree whose trunk, as we mentioned in chapter 5, is one of the symbols of the World

17. One might say that this is a picturesque account of how the Divine influence was handed down from generation to generation, a matter we discussed in chap. 2.

18. Cf. *The Book of the Bee* tr. Earnest A. Wallis Budge (Oxford: The Clarendon Press, 1886), chap. xxx, pp50–51. The book was written by a Nestorian Syrian Bishop named Solomon in 1222. Widengren, in his *The King And The Tree Of Life In Near Eastern Religion*, mentions that kings in Mesopotamia were often described as holding a branch from the Tree of Life as their scepter (pp22–32).

Axis. The blossom at the top of the staff signifies either the Sundoor at the top of the cosmos or Being—the Spiritual Sun.

Getting back to Moses' staff as transformed by God, in his hand it is the royal scepter signifying his rulership over the Israelites by Divine right. Moses, through his brother Aaron who, as we said earlier, functions as his alter ego, is priest as well as ruler and thus exemplifies the ideal of the priest-king as the Divine center (or place-holder for God) of his kingdom. The serpent in this instance symbolizes immortality and thus complements the Divine rod. The Divine serpent swallows the worldly serpents of Pharaoh's magicians in an incident symbolizing the hegemony of God over the created world. It also signifies the idea that God engulfs the universe which is but a drop in the Divine ocean.[19]

In a passage whose symbolic meaning is almost the reverse of its literal meaning Moses complains that he is 'slow of speech and slow of tongue' and by implication incapable of transmitting God's message to the Israelites (Exod. 4:10). It is here that God appoints Aaron to be the spokesman for his brother (4:14–16). On the symbolic level there is really no lack in Moses. His inability with words first of all refers to the difficulty involved in expressing the nature of spiritual realization. It is one thing to visit paradise and quite another to talk about it. We must remember that the distinctions on which our conceptual frameworks are built tend to merge as we approach the Divine. Thus the further into the center we go the more difficult it becomes to describe our journey. Then too, spiritual realization is in a sense dumb. It must be experienced to be really understood, words being only of help in leading people to have the experience. It is not so much that nothing descriptive can be said, but that what can be said is of limited value for those who have not yet attained realization. We are thinking of such phrases as 'I am that I am' and 'Being is Being'.

As to the relationship between Moses and Aaron we must keep in mind the statement of Exod. 4:16, 'Thus he shall be your spokes-

19. We might mention in passing that the source of Moses' power is the World Spirit, while the source of the magicians' power is most likely the psychic or intermediate world.

man, and you shall be an oracle to him.' As an oracle of God, Moses' individuality is effectively negated and his voice becomes the voice of God. In other words, for the Israelites he becomes the Spirit. Aaron, the priest, then becomes a mediator or funnel of the Divine influence for the people, and this is indeed the priestly function. One might compare Moses to the sun and Aaron to the moon which reflects the sunlight. While the Israelites cannot look directly at the sun, they can look at the moon which mediates the sun's light. That is to say, while the Israelites are not yet open to receiving the Divine influence directly, they can be uplifted by the mediation of one who is open.

On the level of the individual, Aaron as spokesman symbolizes the outer or external aspects of a person. As older brother he represents the lower centrifugal tendencies which, as we have said, are the first to develop. And we must remember, it is Aaron who is prevailed upon to construct the golden calf, a symbol of one of these tendencies. Moses, on the other hand, who is 'slow of speech', symbolizes the inner aspect of a person. As younger brother he represents the higher centripetal tendencies which are the last to develop. And finally, in this connection, we can say that Moses portrays the spirit or heart of a person, while Aaron depicts the soul which is the seat of the mental processes. The point is that the heart can speak only through the mind.

12

Moses and Pharaoh

CHAPTER 5 OF EXODUS records the beginning of the great tug-of-war between Moses and Pharaoh for control of the Israelites. In symbols, it is the battle between the spirit and the body for possession of the soul. As soon as Moses comes to Pharaoh with his request that the Israelites be allowed to worship God in the wilderness the battle is joined. Pharaoh immediately instructs the taskmasters and foremen to make the work of the Israelites even harder (Exod. 5:6–9). To those on the spiritual path it is well known that in the inner holy war as soon as there is a tug in the direction of God there will be an opposite tug in the direction of the world. The world works like the force of gravity: every attempt to gain freedom by jumping higher is opposed by the forces of slavery pulling us lower. Like gravity, the pull of the world is always present but it is usually unfelt and unnoticed, showing itself only when opposed.[1]

As if in answer to Pharaoh's harsh measures God reveals His name to Moses: 'I am the Lord. I appeared to Abraham, Isaac, and Jacob as El Shaddai, but I did not make myself known to them by My name YHVH' (Exod. 6:2–3). The significance of this little episode must not be overlooked, and Maimonides spends a whole chapter of his *Guide* on it. He writes:

> All the names of God, may He be exalted, that are to be found in any of the books derive from action. There is nothing secret in this matter. The only exception is one name: namely, *Yod, He, Vav, He.* This is the name of God, may He be exalted, that has

1. The pull of the world is really the pull of *Prakriti*, the substance of the world and the passive pole of Existence.

been originated without any derivation, and for this reason it is called the *articulated name.* This means that this name gives a clear unequivocal indication of His essence, may He be exalted.[2]

The point is that while a name like 'El Shaddai' is descriptive and from a human source, the name 'YHVH' is from a non-human source, namely from the Source of everything. Giving the name of the essence is tantamount to transmitting Divine power, for in this case we have a real example of the adage, 'Knowledge is power'. Symbolically, the giving of the name to Moses after his rebuff by Pharaoh signifies the granting of Divine influence to help the higher tendencies in their fight with the lower tendencies.[3]

In the next skirmish of the war Moses' snake swallows the snakes of the Egyptian magicians (Exod. 7:12), 'Yet Pharaoh's heart stiffened and he did not heed them, as the Lord had spoken' (7:13). The Lord had already said He would harden Pharaoh's heart in order to enable Him to show His power (7:3), but we must not take this literally. The reaction of Pharaoh is the normal reaction of the lower tendencies.

We come now to the episode of the ten plagues starting with the turning of the Nile into a river of blood (Exod. 7:20) and continuing with the frogs, lice, insects, pestilence, boils, hail, locusts, darkness, and death of the first born. There is in this episode something of Dante's descent into the various hells, the recapitulation of the lower states of Existence which a person must go through before his spiritual ascent. And in the *Divine Comedy* we find Virgil playing a similar role to that of Moses. It is doubtful that one could tie down each of the plagues as specific symbols. However, we can speak of them as a whole with individual references now and then. The plagues symbolize the attack of the higher tendencies on the lower tendencies under the guidance of the Spirit. The lower tendencies fall into two categories: the lusts for worldly things and the negative emotions such as fear, anger and jealousy. There are also two ways of

2. *The Guide of the Perplexed*, pt. 1, chap. 61, p147.

3. The four letters of the Divine name may well correspond to the 'three worlds' of the cosmos plus God (beyond manifestation) and in this regard cf. the *Mandukya Upanishad* with its analysis of *AUM*.

dealing with these tendencies: education and abstinence, the first being preparatory for the second. The former is symbolized by the plagues and the latter by the wandering in the wilderness.

It is almost a truism that if one finds nothing wrong with the lower tendencies one will do nothing about them. The plagues symbolize the effort to investigate their true nature and ramifications. The lice, boils, and pestilence symbolize the ills to which the flesh is prey, lest we be too concerned with the body. The hail and locusts symbolize the all-consuming nature of desires and negative emotions. The swarming insects indicate the nature of a negative emotion like anger. The first plague, turning the Nile waters into blood and causing death, foreshadows the last plague. The frogs are a symbol not so easily dealt with, although no doubt St Gregory is correct in stressing their amphibious nature (bk II, sects. 68–72). In the water the frogs are no problem, but during the plague they come up on the land. Bodily desires, when they are confined to serving real bodily needs, are not inimical to a person. But when they forget their rightful place and come to dominate life they are definitely a problem.

The plague of darkness, besides symbolizing the debilitating effects of fear, also stands for the situation of a soul completely given over to the lower tendencies. It wanders in darkness instead of in the light of the Spirit. One could say that this plague summarizes all of the eight we have just discussed.

The last plague, death of the first born, is the most obvious symbol of all and, not surprisingly, it tips the balance in favor of the higher tendencies. The specter of death looms over everyone as much as we may wish to forget it. The last plague puts a question: Do we wish to spend our lives in darkness or in light? It is a matter of choosing the worldly life, which is death, or the spiritual life in which we can attain the sense of eternity. This is the meaning of the well-known passage in Deuteronomy:

> I call heaven and earth to witness against you this day: I have put before you life and death: blessing and curse. Choose life—if you and your offspring would live—by loving the Lord your God, heeding His Commands, and holding fast to Him. For thereby

you shall have life and shall long endure upon the soil that the Lord your God swore to Abraham, Isaac, and Jacob to give to them. (Deut. 30:19–20)

This matter of choosing eternal life (in the sense indicated) is intimately connected with the method used by the Israelites to save themselves from the effect of the tenth plague: viz., the daubing of their door-posts and lintels with the blood of sacrificial lambs (Exod. 12:7). Blood is the most obvious symbol of life, from which we derive the phrase 'life blood'. But the door-posts and lintel function symbolically in a way comparable to that of the initiatic ladder and thus signify the World Axis or Spirit. The sacrificial blood of the lambs is the antitype of the influence of the Spirit, which is sometimes symbolized by drops of blood. And we can recall here the blood of the sacrificial bull in Mithraic initiation ceremonies. The flow of this nectar of immortality can be seen as due to the self-sacrifice of the Spirit which must be emulated on an individual level if spiritual advancement is to be possible.[4]

If we wish to obtain the promised land mentioned in the verses just quoted, we must hold fast to God as Moses held fast to his staff, and to do this we must first escape the pull of the lower tendencies. But it is practically impossible to escape the pull of these tendencies on the first attempt. One tries to get free, and one is pulled back. One tries again and perhaps gets a little further, but one is pulled back again. And so it goes, over and over, and a certain tension is built up. One reaches the stage where one can no longer give up the attempts but where one is still not making any progress. At last the energy of the tension is built up to such an extent that the next attempt succeeds, and one is on the road to the promised land. To use a contemporary analogy, we can compare this process to that of getting a rocket off the earth and beyond the earth's gravitational pull into space. The first rockets hardly had enough power to get off the ground. Others were developed which got further and further

4. René Guénon has written about the symbolism of blood in 'Symbolic Flowers', which is chap. 9 of *Symbols of Sacred Science*. We have alluded the significance of sacrificial actions in chaps. 3 and 8.

off the ground but which still fell back to earth. Finally one was developed with sufficient power to overcome the gravitational pull and fly off into space. It takes this much effort to accomplish what is called repentance in the West, and only when this has taken place can an aspirant claim to be on the spiritual path.

But far from being the end it is only the beginning, and any baggage we take with us from our old life hinders us on the way. This is shown by the story of the jewelry which the departing Israelites were given by the Egyptians (Exod. 12:35). As soon as Moses leaves the people to ascend Mt Sinai and receive the Ten Commandments the trouble begins. The absence of Moses symbolizes the disassociation of the spirit from the rest of the person. When the action of the spirit (and hence of the World Spirit) is interrupted, a person is prey to the pull of the lower tendencies. Thus, in the present story, the Israelites present their jewelry to Aaron for the construction of a calf (32:1–6). The worship of this calf signifies the worship of wealth, and one cannot avoid this sort of backsliding if one carries along the spiritual path any of the baggage of the worldly path. The old cravings must be utterly destroyed, and this is symbolized by the action of Moses in having the calf burnt up, crushed to powder, and swallowed by the Israelites (32:20).

Returning to our account of the Exodus, after Pharaoh lets the Israelites go, he has second thoughts and chases after them (14:5–9). This episode vividly portrays the fact that the lower tendencies do not go to sleep once repentance has occurred. They hound a person much as Pharaoh hounded the Israelites until the crossing of the Red Sea.[5] This crossing to the other shore is not equivalent to the Buddhist crossing of the ocean of birth and death, although it has some elements in common. The main difference is that, whereas for the Buddhist getting to the other side means reaching the ultimate

5. In two articles, 'The Reed Sea: *Requiescat in Pace*', *Journal of Biblical Literature*, vol. 102 (1983), pp27–35, and 'Red Sea or Reed Sea', *Biblical Archeology Review*, vol. x, no. 4 (July/August 1984), pp57–63, Bernard F. Batto has shown that the reading 'Sea of Reeds' for '*yam sup*' is very questionable. A better translation would be 'Sea of the End (of the world)' and the reference is to the primordial chaos. What we have here, in effect, is another creation story similar to the one in which Marduk cleaved Tiamat in two in order to create the cosmos.

goal, it obviously does not mean this for the Israelites. Nevertheless, it seems to mark an important milestone on the path in that the Egyptian army is swallowed up in the waters (14:27–28) signifying a real defeat for the lower tendencies. And if the Exodus itself represents repentance, this last episode symbolizes the first rebirth. It is as if the higher tendencies have been separated from the lower in the way a purifying fire separates the precious metal from the dross.

The walls of water the Israelites pass through are equivalent to the clashing rocks of ancient myths. They symbolize the dualistic view of reality. We stated earlier that approaching the Divine we must leave the dualistic viewpoint behind. Where all contraries are reconciled, our consciousness must follow suit. Whether represented by the walls of water, or clashing rocks, or even by thorn bushes, the dualistic conception of reality and the patterns of discursive thought which support it are very difficult to pass beyond, especially as we tend to be chain thinkers, taking up one thought as we put down another.[6] The Egyptians, who can be said to represent a person tied to the lower tendencies and hence immersed in dualism, do not make it through. But the Israelites, led by the pillar of cloud in the day and the pillar of fire at night (13:21), both symbolizing the World Axis or Spirit, manage to get through unscathed. Having done so they symbolize a person who has reached the Terrestrial Paradise.

Almost as soon as the Israelites begin their trek through the wilderness they begin to complain about their plight. They lack water, and when they discover some at a place called Marah it turns out to be bitter. They grumble to Moses, 'So he cried out to the Lord, and the Lord showed him a piece of wood; he threw it into the water and the water became sweet' (15:25). However, the troubles continue in the form of lack of food, and the Israelites begin to wish they were back in Egypt (16:1–3). Following St Gregory (bk II, sect. 132) we must remember that the wandering through the wilderness symbolizes a period of abstinence, a period when a whole former way of living is given up. The adjustment is difficult as the new life seems arid

6. On the symbolism of the dualistic standpoint cf. Ananda Coomaraswamy, 'Symplegades', in *Coomaraswamy: Selected Papers*, vol. 1, and Samuel D. Fohr, 'Clashing Rocks', in *Cinderella's Gold Slipper*.

and bitter. But the Lord has ways of sweetening one's plight, as we learn from the example of the wood. The meaning of this becomes clearer in the case of the manna.

The Israelites long for the old life when they 'ate their fill of bread' (16:3). Certainly the new life seems empty and hopeless, but if one perseveres, the Lord will send heavenly food to replace the earthly. The manna that God sends symbolizes the Divine blessing which fulfills a person completely.

> And the Lord said to Moses, 'I will rain down bread for you from the sky, and the people shall go out and gather each day that day's portion—that I may thus test them, to see whether they follow my instructions or not' (16:4).... The Israelites did so, some gathering much, some little. But when they measured it by the omer, he who gathered much had no excess, and he who gathered little had no deficiency. (16:17–18)

When the Divine influence nourishes a person's being it is as if all of his desires have been fulfilled, and the joy it brings is not the fleeting joy of earthly satisfactions.[7]

The Israelites are told, 'Let no one leave any of it over until morning' (16:19), and those who disobey find that it has become rotten with maggots overnight (16:20). St Gregory rightly finds a lesson in this occurrence:

> In this account Scripture after a fashion cries out to the covetous that the insatiable greed of those always hoarding surplus is turned into worms. Everything beyond what they need encompassed by this covetous desire becomes on the next day—that is

7. In a section of *Questions and Answers on Exodus* dealing with the sanctuary Philo has the following to say about Divine blessings:

> If, however, thou art worthily initiated and canst be consecrated to God and in a certain sense become an animate shrine of the Father, (then) instead of having closed eyes, thou wilt cease from the deep sleep in which thou hast been held. Then will appear to thee the manifest One, Who causes incorporeal rays to shine for thee, and grants visions of the unambiguous and indescribable things of nature and the abundant sources of other good things. For the beginning and end of happiness is to be able to see God. But this cannot happen to him who has not made his soul, as I said before, a sanctuary and altogether a shrine of God. (bk II, sec. 51)

> in the future life—a worm to the person who hoards it. He who hears 'worm' certainly perceives the undying worm which is made alive by covetousness. (bk 11, sect. 143)

Evidently St Gregory's Bible mentioned worms instead of maggots, but the point is the same: wealth becomes rotten when hoarded. We have become slaves to its maintenance and augmentation instead of free agents of its distribution.

In a parallel story to that of the manna the Israelites cry out again that they lack what they need for sustenance, this time water (Exod. 17:2–3). The Lord then instructs Moses to go up to Mt Horeb and strike a certain rock with his staff, and water issues from the rock (17:5–6). This water is really no different from the manna and again symbolizes the Divine influence. It quenches the thirst as no earthly water quenches it. The rock from which the water flows is comparable to the rock on which Jacob slept (Gen. 28), and as in the former story symbolizes the connecting link between Heaven and Earth. In addition, the rock is situated on Mt Horeb, the world mountain, which is still another symbol of the World Axis leading up to heaven. In fact, three symbols of the same thing are conjoined in this story: the staff, the rock, and the mountain.

There follows the incident of the war with Amalek in which the Israelites score a major victory. The description of this event is so obviously symbolic that it hardly needs comment. Moses goes up on a hill with the 'rod of God' in his hand, and while he holds up his hand the Israelites prevail but when his hand falls through tiredness Amalek prevails. So Aaron and Hur set him on a rock and hold up his hands for the rest of the battle (Exod. 17:8–13). Here again we have the rod, the rock and the mountain mentioned together. As if the meaning of this isn't sufficiently clear, 17:14–16 explain it explicitly:

> Then the Lord said to Moses, 'Inscribe this in a document as a reminder, and read it aloud to Joshua: I will utterly blot out the memory of Amalek from under heaven!' And Moses built an altar and named it Adonai-nissi [the Lord is my banner]. He said, 'it means, Hand upon the throne of the Lord!' The Lord will be at war with Amalek throughout the ages.

These statements about the Amalekites are amplified in Deut. 25:17–19 where God orders the Israelites to 'blot out the memory of Amalek from under heaven.'

If we were to take these statements literally we would be led to the conclusion that God was quite bloodthirsty, and indeed many people have claimed on the basis of such passages that the God of the Old Testament is stern and cruel—a God of vengeance. This point of view indicates a complete lack of understanding of the inner significance of these passages.[8] There is another section of Deuteronomy which bears on this matter. In Deut. 20 the Israelites are given rules for the conduct of war which preclude the 'blotting out' of a people and even prescribe the offer of terms of peace before any attack is begun. But then an exception is made:

> Thus you shall deal with all towns that lie very far from you, towns that do not belong to nations hereabout. In the towns of the latter people, however, which the Lord your God is giving you as a heritage, you shall not let a soul remain alive. No, you must proscribe them—the Hittites and the Amorites, the Canaanites and the Perrizites, the Hivites, and the Jebusites—as the Lord your God has commanded you, lest they mislead you into doing all the abhorrent things that they have done for their gods and you stand guilty before the Lord your God. (Deut. 20:15–18)

It is the reason given in the last verse which is important for our consideration. The Amalekites and all the other peoples named are symbols of the lower tendencies which have no place in the promised land, the land of the Spirit. A person cannot dwell in paradise and still be subject to these tendencies.

The battle against Amalek is really a doublet of the fleeing from

8. In fact, no archeological evidence has been found to support the idea that Canaan was conquered violently. It seems instead that most of the people in the area were converted to the Israelite religion peacefully. If we would not accept as historical the various legends about the founding of Rome, why accept as historical the corresponding stories about the founding of Israel? All of these legends and stories served a sort of patriotic purpose, but that does not make them true, and of course, the biblical stories also have a symbolic spiritual significance.

Pharaoh. The destruction of the Amalekites is a doublet of the destruction of Pharaoh's forces in the Red Sea. 'The Lord will be at war with Amalek throughout the generations' means that the Lord will always oppose the lower tendencies within a person. Moses, sitting on a rock which is to become an altar (a throne of God), staff in upraised hand, is a conduit of Divine influence to his people. Thus it is really God through the person of Moses functioning as the Spirit who is fighting against the Amalekites. On the personal level it is a picture of the Spirit within fighting against the lower tendencies. When the higher tendencies weaken, i.e., when the hands fall, a person is no longer in touch with the Spirit and the lower tendencies prevail. But when the higher tendencies are revived, i.e., when the hands are held up, the outcome of the battle is not in doubt.

Wiping out the Amalekites is obviously related to swallowing the remains of the golden calf, a matter we have already discussed. Immediately following the latter occurrence we are told: 'Moses stood up in the gate of the camp and said, "Whoever is for the Lord, come here"' (Exod. 32:26). There comes a point on the spiritual path where one must make a decision: to go forward or back. One cannot go in two directions at once, or in the words of Sri Ramakrishna[9] one cannot have both *yoga* and *bhoga*, the life of God and the life of the senses. The call of Moses to rally to the banner of God is really the call of the Spirit within to commit oneself to going forward in the path of abstinence (or renunciation). More precisely, it is the call for the higher tendencies to separate themselves utterly from the lower tendencies. And this is another of the meanings of the saying 'Do not let your left hand know what your right hand is doing' (Matt. 6:3).

Soon after this incident come two appeals by Moses: 'Now, if I have truly gained Your favor, pray let me know Your ways, that I may know You and continue in Your favor' (Exod. 33:13), and 'Oh, let me behold Your Presence' (33:18). God answers,

> I will make all my goodness pass before you, and I will proclaim before you the name Lord, and the grace that I grant and the

9. See chap. 1, n11.

> compassion that I show. But . . . you cannot see My face, for man may not see Me and live (33:19–20). [He goes on] See, there is a place near Me. Station yourself on the rock and, as My Presence passes by, I will put you in a cleft of the rock and shield you with my hand until I have passed by. Then I will take My hand away and you will see My back; but My face must not be seen (33:21–23).

In 34:6 we are told that the Lord passed before Moses proclaiming His name and His compassion. There are well-known parallels in Greek mythology to the idea that a human being cannot survive a face-to-face meeting with the Divine radiance, but there is no reason to lay great stress on this, especially as the significance is quite different in the two cases. In the biblical case there is no question of harm but rather impossibility.

Maimonides comments on these passages throughout Part I of *The Guide of the Perplexed*:

> Know that the master of those who know, *Moses our Master*, peace be upon him, made two requests and received an answer to both of them. One request consisted in his asking Him, may He be exalted, to let him know His essence and true reality. The second request, which he put first, was that He should let him know His attributes. The answer to the two requests that He, may He be exalted, gave him consisted in His promising him to let him know all His attributes, making it known to him that they are His actions, and teaching him that His essence cannot be grasped as it really is.[10]

In another place he comments, 'In this sense it is also said: *But my face shall not be seen*, meaning that the true reality of my existence as it veritably is cannot be grasped.'[11] And he relates elsewhere:

> Scripture accordingly says in this passage that God, may He be exalted, hid from him the apprehension called that *of the face* and made him pass over to something different; I mean the

10. *The Guide of the Perplexed*, pt. 1, chap. 54, p123.
11. Ibid., pt. 1, chap. 37, p86.

> knowledge of the acts ascribed to Him, may He be exalted, which, as we shall explain, are deemed to be multiple attributes. When I say He hid from him, I intend to signify that this apprehension is hidden and inaccessible in its very nature.[12]

The verses we are discussing deal with the supreme and final realization of Moses, for he has reached the end of the vertical path to God which he began to climb at the time of the theophany of the burning bush. It describes the result of what we have called the second rebirth: a person's realization of his essential identity with God. This is indicated by Exod. 34:29–30:

> So Moses came down from Mount Sinai. And as Moses came down from the mountain bearing the two tablets of the Pact, he was not aware that the skin of his face was radiant, since he had spoken with Him. Aaron and all the Israelites saw that the skin of Moses' face was radiant; and they shrank from coming near him.

According to this description Moses has become a medium through which the Divine Sun can be refracted on earth. This is possible only when one has reached the height of realization and one's ego, which blocks the Divine light, has been completely transcended. Moses has become empty of himself and thereby he has become full of God.

Even so, there is a limit to what can be experienced and apprehended at these heights. God's face, His essential nature, that Ultimate Mystery or Darkness which is symbolized in Exodus by the Divine cloud, is beyond all experience and description. This is the significance, as Maimonides explains so well, of God's denial of Moses' second request. And St Gregory, too, sheds some light on this subject in his comments on Exod. 20:21. Speaking of the mind set on the spiritual path he says the following, quoting from John 1:19, Exod. 20:21, and Ps. 17:12:

> For leaving behind everything that is observed, not only what sense comprehends but also what the intelligence thinks it sees, it keeps on penetrating deeper until by the intelligence's yearning for understanding it gains access to the invisible and the incom-

12. Ibid., pt. 1, chap. 21, pp48–49.

prehensible, and there it sees God. This is the true knowledge of what is sought; this is the seeing that consists in not seeing, because that which is sought transcends all knowledge, being separated on all sides by incomprehensibility as by a kind of darkness. Wherefore John the sublime, who penetrated into luminous darkness, says *No one has ever seen God*, thus asserting that knowledge of the divine essence is unattainable not only by men but also by every intelligent creature.

When, therefore, Moses grew in knowledge, he declared that he had seen God in the darkness, that is, that he had come to know that what is divine is beyond all knowledge and comprehension, for the text says, *Moses approached the dark cloud where God was.* What God? *He who made darkness his hiding place*, as David says, who also was initiated into the mysteries in the same inner sanctuary. (bk II, sects. 163–164)

Gregory also shows how the plan of the earthly tabernacle reflects Divine realities:

The curtains divided the tabernacle into two parts: the one visible and accessible to certain of the priests and the other secret and inaccessible. The name of the front part was the Holy Place and that of the hidden part was the Holy of Holies. (bk II, sect. 172)

On the granting of the first request Maimonides has something very interesting to say:

For he was told: *I will make all my Goodness pass before thee....* This dictum—*All my goodness*—alludes to the display to him of all existing things of which it is said: *And God saw every thing that he had made, and behold it was very good*. By their display, I mean that he will apprehend their nature and the way they are mutually connected so that he will know how He governs them in general and in detail.[13]

According to this explanation Moses was granted the experience of

13. *The Guide of the Perplexed*, pt. I, chap. 54, p124.

the unity of Existence. And if we may distinguish between the goodness and the back of God, in the case of the latter Moses was granted the experience of the oneness of Being, one step below the Divine essence. In effect, Being is the outside of God which veils the inside—the essential infinite nature of God.

On the matter of the niche in the rock where Moses positioned himself during the theophany we defer to St Gregory:

> For the same thing which is here called an opening in the rock is elsewhere referred to as 'pleasure of paradise', 'eternal tabernacle', 'mansion with the Father', 'bosom of the patriarch', 'land of the living', 'water of refreshment', 'Jerusalem which is above', 'kingdom of heaven', 'prize of calling', 'crown of graces', 'crown of pleasure', 'crown of beauty', 'pillar of strength', 'pleasure on a table', 'councils of God', 'throne of judgment', 'place of name', 'hidden tabernacle'. (bk 11, sect. 247)

In sum, it is the Celestial Paradise, which should not be surprising in light of all we have said concerning the symbolism of the rock on the mountain.

This story of the spiritual progress of Moses does not exactly parallel the story of the progress of the Israelites. If we take the Israelites as symbolizing a person on the spiritual path, the first rebirth, as we have said, occurs at the crossing of the Red Sea, and the second and final rebirth occurs at the crossing of the Jordan River into the promised land which is described at the beginning of Joshua. That the second crossing is meant to be analogous to the first is shown by the description of the waters of the Jordan piling up to allow the Israelites to walk on dry land (Josh. 3:14–17). In the two crossings we are thus witnessing the two turning points of the same drama, the human drama of the spiritual journey with all its pitfalls. For the journey to be a success the old ways must be left behind. This is symbolized not only by the swallowing of the Egyptian gold but also by the dying in the wilderness of the generation of the first crossing.[14]

14. This dying of the generation of the Exodus also symbolizes the second death which must occur before the second and final rebirth.

The whole journey can also be likened to approaching and ascending a mountain, and St Gregory does just this in his discussion (bk II, sects. 152–161) of the ascent of Moses just described in Exod. 19 and 20. Corresponding to crossing the Red Sea would be arriving at the foot of the mountain, and corresponding to conquering the promised land would be arriving at the top. In fact, the two rebirths and corresponding attainments are also symbolized by the structure of the tabernacle. On the one hand we have the far side of the Red Sea, the foot of the mountain, and the front part of the tabernacle. On the other we have the promised land, the top of the mountain, and the rear part of the tabernacle. The two parts of this journey are described very beautifully by Origen in his explanation of why the stages of the journey of the Israelites are repeated twice in the Torah (in Numbers and Deuteronomy):

> The stages are repeated twice in order to show two journeys for the soul. One is the means of training the soul in virtues through the Law of God when it is placed in flesh; and by ascending through certain steps it makes progress, as we have said, from virtue to virtue, and uses these progressions as stages. And the other journey is the one by which the soul, in gradually ascending to the heavens after the resurrection, does not reach the highest point unseasonably, but is led through many stages. In them it is enlightened stage by stage; it always receives an increase in splendor, illumined in each stage by the light of wisdom, until it arrives at the Father of lights Himself. (Cf. Jas. 1:17.)[15]

Looking at matters from a somewhat different perspective, we can say that the spiritual journey involves emulating Enoch. We are told (Gen. 5:23–24) that Enoch lived 365 years before 'God took him' without his actually dying. Anyone reading the genealogical lists of Genesis 5 carefully is bound to be struck by the fact that the earthly lifetime of Enoch is totally incommensurate with the longer lifetimes of all the other early humans. As everyone knows, 365 is the number of the days in a solar year. As such it symbolizes complete-

15. From 'Homily XXVII on *Numbers*' in *Origen*, tr. Rowan A. Greer (New York: Paulist Press, 1979), p253.

ness, like a circle which is usually divided into 360 degrees, an approximation or rounding off of the number of days in a year. The completeness of Enoch contrasts with the incompleteness of Adam and Eve after the separation of Eve from Adam. The symbolism here is that if we can regain our completeness we can be taken to God without physically dying. As we mentioned earlier, this is the very journey Dante describes himself as making in the *Divine Comedy.* That 365 days constitute a solar year connects Enoch with the sun as well. In effect, he is taken to the Spiritual Sun or Being.[16]

In chapters 1 and 7 we remarked that the spiritual journey involves two main deaths and rebirths (though there may be many small deaths and rebirths along the way). With this in mind we end with a combination of two quotations from Heraclitus of ancient Greece:

> For better deaths gain better portions according to Heraclitus (Fr. 25).
>
> ... they rise up and become guardians, wakefully, of the living and the dead (Fr. 63).[17]

16. In *The City of God*, bk xv, chap. 19, St Augustine mentions that Enoch was of the seventh generation of humans, counting Adam (Gen. 5:1–18), and thus symbolizes the sabbath. As we pointed out in the last part of chapter 3, observing the sabbath involves returning to God.

17. *The Presocratic Philosophers*, p207.

Bibliography

Abu Bakr Siraj Ed-Din (Martin Lings). *The Book Of Certainty.* New York: Samuel Weiser, 1970.

Al-Ghazali, Abu Hamid Muhammad. *The Niche for Lights.* Translated by W.H.T. Gairdner. Lahore: Sh. Muhammad Ashraf, 1968.

______. *The Mysteries of Fasting.* Translated by N.A. Faris. Lahore: Sh. Muhammad Ashraf, 1968.

Al-Hujwiri, Ali Be Uthman Al-Jullabi. *The Kashf Al-Mahjub.* Translated by Reynold A. Nicholson. London: Luzac & Company, 1976.

Anshen, Ruth Nanda. *The Reality of the Devil: Evil In Man.* New York: Dell Publishing Company, 1972.

Aquinas, Saint Thomas. *Summa Theologiae.* Translated by the Fathers of the English Dominican Province.

Aristotle. *Metaphysics.* Translated by Richard Hope. Ann Arbor: University of Michigan Press, 1963.

Augustine, Saint. *Confessions.* Translated by R.S. Pine-Coffin. Baltimore: Penguin Books, 1961.

______. *City of God.* Translated by Henry Bettenson. New York: Penguin Books, 1972.

______. *The Literal Meaning of Genesis.* Translated by John Hammond Taylor, S.J. New York: Newman Press, 1982.

Austin, R.W.J., trans. *Ibn Al'Arabi: The Bezels of Wisdom.* New York: Paulist Press, 1980.

Batto, Bernard F. 'Red Sea or Reed Sea'. *Biblical Archeology Review* (July/August 1984):56–63.

______. 'The Reed Sea: Requiescat in Pace'. *Journal of Biblical Literature* (volume 102): 27–35.

Benda, Julian. *The Treason of the Intellectuals.* New York: W.W. Norton, 1969.

Berlin, Isaiah. *The Proper Study of Mankind.* New York: Farrar, Straus and Giroux, 1998.

Bernard of Clairvaux, St. *Five Books On Consideration.* Translated by John

D. Anderson and Elizabeth T. Kennan. Kalamazoo, MI: Cistercian Publications, 1976.

Bosch, Frederick D.K., *The Golden Germ*. The Hague: Mouton & Co., 1960.

Brandes, Stanley. *Forty The Age And The Symbol*. Knoxville: University of Tennessee Press, 1985.

Brenner, Louis. *West African Sufi*. Berkeley: University of California Press, 1984.

Broudy, Harry. *Truth and Credibility*. New York: Longman, 1981.

Buhler, Georg, trans. *The Laws of Manu*. New York: Dover Publns, 1969.

Burckhardt, Titus. *An Introduction to Sufi Doctrine*. Translated by D. M. Matheson. Lahore: Sh. Muhammad Ashraf, 1959.

———. *Mirror of the Intellect*. Translated by William Stoddart. Albany: State University of New York Press, 1987.

Cahill, Thomas. *The Gifts of the Jews*. New York: Doubleday, 1998.

Cerny, Ladislav. *The Day of Yahweh and Some Relevant Problems*. Prague: Karlovy University, 1948.

Cervantes, Miguel de. *Don Quixote*. Translated by John Rutherford. New York: Penguin Books, 2001.

Chan, Wing-tsit, trans. *The Way of Lao Tzu*. Indianapolis: Bobbs-Merrill, 1963.

Cherry, Conrad, Deberg, Betty A. and Porterfield, Amanda. 'Religion on Campus'. *Liberal Education*, vol. 87, no. 4, Fall 2001.

Chittick, W.C. and Wilson, P.L., trans. *Fakhruddin Iraqi: Divine Flashes*. New York: Paulist Press, 1982.

Coomaraswamy, Ananda. *What Is Civilization*. Great Barrington, MA: Lindisfarne Press, 1989.

Dante Alighieri. *Convivio*. London: J.M. Dent & Sons, 1924.

———. *Paradiso*. Translated by Robert Hollander and Jean Hollander. New York: Anchor Books (Random House), 2008.

———. *Purgatorio*. Translated by Robert Hollander and Jean Hollander. New York: Anchor Books (Random House), 2004.

Deutsch, Eliot, trans. *The Bhagavad Gita*. New York: Holt, Rinehart and Winston, 1968.

Dogen, Eihei. *Shobogenzo*. Translated by Kosen Nishiyama and John Stevens. Tokyo: Nakayama Shobo, 1977.

Bibliography

Donniger, Wendy, with Smith, Brian K., trans. *The Laws of Manu*. New York: Penguin Books, 1991.

Dostoevsky, Fyodor. *The Brothers Karamazov*. Translated by Richard Pevear and Larissa Volokhonsky. New York: Vintage Classics, 1991.

Douglas, Mary. *Natural Symbols*. New York: Pantheon, 1982.

Dunbar, H. Flanders. *Symbolism In Medieval Thought*. New York: Russell & Russell, 1961.

Dundes, Alan. *Holy Writ as Oral Lit*. Lanham, MD: Roman & Littlefield, 1999.

Eliade, Mircea. *The Two and the One*. Translated by J.M. Cohen. New York: Harper & Row, 1965.

Ellul, Jacques. *The New Demons*. Translated by C. Edward Hopkin. New York: The Seabury Press, 1973.

______. *The Technological Society*. Translated by John Wilkinson. New York: Vintage Books, 1964.

Feiler, Bruce. *Abraham*. New York: William Morrow, 2002.

Fohr, Samuel D. *Cinderella's Gold Slipper: The Spiritual Symbolism of Folk & Fairy Tales*. Fourth, retitled and revised edition. Peterborough: Philosophia Perennis, 2017.

______. 'Shamanism for the Twenty-First Century: Spirituality and the Quest for Special Experiences'. *Journal of Drug Education and Awareness*, vol. 1, no. 1, 2003, pp 13–34.

Fraenger, Wilhelm. *Hieronymous Bosch*. Amsterdam: Overseas Publishing Association, 1999.

Frye, Northrup. *The Great Code*. New York: Harcourt, Brace and Jovanovich, 1982.

Gaster, Theodor H. *Myth, Legend and Custom in the Old Testament*, volume 1. New York: Harper & Row, 1975.

Greer, Rowan A., trans. *Origen*. New York: Paulist Press, 1979.

Grube, G.M.A. trans., revised by C.D.C. Reeve. *Plato/Republic*. Indianapolis: Hackett Publishing Company, 1992.

Guénon, René. *The Crisis of the Modern World*. Translated by Arthur Osborne, Marco Pallis, and Richard C. Nicholson. Hillsdale: Sophia Perennis, 2001.

______. *The Great Triad*. Translated by Henry D. Fohr. Hillsdale: Sophia Perennis, 2004.

———. *Insights into Christian Esoterism*. Translated by Henry D. Fohr. Hillsdale: Sophia Perennis, 2004.

———. *The King of the World*. Translated by Henry D. Fohr. Hillsdale: Sophia Perennis, 2004.

———. *Man and His Becoming according to the Vedānta*. Translated by Richard C. Nicholson. Hillsdale: Sophia Perennis, 2004.

———. *Miscellanea*. Translated by Henry D. Fohr, Cecil Bethell, Patrick Moore, and Henry Schiff. Hillsdale: Sophia Perennis, 2003.

———. *Perspectives on Initiation*. Translated by Henry D. Fohr. Hillsdale: Sophia Perennis, 2004.

———. *The Reign of Quantity and the Signs of the Times*. Translated by Lord Northbourne. Hillsdale: Sophia Perennis, 2004.

———. *Studies in Hinduism*. Translated by Henry D. Fohr. Hillsdale: Sophia Perennis, 2004.

———. *Symbols of Sacred Science*. Translated by Henry D. Fohr. Hillsdale: Sophia Perennis, 2004.

———. *Symbolism of the Cross*. Translated by Angus McNab. Hillsdale: Sophia Perennis, 2004.

———. *Traditional Forms and Cosmic Cycles*. Translated by Henry D. Fohr. Hillsdale: Sophia Perennis, 2004.

Guillaumont, A. et al. *The Gospel According to Thomas*. New York: Harper & Row, 1959.

Halkin, A.S. 'Yedaiah Bedershi's Apology'. In *Jewish Medieval and Renaissance Studies*, ed. by Alexander Altmann. Cambridge: Harvard University Press, 1967.

Hamilton, Edith and Cairns, Huntington, eds. *The Collected Dialogues of Plato*. Princeton: Princeton University Press, 1961.

Heidel, Alexander. *The Gilgamesh Epic And Old Testament Parallels*. Chicago: Phoenix Books, 1963.

Herbrechtsmeier, William. 'Buddhism and the Definition of Religion: One More Time'. *Journal for the Scientific Study of Religion*, 1993, vol. 32, no. 1, p1.

Herman, Arthur. *The Idea of Decline in Western History*. New York: The Free Press, 1997.

Heschel, Abraham Joshua. *The Circle of the Baal Shem Tov*. Edited by Samuel H. Dresner. Chicago: The University of Chicago Press, 1985.

———. *The Earth is the Lord's* and *The Sabbath*. Cleveland: The World Publishing Company, 1963.

Hesse, Hermann. *My Belief.* Edited by Theodore Ziolkowski, and translated by Denver Lindley. New York: Farrar, Straus, and Giroux, 1974.

Hillers, Delbert R. *Covenant: History of a Biblical Idea.* Baltimore: The Johns Hopkins Press, 1969.

Hügel, Friedrich von. *Mystical Elements in Religion*, volume 1. London: Dent & Son 1923.

Hugh of St Victor. *De Sacramentis.* Medieval Academy of America, 1976.

Ionesco, Eugene. *Fragments of a Journal.* New York: Grove Press, 1969.

Israel, Manasseh ben. *Conciliator.* Translated by E.H. Lindo. New York: Hermon Press, 1972.

Izutsu, Toshihiko. *A Comparative Study of the Key Concepts in Sufism and Taoism.* Tokyo: Keio Institute of Cultural and Linguistic Studies, 1966.

Jacobsen, Thorkeld. *The Sumerian King List.* Chicago: University of Chicago Press, 1939.

Jaffee, Martin S. 'One God, One Revelation, One People: On the Symbolic Structures of Elective Monotheism'. *Journal of the American Academy of Religion*, vol. 69, no. 4, Dec. 2001.

Josephson, Jason Ananda. *The Invention of Religion in Japan.* Chicago: University of Chicago Press, 2012.

Kalupahana, David J. *Buddhist Philosophy: A Historical Analysis.* Honolulu: The University Press of Hawaii, 1976.

Kaminer, Wendy. 'The Last Taboo'. *The New Republic*, vol. 215, no. 16, Oct. 14, 1996.

———. *Sleeping With Extra-Terrestrials.* New York: Pantheon Books, 1999.

Keown, Damian. *The Nature of Buddhist Ethics.* New York: Palgrave, 2001.

Kirk, G.S., Raven, J. E., and Schofield, M. *The Presocratic Philosophers*, Second Edition. Cambridge: Cambridge University Press, 1983.

Kunsang, Erik Pema, trans. *Dakini Teachings.* Kathmandu: Ranjung Yeshe Publications, 1999.

Lal, P., trans. *Dhammapada.* New York: Farrar, Straus & Giroux, 1967.

Lama Lodo. *Bardo Teachings.* Ithaca, NY: Snow Lion, 1982.

Leach, Edmund. 'Nobody Lives in the Real World'. *Psychology Today* (July 1974): 61–70.

———. and Aycock, D. Alan. *Structuralist Interpretations of Biblical Myth*. New York: Cambridge University Press, 1983.

Lewis, C.S. *The Abolition of Man*. San Francisco: Harper Collins, 2001.

Lings, Martin. *Ancient Beliefs and Modern Superstitions*. London: Unwin Paperbacks, 1980.

———. *The Eleventh Hour*. Cambridge: Quinta Essentia, 1987.

Lipsey, Roger, ed. *Coomaraswamy: Selected Papers*, volume 1. Princeton: Princeton University Press, 1977.

Luk, Charles. *Secrets of Chinese Meditation*. London: Rider & Co., 1964.

Maimonides, Moses. *The Guide of the Perplexed*. Translated by Shlomo Pines. Chicago: The University of Chicago Press, 1963.

Malherbe, Abraham J. and Ferguson, Everett, trans. *Gregory of Nyssa: The Life of Moses*. New York: Paulist Press, 1978.

Marty, M.E. 'Literalism And Everything Else'. *Bible Review*, April 1994.

Marx, Karl and Engels, Frederick. *Selected Works*, Two Volumes. Moscow: 1958 and 1969-70.

Matt, Daniel C., trans. *The Zohar: Pritzker Edition*. Stanford: Stanford University Press, 2004.

Meier, Fritz. 'The Mystery of the Ka'ba Symbol and Reality in Islamic Mysticism'. In *The Mysteries*, ed. by Joseph Campbell. Princeton: Princeton University Press, 1971.

Meister Eckhart. *The Essential Sermons, Commentaries, Treatises and Defence*. Translated by Edmund Colledge and Bernard McGuin. New York: Paulist Press, 1981.

———. *Teacher and Preacher*. Translated by Bernard McGuin, Frank Tobin and Elvira Borgstadt. New York: Paulist Press, 1986.

Mencken, H.L. *Minority Report*. Baltimore: The Johns Hopkins University Press, 1997.

Middleton, John, ed. *Myth and Cosmos*. Garden City: The Natural History Press, 1967.

Namkai Norbu, Chogyal. *Dzogchen: The Self-Perfected State*. Ithaca, NY: Snow Lion, 1996.

Nasr, Seyyed Hossein. 'The Gnostic Tradition'. In *Science and Civilization in Islam*. New York: New American Library, 1968.

———. 'Post-Avicennan Islamic Philosophy and the Study of Being'. In *Philosophies of Existence*, ed. by Parviz Morewedge. New York:

Fordham University Press, 1982.

Nikhilananda, S., trans. *The Gospel of Sri Ramakrishna*. New York: Ramakrishna-Vivekananda Center, 1973.

O'Flaherty, Wendy Doniger, trans. *The Rig Veda*. New York: Penguin Books, 1981.

Ono, Sokyo. *Shinto: The Kami Way*. Rutland, VT: Charles E. Tuttle, 1962.

Origen. *On First Principles*. Translated by G.W. Butterworth. Gloucester: Peter Smith, 1913.

Orwell, George. *Collected Essays, Journalism & Letters*, volumes 1–4. Edited by Sonia Orwell and Ian Angus. New York: Harcourt, Brace, Jovanovich, 1968.

Pallis, Marco. *A Buddhist Spectrum*. New York: Seabury Press, 1981.

______. *Peaks and Lamas*. New York: Alfred A. Knopf, 1949.

Peters, F.E. *Greek Philosophical Terms*. New York: New York University Press, 1967.

Philo. *Concerning Noah's Works as a Planter*. Translated by F.H. Colson and G.H. Whitaker. Cambridge: Harvard University Press, 1968.

______. *On Dreams* [De Somnis]. Translated by F. H. Colson and G. H. Whitaker. Cambridge: Harvard University Press, 1968.

______. *On Flight and Finding*. Translated by F.H. Colson and G.H. Whitaker. Cambridge: Harvard University Press, 1968.

______. *On the Account of the World's Creation Given by Moses*. Translated by F.H. Colson and G.H. Whitaker. Cambridge: Harvard University Press, 1971.

______. *Questions and Answers On Exodus*. Translated by Ralph Marcus. Cambridge: Harvard University Press, 1970.

______. *Who is the Heir of Divine Things*. Translated by F.H. Colson. Cambridge: Harvard University Press, 1968.

Picker, Stuart D.B. *Shinto: Japan's Spiritual Roots*. Tokyo: Kodansha International, 1980.

Plato. *The Dialogues of Plato*, Fourth Edition, translated by Benjamin Jowett. Oxford: Oxford University Press, 1953.

Plotinus. *The Enneads*. Translated by Stephen MacKenna. New York; Penguin Books, 1991.

Plutarch. 'Concerning the Face Which Appears in the Orb of the Moon'.

Translated by Harold Cherniss and William C. Hembold. In *Moralia*, Volume XII. Cambridge: Harvard University Press, 1968.

———. 'On the Sign of Socrates'. Translated by Phillip H. DeLacy and Benedict Einerson. In *Moralia*, Volume VII. Cambridge: Harvard University Press, 1968.

Pritchard, James B., ed. *Ancient Near Eastern Texts*, Third Edition. Princeton: Princeton University Press, 1969.

Radhakrishnan, Sarvepalli. *Eastern Religion and Western Thought*. New York: Oxford University Press, 1959. trans. The Principle Upanishads. London: George Allen & Unwin, 1974.

———. trans. *The Dhammapada*. New Delhi: Oxford Univ. Press, 1966.

———. trans. *The Principal Upanishads*. London: George Allen & Unwin, 1953.

Rahner, Karl. *Theological Investigations*, vol. iv. Translated by Kevin Smyth. London: Darton, Longman & Todd, 1966.

Rambam (Nachmanides). *Commentary of the Torah: Deuteronomy*. New York: Shilo Publishing House, 1971.

Reynolds, John Myrdin, trans. *The Golden Letters*. Ithaca, New York: Snow Lion Publications, 1996.

Rumi, Jalaluddin. *The Mathnawi*. Translated by Reynald A. Nicholson. London: Luzac & Co., 1977.

———. *Signs of the Unseen: The Discourses of Jalaluddin Rumi*. Translated by W.M. Thackston Jr. Putney, VT: Threshold Books, 1994.

Schimmel, Annemarie. *Mystical Dimension of Islam*. Chapel Hill: The University of North Carolina, Press 1975.

Scholem, Gershom. 'Kabbalah'. In *Encyclopaedia Judaica*, Volume 10. Jerusalem: Keter, 1972.

———. *Kabbalism*. New York: Meridian, 1978.

———. 'Magen David'. In *Encyclopaedia Judaica*, Volume 11.

———. *Major Trends in Jewish Mysticism*. New York: Schocken Books, 1954.

Schuon, Frithjof. 'Alternations In Semitic Monotheism'. In *Christianity/Islam: Essays on Esoteric Ecumenicism*. Bloomington, IN: World Wisdom Books, 1985.

———. *Esoterism as Principle and as Way*. Translated by William Stoddart. Hillsdale: Sophia Perennis, 1981.

———. *Gnosis: Divine Wisdom*. Translated by G. E. H. Palmer. Hillsdale: Sophia Perennis, 1990.

———. *In the Tracks of Buddhism*. Translated by Marco Pallis. London: George Allen & Unwin, 1968.

———. *Islam and the Perennial Philosophy*. Translated by J. Peter Hobson. Hillsdale: Sophia Perennis, 1976.

———. *Logic and Transcendence*. Translated by Peter N. Townsend. Hillsdale: Sophia Perennis, 1984.

———. *Spiritual Perspectives and Human Facts*. Translated by P. N. Townsend. Hillsdale: Sophia Perennis, 1987.

Senzaki, Nyogen and McCandless, Ruth Strout, trans. *The Iron Flute*. Tokyo: Charles E. Tuttle Company, 1961.

Shoper, Rev. Donna. 'Me-First "Spirituality" is a Sorry Substitute for Organized Religion on Campuses'. *Chronicle of Higher Education*, August 18, 2000.

Smith, Jonathan Z. 'A Matter of Class: Taxonomies of Religion', *Harvard Theological Review*, Oct. 1996, vol. 89, no. 4, pp387–404.

Smith, Wilfred Cantwell. *Faith and Belief*. Oxford: Oneworld Publications Ltd., 1998.

———. *The Meaning and End of Religion*. Minneapolis: Fortress Press, 1991.

Speiser, E. A., trans. *Genesis*. Garden City: Doubleday & Company, 1964.

Sperling, Harry and Simon, Maurice, trans. *The Zohar*. London: The Soncino Press, 1978.

Tishby, Isaiah. *The Wisdom of the Zohar*, Two Volumes. Oxford: Oxford University Press, 1991.

Tucci, Giuseppi. *The Religion of Tibet*. Berkeley: University of California Press, 1980.

Wallis Budge, Earnest A., trans. *The Book of the Bee*. Oxford: The Clarendon Press, 1886.

Watson, Burton, trans. *Chuang Tzu*. New York: Columbia University Press, 1968.

Watt, James and Harper, Prudence. *China: Dawn Of A Golden Age*. New Haven: Yale University Press, 2004.

Widengren, Geo. *The King And The Tree Of Life In Ancient Near Eastern Tradition*. Uppsala: A-B Lundequistska Bokhandlen, 1945.

Wilmshurst, W.L. *The Meaning of Masonry.* New York: Crown, 1980.

Wolf, Rabbi Arnold Jacob. 'Against Spirituality'. *Judaism*, vol. 50, no. 199, Summer 2001.

Yampolsky, Philip B., trans. *The Platform Sutra of the Sixth Patriarch.* New York: Columbia University Press, 1967.

The author received his B.A. in Philosophy from Brooklyn College and his M.A. and Ph.D. in Philosophy from the University of Michigan. His thesis was in the field of Philosophy of Religion. He began his career at Virginia Polytechnic Institute and State University and went on to the University of Pittsburgh at Bradford, where he taught for many years and is currently Professor Emeritus of Philosophy. Becoming interested in Zen Buddhism while still an undergraduate he proceeded to investigate most of the spiritual traditions of the East. Realizing that many Biblical verses could be interpreted as expressing what are normally considered Eastern ideas, he began systematic research into the question of whether Eastern and Western spiritual traditions really expressed the same basic truths. *Adam & Eve* was the first fruit of this endeavor, and this newer edition greatly expands on his research. In between writing these two editions he presented papers at meetings of the American Academy of Religion and wrote *Cinderella's Gold Slipper,* in which he analyzed the spiritual symbolism of folktales from around the world.

Index

Index

Index

Index

Index

Index

Index